C. G. JUNG AND THE DEAD

C. G. Jung and the Dead: Visions, Active Imagination and the Unconscious Terrain offers an in-depth look at Jung's encounters with the dead, moving beyond a symbolic understanding to consider these figures a literal presence in the psyche. Stephani L. Stephens explores Jung's personal experiences, demonstrating his skill at visioning in all its forms as well as detailing the nature of the dead.

This unique study is the first to follow the narrative thread of the dead from *Memories, Dreams, Reflections* into *The Red Book*, assessing Jung's thoughts on their presence, his obligations to them, and their role in his psychological model. It offers the opportunity to examine this previously neglected theme unfolding during Jung's period of intense confrontation with the unconscious, and to understand active imagination as Jung's principle method of managing that unconscious content. As well as detailed analysis of Jung's own work, the book includes a timeline of key events and case material.

C. G. Jung and the Dead will offer academics and students of Jungian and post-Jungian studies, the history of psychology, Western esoteric history and gnostic and visionary traditions a new perspective on Jung's work. It will also be of great interest to Jungian analysts and psychotherapists, analytical psychologists and practitioners of other psychological disciplines interested in Jungian ideas.

Stephani L. Stephens holds a PhD from the University of Kent, Canterbury, UK, in Jungian Psychology. Between 2004 and 2013 she served on the Executive Committee of the International Association of Jungian Studies. She teaches psychology in the International Baccalaureate programme and is a practising counsellor in Canberra, Australia. She is the recipient of the 2018 Frances P. Bolton Fellowship.

'This bold and fascinating book not only provides the most thorough examination to date of Jung's dreams and visions of the dead but also argues provocatively that at least some of these experiences, rather than just symbolising processes of the psyche, really were encounters with the dead. Beyond just presenting the evidence for this, Stephens demonstrates through her detailed analyses of specific dreams and visions, especially those contained in *The Red Book*, how Jung's encounters with the dead helped to shape his psychological concepts and therapeutic techniques. Needless to say, Stephens' argument also has far-reaching implications for understanding Jung's epistemological and ontological views of the psyche.'

– Professor Roderick Main, Department of Psychosocial and Psychoanalytic Studies, University of Essex, UK

'That the unconscious persists in developing spaces for the dead convinced Jung that what we owe them cannot be expiated by recognizing them as intergenerational complexes standing in for archetypes. Stephani L. Stephens details the visions that led Jung to identify more precisely what his own dead were demanding. How Jung paid this debt to psychological ancestors has never been so thoroughly accounted for. We see Jung going to hell to rescue their narratives and granting their concerns transcendent meaning when he takes up their projects as subjects of his own psychology.'

– John Beebe, C. G. Jung Institute of San Francisco, USA

C. G. JUNG AND THE DEAD

Visions, Active Imagination and the Unconscious Terrain

Stephani L. Stephens

LONDON AND NEW YORK

First published 2020
by Routledge
2 Park Square, Milton Park, Abingdon, Oxon OX14 4RN

and by Routledge
52 Vanderbilt Avenue, New York, NY 10017

Routledge is an imprint of the Taylor & Francis Group, an informa business

© 2020 Stephani L. Stephens

The right of Stephani L. Stephens to be identified as author of this work has been asserted by her in accordance with sections 77 and 78 of the Copyright, Designs and Patents Act 1988.

All rights reserved. No part of this book may be reprinted or reproduced or utilised in any form or by any electronic, mechanical, or other means, now known or hereafter invented, including photocopying and recording, or in any information storage or retrieval system, without permission in writing from the publishers.

Trademark notice: Product or corporate names may be trademarks or registered trademarks, and are used only for identification and explanation without intent to infringe.

British Library Cataloguing-in-Publication Data
A catalogue record for this book is available from the British Library

Library of Congress Cataloging-in-Publication Data
Names: Stephens, Stephani L., author.
Title: C.G. Jung and the dead : visions, active imagination and the
    unconscious terrain / Stephani L. Stephens.
Description: 1st edition. | Milton Park, Abingdon, Oxon ; New York, NY :
    Routledge, 2019. | Includes bibliographical references and index.
Identifiers: LCCN 2019009302 (print) | LCCN 2019011958 (ebook)
    | ISBN 9781351259897 (Master E-Book) | ISBN 9780815366126
    (hardback : alk. paper) | ISBN 9780815366140 (pbk. : alk. paper)
Subjects: LCSH: Jung, C. G. (Carl Gustav), 1875–1961. | Jung, C. G.
    (Carl Gustav), 1875–1961. Erinnerungen, Trèaume, Gedanken. |
    Death—Psychological aspects. | Visions.
Classification: LCC BF109.J8 (ebook) | LCC BF109.J8 S735 2019 (print)
    | DDC 128/.5—dc23
LC record available at https://lccn.loc.gov/2019009302

ISBN: 978-0-8153-6612-6 (hbk)
ISBN: 978-0-8153-6614-0 (pbk)
ISBN: 978-1-351-25989-7 (ebk)

Typeset in Bembo
by Swales & Willis Ltd, Exeter Devon, UK

 Printed in the United Kingdom by Henry Ling Limited

This book is for family: For my grandmother who knew no bounds and cleverly planted the seed. For my parents who lovingly paved my way. For David who knew early this all needed a container and patiently supported me when I could not see it clearly. For Kalu and Ephrim who are each their own miracles. For my sister, niece and nephew who treat their creativity like a gift and continue to produce unique contributions in the world. For Leon who walked this journey with me. For Constance and Russ whose love and perspective have grown me over many, many years. And for the readers who also walk with ancestors and do so in secret.

The dead are invisible, they are not absent.

– *Saint Augustine*

Dine hunc ardorem mentibus addunt

. . . sua cuique deus fit dira cupido?

[Do the gods light this fire in our hearts or does each man's mad desire become his god?]

– *Aen. Bk. 9.184–185*

CONTENTS

Acknowledgements	*ix*
Concurrent timeline	*xi*

PART I
Defining the terrain   **1**

1 Introduction	3
2 The literal and the symbolic	11
3 Jung's ways of seeing	20
4 Jung's primary orientation to the dead	29
5 The big dream	31
6 Death dreams	40

PART II
Liber Primus   **55**

7 *The Red Book*	57
8 Introduction to *Liber Primus*	62

viii Contents

9 Descent into hell in the future: Jung's first active imagination   69

10 Siegfried and the merry garden   80

11 Mysterium Encounter: Elijah and Salome   85

PART III
Liber Secundus   **97**

12 The Red One, the tramp and Death   99

13 Divine Folly   112

14 Philemon and the poisoner   128

PART IV
Scrutinies   **133**

15 *Scrutinies*   135

16 The *Septem Sermones*   147

17 After the last sermon: Death, Elijah and Salome   160

PART V
Beyond *The Red Book*   **163**

18 Post-*Red Book* implications   165

19 Contemporary context   168

20 Concluding thoughts   171

Bibliography   *173*
Index   *180*

ACKNOWLEDGEMENTS

This project has been many years in the making. It grew from an intense personal interest into doctoral research and finally into this book. During this time I became a mother and moved internationally, twice. I have had assistance along the way and at times people were unaware of the support they offered just at that moment of most need.

I must offer deep thanks to the various libraries and librarians who helped, guided, assisted and directed me in the formulation of the topic and terrain over the years. These spaces served many purposes not the least of which was to augur a sense of intention absent of the lures and distractions of modern life. They offered me a chance to gather and grow my thoughts until they were ready to find the page.

The library at the American Academy in Rome might be where the inspiration for this project began, where as a young Latin teacher I befriended many classics scholars who brought the ancient city and letters to life. It was there that I saw the first threads that ran from the ancient mind to modern depth psychology and where I felt called to dig deeper into the vestiges of the classics on the contemporary psyche.

When it looked like this project was more Jung than Virgil, the Pacifica Graduate Institute library offered me a corner where I gathered material that set me on course. I found Pacifica extremely helpful with their impressive trove of the discipline. The Scottsdale Public Library librarians in the interlibrary loan department performed miracles in obtaining books from far-flung shores and delighted in doing so. The Petherick Reading Room for advanced research at the National Library of Australia more recently offered a welcoming space to pull the writing together and to share my research with interested scholars. A special thank you to librarians Andrew Sergeant and Michael Herlihy for their supportive collegiality during the project.

x Acknowledgements

I must offer my deepest gratitude to my supervisor, Dr Leon Schlamm, who was a convivial and wise guide from the beginning and whose lengthy conversations over eleven years broadened my mind on Jung and prepared me well to enter the space of *The Red Book*. I am aware of being in that moment of hoping my teacher would be pleased, and as I type this I hear his jovial laugh and know there would be many points he would want to argue. While writing, I have missed being able to ask him his thoughts. And then I remember what this book is about and think 'isn't honouring the dead knowing what the dead would say'? The parts of this book that have worked particularly well are Leon's influence and at times during this process I have felt his deep understanding and love for Jung.

I must thank two wonderful teachers, Julie Soskin and Penny Brownjohn who with grace, discipline and knowing guided me to understand the subtleties of my awareness and helped me refine them at just the right time.

A special thank you to Jon Mills whose encouragement and professional conversation helped me articulate experiences that I had long ago put aside and he did so in a skillful documentary made in Capetown South Africa in 2017. When the time is right the teacher does come and usually with the message to get on with your work, thank you for that.

I'd also like to thank the International Association of Jungian Studies whose discussion group has been a wonderfully dynamic and consistent conversation for almost fourteen years. I have grown to love the discourse, disagreements and scholarly gems that members share openly and committedly with a wealth of perspectives. We are very lucky indeed to have this community. In particular, the friendship of both Marybeth Carter and Liz Brodersen has encouraged me more than they know. I have valued how each of you live your Jungian ideas and I have learned from you both.

I want to express deep thanks to Lisette Coly and the Parapsychological Foundation for the 2018 Frances P. Bolton fellowship award and for their financial assistance, which enabled me time and resources to finish the project.

To both my parents who each have led deeply scholarly lives and their love of curiosity was their biggest gift.

And finally, thank you to my beautiful family who have had more patience with me than I deserve and who can finally say, 'So this is what you were doing, this is what has taken so long?' With deep love, thank you.

CONCURRENT TIMELINE

		Personal	Professional
1875	26 July	Birth	
1878		Illness, memories of parents' troubled marriage, mother's absence First memory of father, finding the corpse of a deceased child	
1896	28 January March November	Father dies Two death dreams	Freud's father dies the same year Delivers Zofingia lecture
Summer 1899 1899–1900		Meets Emma Rauschenbach Seances with Helly	
1900			Finishes medical school Begins work at Burghölzli
1901	6 October	Betrothal to Emma	
1902			Dissertation: *On the Psychology and Pathology of So-Called Occult Phenomena*
1903	14 February	Marries Emma Rauschenbach	
1904	17 August	Sabina Spielrein is admitted to the Burgholzli	
1905	1 June	Sabina leaves Burgholzli	
	21 October		Delivers his first lecture at the University of Zurich 'The Psychopathological Significance of the Association Experiment'

(continued)

(continued)

		Personal	Professional
1906			Begins correspondence with Freud
1907	March		Meets Freud in Vienna
1908	Summer–November	Sabina and Jung become close	
1909	15 April		Resigns from the Burgholzli and opens private practice in Kusnacht
	21 August	Mummies/corpse conversation	Jung, Freud, Ferenczi to Clark University (seven-week trip)
1910	20 September	Toni Wolff meets Jung	
1911	21–22 September		Weimar Congress
	13 November	Helly Preiswerk dies age 30	
		Ancestral spirits dream	*Psychology of the Unconscious/Symbols of Transformation*
1912	December	Austrian customs official dream	
		Loggia dream	
		Row of tombs dream[1]	
1913	September		Jung's last correspondence with Freud
	October	Visions of Europe flooding	
	27 October		Resigns from the *Jarbuch* editorship
	12 December	First active imagination	
	18 December	Siegfried dream/vision	
	22 December	Elijah and Salome episodes	

	25 December	Last entry of *Liber Primus*	
	26 December	*Liber Secundus* begins; the Red One	
	29 December	'One of the Lowly' (the tramp)	
1914	2 January	'Death' (episode)	
	12 January	Hell	
	13 January	'Sacrificial Murder'	
	14 January	'Divine Folly': to the madhouse	
	17 January	'Nox Secunda'	
	18 January 19 January	'Nox Tertia' 'Nox Quarta': back to the kitchen	
1914	27 January	'The Magician', Philemon	
	2 February	'The Poisoner'	
	19 April	*Liber Secundus* ends and *Scrutinies* begins Jung's 'I' appears	
	8–24 May	Jung's soul returns and they speak	
	25 May	The old man spoke Jung's 'I' burdened to carry the dead	
	April, May, June	Dream of Arctic cold freezing land	
	20 April		Resigns as president of the International Psychological Association

(continued)

(continued)

		Personal	Professional
	30 April		Resigns from the Medical faculty at the University of Zurich
	24 June	Last the soul spoke before the war breaks out	
	28 July		Delivers a lecture to the British Medical Association in Scotland: 'The Importance of the Unconscious in Psychopathology'
1914	1 August		World War I begins
	9–22 August		Military service in Luzern
1915	January–March		Military service in Olten
1915	3 June	'[V]oices of the depths remained silent for a whole year'[2] Sign of an osprey	
	14 September	Philemon returns	
	2 December	The deceased shade; Helly	
	20 December	The Mass	
	14 January	Soul returns to perform an alchemical incubation	
1916	29 January	Jung's house is haunted: the dead return from Jerusalem The start to the *Sermones*	
	31 January	Second sermon	
	8 February	Last sermon	
	1 June	Last dated entry to *The Red Book*: Philemon walks in the garden with Christ	
		First mandala	
1922	September	Jung's mother dies	

Notes

1 There is no date indicated for the row of tombs dream, but it appears in *Memories, Dreams, Reflections* between the loggia dream of 1912 and Jung's visions of the flooding in October of 1913.
2 Shamdasani suggests the gap in entries is due to Jung's time spent writing the *Draft* for *Liber Novus*.

PART I
Defining the terrain

1

INTRODUCTION

The unconscious terrain: setting the stage for the dead

Seeing the dead is as old as death itself. Whether in a dream, a vision, in the corner of the room or the corner of one's eye, the dead return. The encounters are often significant, moving and life altering, and they demand something from both parties, what that is exactly is the mystery of their appearance in the first instance. Jung knew and understood as much.

When I first read *Memories, Dreams, Reflections*, it became clear the extent to which Jung grappled with his visionary experiences and how he struggled to understand the dead from a psychological perspective. His direct encounters with figures of the unconscious, some of whom he specifically identified as the dead, proved seminal to his experiences of the unconscious as a whole and appear to have assisted him in conceptualising both the unconscious and the figures who occupied the same psychic space as the dead.

This book arises from my fascination with Jung's descriptions of the dead in *Memories, Dreams, Reflections* and *The Red Book* and is intended to guide the reader through the content of Jung's visionary experiences as well as the methods by which he discovered the unconscious terrain. Active imagination assisted Jung in dealing with his own emotional and psychological imbalance. This process permitted him to mine visionary content that lay under the surface of consciousness and prompted him to refine and define a method that would include the interplay between the two. Yet, Jung also visioned in several other specific ways. In one sense, active imagination sits as the cornerstone of Jung's entire psychological model.[1] The work here speaks to Jung's ability to visualise material, describe these experiences and do something unique; determine a model of how consciousness and the unconscious exist as a dynamic in the personality. I argue that specifically Jung's encounters with the dead assisted with his project. The premise here looks

4 Defining the terrain

beyond the symbolic nature of the dead's appearance, which signifies a departure from the traditional Jungian approach, and examines the implications of Jung's psychological model as a result of considering the dead as a literal presence in the psyche. Offering an alternative to the symbolic approach allows the dead to point to themselves as psychic material and thus enhances the timing and psychological effect of their appearance. By formulating a picture of what Jung's relationship with his dead actually entailed, this book argues the central yet neglected role the dead played in pointing Jung toward themselves and toward the formulation of the unconscious dynamic.

This work does not attempt to build an argument that the dead exist *in se*, parapsychologists have been at that for a while now. But rather to raise a question that if we understand the dead to exist literally, as I propose Jung did, what do we learn about the dead, the unconscious and how we live with both? What do Jung's accounts of the dead teach us?

Where my focus in the article 'Active Imagination and the Dead'[2] was to suggest and then attempt to support that Jung was experiencing a different type of unconscious material when he labelled the experience as being with the dead, my project here is different. Here, I wish to illustrate the variety and scope of Jung's visual encounters with (and as a result of) the dead. These would later inform and expand episodes that he recounted in *Memories, Dreams, Reflections*. The assumption here is that Jung is speaking with the dead when he says as much, and thus the focus can now be on the skills he develops as a result of such encounters. This raises the fundamental question as to how the dead informed his understanding of the visioning process. I wish this question to stand apart from examining if Jung was a visionary because I feel this is a different question and one handled by previous authors.[3] Rather, Jung's experiences reveal he was skilled at visioning and in turn became even more so as he used it.

I have adopted the term 'visioning' because the word communicates both active engagement and interactivity. Jung did not simply 'have visions', as this would imply that he became distracted by flashes of visionary material. Rather, Jung engaged in a process of entering the space of the unconscious perceiving, seeing and then seeing more and further. This layered journeying entailed a type of sustained visioning/seeing/sight in which what he saw informed him further, not only in understanding but in process.[4] When Jung came to understand what he witnessed, his ability to sustain visioning assisted him further. Thus, 'The focus is not on what Jung sees or on his attempts to formulate what he sees, but rather on his manner of seeing, that is his approach and method.'[5] Visioning therefore refers not only to Jung's capacity to see, but also his ability to manage his unconscious content for further exploration.[6]

The theme of the dead began in Jung's childhood, and manifested in provocative form in 1896 with the dream of his deceased father six weeks after his death and to brief resolution with the dead's appearance when writing *Septem Sermones ad Mortuos* (*Seven Sermons to the Dead*) in 1916. During this time it was the dead who showed Jung the nature of 'figures of the unconscious' in a series of death dreams and visions. He made this distinction in his chapter 'On Life After Death', when he speaks about both figures of the unconscious and 'that other group . . . often indistinguishable from them, the "spirits of the departed"'.[7] In their role, they not only pointed Jung toward the unconscious as a venue of exploration, but they also pointed to themselves as separate and distinct entities. They guided him to discover layers of the unconscious both personal and collective, and to the lively countenance of the unconscious itself. The dead remained a consistent presence in his discoveries and facilitated for him the ability to explore and define its workings.

The approach

The book's approach is principally chronological and draws conclusions about the experiences of the dead themselves. The discussions treated here examine Jung's personal material in visions and dreams in both *Memories, Dreams, Reflections* and *The Red Book* and includes the seminal dream of Paul Jung six weeks after his death in 1896 and continues to examine the death dreams occurring between 1911 to 1912, which served as a preparatory phase before Jung's full confrontation with the unconscious between 1913 and 1914. This discussion sets the background for the emergence of *The Red Book* material. Much of the content here includes encounters with the dead as well as pointing to instances in which death is a prominent theme. As Jung recounted his dreams and visions with graphic descriptions of terrain, climate and even time, he reveals the unconscious as a process in which dynamic transformations occur and in which he became a more active participant.

It has been a challenge for the Jungian community to approach *The Red Book* as a text, its form seems to have dictated the way it has been discussed, argued, advocated and in some cases (perhaps few) dismissed.[8] As such, previous scholarly approaches have attempted to tackle the work as a whole and in terms of a narrative, which have lent the work a broad appeal in an attempt to make it more accessible and understood. Attempts to determine what *The Red Book* is have fallen short in acknowledging specific details, which prove it masterly in terms of what Jung learns about himself and the unconscious as he describes it. Where *Memories, Dreams, Reflections* reveals the recurrent appearance of the dead in Jung's personal material, *The Red Book* confirmed and in some instances elaborated these accounts.

Spirits and the dead

During Jung's lifetime he vacillated as to whether spirits could be defined as split-off parts of a subjective psyche or whether they actually existed unto themselves, *in se*.[9] This is best demonstrated when he asks if 'the ghost or the voice is identical with the dead person or is a psychic projection' and if what we attribute as information coming from the dead might be content that already exists in the unconscious.[10] That is whether emerging knowledge is derived from a discarnate as such or if details remain in an unconscious readily accessible by some.

6 Defining the terrain

But, Jung's professional position on after-death survival was indecisive not because personally he was unsure if there existed life after death,[11] but rather because of the challenges the dead posed to his psychological model. Did they fit into a psychological framework and if so how? What kind of unconscious accommodates for the dead? One can see Jung's intentional ambiguity in affirming the topic of 'spirits' in relation to his established psychological ideas when in a letter about spiritualism, he states:

> I am inclined to assume that she is more probably a spirit than an archetype, although she presumably represents both at the same time. Altogether, it seems to me that spirits tend increasingly to coalesce with archetypes. For archetypes can behave exactly like real spirits, so that communications like Betty's could just as well come from an indubitably genuine archetype.[12]

Here Jung is attempting to bring his psychological concept of the archetype in alignment with the querant's understanding of a spirit. The significance of this detail rests with Jung's consideration of spirits *alongside* his concept of archetypes and therefore confirms that he, at the very least, considered the existence of spirits or the dead as a separate category of experience. By attempting to link the two ideas, Jung falls short in an attempt to clarify. He was aiming not to dismiss the experience of a spirit, but rather to highlight that the symbolic appearance of a ghostly form can be archetypal and this consideration is meant to accommodate the concepts of both. Does this clarify? Not really, but it allowed him to justify each occasion and to frame Betty's ghostly appearance into a psychological context. What appears certain is Jung's position on how 'real spirits' behave.

Defining the dead

For Jung, the dead proved themselves to be souls without bodies (discarnates) and this is revealed in a scene from the *Sermones* when the dead leave for Jerusalem. Jung has an exchange with the figure Ezechiel and asks where they are going and might he join them. Ezechiel responds, 'You cannot join us, you have a body. But we are dead.'[13] It is this exchange that makes clear the speculation as to what Jung meant when he designated experiences to be with 'the dead'.[14] At the heart of not only this encounter but all his exchanges with the dead is the notion that the human being is both soul and body and that the soul possesses immortal qualities.[15] I suggest this seminal moment informed Jung's future encounters with the dead. Although the distinction was pointed out by Ezechiel, this pivotal revelation shows that Jung experienced the dead as souls divorced from their physical bodies, who appear in the same psychic space as all other figures of the unconscious.

THE DEAD AND THE TRANSCENDENT FUNCTION

As a part of defining the dead, I have previously suggested them to be a separate experience to figures of the unconscious who also emerge visually and are projections or split-off parts of the psyche. For figures, the visioning process is about objectification so as to manage them as contents of the unconscious that will, as the process occurs, be reintegrated into the personality as a result. Their appearance in the first instance emerges from Jung's psyche and therefore is supported by somewhat of an energetic extension of Jung himself. Jung identified this dynamic as the transcendent function or the process of reintegrating split-off parts of the psyche back into the personality. I have argued that this process, although appearing the same for the dead, does not include the final part of the function, which would have the dead absorbed back into the personality. This cannot occur if the dead appear in the psyche *in se* and presumably have their own energetic and psychological integrity that has no interest in absorbing or reintegrating into the personality of another.

Although *Memories, Dreams, Reflections* points to substantial discussions about the nature of life and death and highlights Jung's personal material on the question, this exchange is by far the clearest in terms of how Jung discovers and defines the dead. Therefore, when evaluating Jung's experiences, I suggest abandoning a metaphorical understanding for a literal one. That is, it is necessary to leave aside the idea that the dead appear solely as symbolic of the unconscious itself and move toward the notion of the dead as disembodied souls, yet, no less psychological. When I emphasise the psychological relationship to the dead, this does not allocate them to a projection. Rather, primarily and most intimately this psychological approach poses the questions: 'How do we live with the dead?' and 'What do the dead teach us about them, ourselves and the unconscious?' Or, most critically, 'What do the dead teach Jung about the unconscious through his visioning process?'

Jungians on the dead

Jungian scholarship traditionally has framed the discussion of the dead in relation to the bereavement process. Analysts have suggested that the return of the dead is manifested by a mourning psyche adjusting to a lost object.[16] One approach has been to view the history of spiritualism and its influence on the genesis of Jungian psychology.[17] A recent theme has treated spirit possession as a psychological dynamic.[18] Yet, little research has focused the discussion on the dead themselves and their specific role in Jung's personal material. By focusing attention on Jung's interactions and experiences, a novel perspective emerges; the dead illuminated the possibility that this relationship was anything but pathological. The dead extended

8 Defining the terrain

beyond the problematic issue of after-death survival to become a profound psychological agency whose main purpose was to assist Jung with his understanding of the dynamic of the unconscious itself. Jung attempted to address a similar issue in his dissertation when he suggested, 'It is, in fact, exceedingly difficult, and sometimes impossible, to distinguish these states from the various types of neurosis, but on the other hand certain features point beyond pathological inferiority'.[19]

The appearance of the dead raises some seminal questions, 'Who are [they] and what does it mean to answer them?' and 'What do the dead want?'[20] Analyst Paul Kugler asks, 'What is the significance of this realm between the living and the dead and why are the dead so intent upon getting our attention?'[21] Analyst Susan Olson asks, 'Do [the dead] grieve as we do? Does the process of individuation continue after death?'[22] And analyst Greg Mogenson suggests the possibility of what he calls the 'life of the dead'.[23] Most recently Peter Moore considers that we have not done justice to the obvious question of how the dead might survive by limiting the possibility to either incarnate or discarnate options. Rather, he proposes the possibility of a post-mortem form of survival of consciousness, which maintains a type of form, simply not a physical one.[24]

These types of speculations reflect the possibility that the consideration of the dead apart from previously held assumptions of being personal projections or split-off parts of a mourning psyche might yield some surprising directions of inquiry. By considering the dead as Jung experienced them, as discarnates or souls without bodies inhabiting the very same psychic space as other figures of the unconscious, the full extent of their influence on Jung can be understood.[25]

Scholars have charted some of these difficulties and inconsistencies regarding spirits in Jung's professional writings, but lacking until recently, has been a concentrated focus on the presence of the dead in Jung's personal accounts. Jung's vacillation is apparent in the Zofingia lectures, which contain an, 'impassioned and informed appeal for the serious scientific study of spiritualistic [i.e. paranormal] phenomen' to his 'cautious position' regarding 'the objective existence of spirits' in 1919.[26] This back and forth would continue throughout his career until his out-of-body experience in 1944, when Jung stated, 'I am absolutely convinced of personal survival, but I do not know how long it persists.'[27] Some think that Jung expressed his conviction in after-death survival later in his life, yet Shamdasani suggests it is more likely that after his mother's death in 1923, he began writing professionally about it and became most certain.[28] With the publication of *The Red Book* not only can the dead be positioned centrally in the discussion of Jung's model of the unconscious, but it also appears that their role challenges the previously held assumption that the dead are simply projections of the personal unconscious. Charet charts how Jung himself analysed the issue of the dead in terms of his personal unconscious thinking the problem rested with his past and then considers: 'Though the dead, as Jung claimed, pressed upon him from within, he still felt he could credibly interpret this psychologically and identify the dead with contents of the unconscious', that is as projections.[29] What *The Red Book* shows is that the dead *are* experienced as contents of the unconscious, as discarnates or disembodied souls *and* they have a psychological relationship.

Introduction **9**

Notes

1 Joan Chodorow, ed., *Jung on Active Imagination* (Princeton, NJ: Princeton University Press, 1997), p. 1.
2 Stephani Stephens, 'Active Imagination and the Dead', *International Journal of Jungian Studies* (2 December 2015): 1–14.
3 See Aniela Jaffé's *Was C. G. Jung a Mystic? And Other Essays* (Einsiedeln, Switzerland: Daimon Verlag, 1989); a sound examination in Gary Lachman's *Jung the Mystic: The Esoteric Dimensions of Carl Jung's Life and Teachings* (New York: TarcherPerigee, 2012); and John Dourley's *Jung and His Mystics: In the End It All Comes to Nothing* (London: Routledge, 2014). Equally, F. X. Charet's *Spiritualism and the Foundations of C. G. Jung's Psychology* (New York: SUNY Press, 1993) is a penetrative pre-*Red Book* discussion.
4 I find this perspective helpful as it is applicable to Jung: 'As shamans make thousands of journeys over the years, some territories become quite familiar to them. Once a shaman has visited a place … he or she knows the workings of that place and how to best navigate it next time. It becomes part of the shaman's map.' Sandra Ingerman, *Soul Retrieval: Mending the Fragmented Self* (New York: HarperSanFrancisco, 1991), p. 33. Also, 'a central feature of shamanism is *control* over trance … in other words, shamans, attain the capacity to re-enter trance states similar to those experienced in their pre-intitiatory illness but without being possessed and overcome'. A quality that Jung begins to demonstrate more as he moves through *The Red Book* material. John Merchant, *Shamans and Analysis: New Insights on the Wounded Healer* (London: Routledge, 2012), p. 31.
5 Roger Brooke, *Jung and Phenomenology* (London: Routledge, 1991), pp. 28–29.
6 Joan Chodorow reminds us that Jung himself used this term at one point to refer to active imagination. I extend the sense here to include how Jung responds to all types of anomalous visionary experiences. Chodorow, *Jung on Active Imagination*, p. 3.
7 C. G. Jung and Aniela Jaffé, *Memories, Dreams, Reflections*, trans. Richard Winston and Clara Winston (London: Fontana, 1961/1995), p. 338 (hereafter cited as *MDR*).
8 Consider these two perspectives; 'It is almost impossible to read this book without thinking about Jung's *Collected Works*. It doesn't diminish the *Collected Works*; on the contrary, *The Red Book* enhances our understanding of Jung's psychology.' Gilda Frantz (2010) 'Jung's *Red Book*: The Spirit of the Depths', *Psychological Perspectives* 53, no. 4: 391–395; and then Geigrich's dismissal: 'As important as the Red Book [*sic*] is for *historical* "Jung studies", *as psychologists* we are well advised to dissociate ourselves from the Red Book [*sic*] and instead base our work on Jung's published psychology, and *critically* so at that' (Giegerich's italics). The irony in this statement represents the desire to distance from the prima materia of Jung's original experiences. Wolfgang Giegerich, 'Liber Novus, That Is, the New Bible: A First Analysis of C. G Jung's *Red Book*', *Spring* 83 (2010): 361–411, at 376.
9 Roderick Main, *The Rupture of Time: Synchronicity and Jung's Critique of Modern Western Culture* (Hove, UK and New York: Brunner-Routledge, 2004), p. 70. Olson also discusses Jung's back and forth position regarding his subjective vs objective interpretations: 'The tension between these two positions runs throughout his work.' Susan Olson, *By Grief Transformed; Dreams and the Mourning Process* (New Orleans, LA: Spring Journal Books, 2010), p. 64.
10 *MDR*, p. 332.
11 There is now evidence that after his heart attack, Jung felt certain about after-death survival. Shamdasani discovered: 'In 1947 in private conversation [Jung] shared with E.A. Bennet, "I am absolutely convinced of personal survival … I am absolutely convinced of the survival of the personality – for a time, + the marvellous experience of being dead."' Shamdasani, Sonu, 'The Boundless Expanse: Jung's Reflections on Death and Life', *Quadrant* 38, no. 1 (Winter, 2008): 9–30, at 23.
12 C. G. Jung, *Letters: 1951–1961*, Vol. 2 (Princeton, NJ: Princeton University Press, 1975), p. 432.
13 C. G. Jung, *The Red Book*, ed. Sonu Shamdasani, trans. Mark Kyburz (New York: W. W. Norton, 2009), p. 294b (hereafter cited as *RB*). These are the same dead who two years later will return from Jerusalem having not found what they sought and will prompt Jung to produce *Septem Sermones ad Mortuos*. The following references confirm Jung's experience

10 Defining the terrain

of the dead in the unconscious as discarnate souls: *RB*, pp. 297b, 299 n. 197 (considered a mark); p. 322b; and, by deduction, p. 339b.

14 In *The Red Book*, Jung further clarifies content from the *Sermones*, that the dead who haunt are those who have not individuated during their lifetime (*RB*, p. 370b).

15 C. G. Jung, *The Zofingia Lectures*, trans. Jan Van Heurck, in *The Collected Works, Supplementary Volume A* (London: Routledge, 1896).

16 Jungian work on bereavement is almost solely focused on bereavement dreams in which the deceased appear to the mourning dreamer. The literature has not addressed the dead who appear in either active imagination or non ordinary states of consciousness as Jung experiences in *The Red Book* material. Geri Grubbs believes: 'It is only in your dreams, however, that you have emotional and apparent physical contact with them' (p. vvii). Geri Grubbs, *Bereavement Dreaming and the Individuating Soul* (Berwick, ME: Nicolas Hays, 2004). The literature is principally limited to the following: Verena Kast, *A Time to Mourn* (Einsiedeln, Switzerland: Daimon Verlag, 1988); Olson, *By Grief Transformed*; Charlotte Mathes, *And the Sword Shall Pierce My Heart: Moving from Despair to Meaning After the Death of a Child* (Ashville, NC: Chiron, 2006); James Hollis, *Dispelling the Ghosts Who Run Our Lives* (Ashville, NC: Chiron 2013).

17 Charet, *Spiritualism*, pp. 171–227.

18 See Lucy Huskinson, 'Analytical Psychology and Spirit Possession: Towards a Non-Pathological Diagnosis of Spirit Possession', in *Spirit Possession and Trance: New Interdisciplinary Perspectives*, eds. Bettina Schmidt and Lucy Huskinson (London: Continuum, 2009), pp. 71–95; Craig Stephenson, *Possession Jung's Comparative Anatomy of the Psyche* (Hove, UK: Routledge, 2009).

19 C. G. Jung, 'On the Psychology and Pathology of So-Called Occult Phenomena', in *Psychiatric Studies*, trans. R. F. C. Hull, *The Collected Works*, Vol. 1 (Princeton, NJ: Princeton University Press, 1957), §3 (hereafter cited as *CW*, vol. 1).

20 Shamdasani, 'The Boundless Expanse', p. 25.

21 Paul Kugler, *Raids on The Unthinkable: Freudian and Jungian Psychoanalyses* (New Orleans, LA: Spring Journal Books, 2005), p. 114.

22 Olson, *By Grief Transformed*, p. 6.

23 Greg Mogenson, *Greeting the Angels: An Imaginal View of the Mourning Process* (New York: Baywood, 1992).

24 Peter Moore, *Where Are the Dead? Exploring the Idea of an Embodied Afterlife* (London: Routledge, 2016).

25 The following pages indicate encounters Jung had with the literal dead: *RB*, pp. 294b, 297b, 299 n. 197 (discusses one having a 'mark' if one was sympathetic to the dead); p. 322b; and, by deduction, p. 339b.

26 Main, *The Rupture of Time*, pp. 67, 70. Also Charet's chapter, 'Jung, Freud and the Conflict over Spiritualistic Phenomena' in *Spiritualism*, pp. 171–227 is of interest here.

27 Shamdasani, 'The Boundless Expanse', p. 23, interview with E. A. Bennett.

28 Kugler, *Raids on The Unthinkable*; Roger Woolger, *Other Lives, Other Selves* (New York, Bantam Books, 1988); Jenny Yates, ed., *Jung on Death and Immortality* (Princeton, NJ: Princeton University Press, 1997); Shamdasani, 'The Boundless Expanse', p. 20.

29 Charet, *Spiritualism*, p. 240.

2

THE LITERAL AND THE SYMBOLIC

Historically, the symbolic interpretation of the dead has been the traditional Jungian method of approach. This entails the dead *representing* many things including transitions, death, beginnings, endings, rebirth, projections, as well as the unconscious itself, not to mention the actual relationship of the deceased to the experient. Yet, Jung emphasised in *Memories, Dreams, Reflections* that these encounters, these conversations with the dead served as a precursor to what he wanted to convey about the unconscious and in turn his psychological model.[1] The dead showed Jung the way to understand his visioning, the unconscious and himself.

The literal approach to the dead is both controversial and potentially, if not obviously, problematic. The dead raise problems for therapists who might be understandably disbelieving and wholly unwilling to admit to such possibilities.[2]

The dead in the consulting room

There is what could be considered burgeoning research in the counselling and psychotherapy fields addressing the needs of clients who present with paranormal, exceptional or spiritually transformative experiences. Although this research shows clearly a positive move toward addressing client needs, there is still much work that can be done.

Research has found 'a substantial number of [spiritually transformative experients] were harmed by disclosing their [experiences] to health care providers – including counsellors'.[3] Elisabeth Roxburgh's study describes experients of STE's feeling 'dismissed' and 'closed down' by their counsellor. She addresses the challenges of attempting to explore the meaning of the experience. Often they 'fear being ridiculed or pathologised [but] are eager to explore the meaning of the experience with an open-minded therapist'.[4] Psychologist M. Belz raises concern about the 'pathologization of ExE [exceptional experiences]' even when 'others . . . consider them to

12 Defining the terrain

be signs of an individuals' spiritual development and growth, there is a profound lack of interest and ignorance within the mainstream arenas of clinical psychology and psychotherapy'.[5] Further research shows that

> clients feel that they are not taken seriously, their experiences being categorized as illusions, halluzination [*sic*], or symptoms of craziness or mental disorder. Therefore many clients approach us with caution, fear and mistrust . . . with high hopes that, this time over, they might encounter a competent and understanding expert.[6]

Added to such findings is an account by sociologist Michele Knight in a description of what prompted her, after the deaths of her husband and mother, to pursue doctoral research in after-death communiqué:

> In trying to determine answers to some of the questions that my own experiences of communiqué with my husband and my mother had generated within my mind, I searched exhaustively for guidance. In conjunction with riding my intellectual steed into the battle of the written word, I also contacted the palliative care service which had attended to the palliative care needs of my father, husband and mother. I was directed to a faith support person with whom I eventually spoke on the telephone. A self-confessed expert, I was bluntly told by the individual that communication between the living and the deceased was negatively viewed, and that such things lay in the realm of the occult. I was also told that such ideas did not accord with Christian churches in Sydney. While this individual implied that the phenomenon was akin to a form of possession, I was also told that throughout their counselling of the bereaved very few individuals had reported this. When I told the individual that my encounters actually helped me cope with my being bereaved, they became angry and insistently stated that this was a side issue which had no relation to bereavement and grief whatsoever. They continued arguing that they dealt with the practicalities, what to do when you wake up crying in the middle of the night, that sort of thing. In concluding the conversation, and when I mentioned that I would be undertaking doctoral studies exploring this phenomenon, already agitated, the individual became more so, reiterated that it was something which belonged to the occult, and that in their opinion it would not help the bereaved. In addition to this encounter, I experienced two similar conversations with individuals from alternate faith traditions.[7]

These responses reflect religious advisors as well as mental health professionals who feel unprepared to manage something they themselves have not experienced and perhaps have little exposure to. Roxburgh's further research into therapists who had experienced synchronistic experiences in the consulting session determined 'these experiences came as a shock to the therapists and challenged their concept of reality'.[8] These reactions of course are coupled with the

The literal and the symbolic **13**

professional responsibility to dissuade potentially psychotic clients of an opportunity to aggrandise a possible pathology rather than dismiss the experience because they are disbelieving of its veracity.

Yet, the very first encounter, first sighting, first exchange or first event is a literal one. It is contact with something inexplicable that one attempts to process on a visceral level. Thus, the literal interpretation of the dead need not replace or displace the symbolic, but I suggest absolutely does precede it. Encounters with the dead must be allowed to be literal if metabolising the experience to understand why the dead return is to happen.

It is only after creating the space for the literal event to be understood, that their significance can be managed. In fact, questions such as, 'Why have they come, and what do they want?' necessarily and naturally follow such encounters and look to contextualise the experience for meaning. Inevitably, the symbolic space assists with managing meaning into understanding and can help interpret and usher the literal dead into a position of ancestral wisdom.

A case study: the jelly bean

Psychotherapist Rose Cameron discusses a similar tension regarding paranormal events in the consulting room and suggests 'the concepts of extrasensory perception and the paranormal are embedded in a debate in which therapists need not become involved'.[9] Historically, parapsychology has defined itself alongside science in its attempt at acceptance by the very discipline. But Cameron claims, 'This debate is of no consequence to therapeutic practice; the search for objectivity is irrelevant to understanding what happens in the therapeutic encounter.'[10]

For us, this is important because we are unable to prove that the dead themselves aren't standing there speaking. For our purposes, proving the dead are in fact the dead *in se* is misplaced. The real focus is to assume the experience is as it is related and might just reveal a bigger clue to what's going on than the effort taken to prove what the experience is or is not. As psychologists Dannenbaum and Kinnier state: 'Some people do believe that communication between the living and dead is a reality, and we do not have evidence to the contrary.'[11]

Cameron shares a very useful professional anecdote to meaningful effect. She explains an event that unfolded during a counselling session in which her client (Mary) was relaying some concerns about her workplace:

> I want to say I 'saw' but perhaps 'perceived' might be more accurate . . . I perceived . . . something . . . wiggling across the short distance between us. It was an invisible something, yet I somehow perceived it to have a form. It was rather like an elongated (and wriggly) jellybean: translucent, yet somehow also encased in a slightly opaque shell. It had a very distinct emotional quality of repeated, heart-sinking disappointment . . . The idea that a therapist might access a client's unspoken feelings is fundamental to many schools of counselling and psychotherapy . . . However, my experience with the jellybean . . . cannot

14 Defining the terrain

> be understood as projective identification or as embodied counter-transference as I did not experience Mary's disappointment within myself. The jellybean was most definitely 'out there', wriggling in the space between us [a few inches in front of her chest] . . . I did not feel disappointed.[12]

Now, it might be argued that Cameron indeed *felt* the disappointment because she was able to identify it, but it appears her certainty of 'not' feeling seems to point to her perceiving the emotion contained in it, in the jelly bean. Cameron was able to immediately verify the disappointment with her client who confirmed it to be so. To spend time figuring out what the jelly bean is and why it appeared as such would not have served her client, nor was it timely to do so:

> Had I, in the moment, become interested in whether the jellybean was paranormal or scientifically explicable I would have done so at Mary's expense (literally). The question is irrelevant. Instead I became interested in the disappointment and this led to a very useful piece of work.[13]

She goes on to build the point that the paranormal as defined as 'phenomena which in one or more respects conflict with accepted scientific opinion as what is physically possible'[14] is not helpful in the consulting room, nor would it be when speaking with someone who had just seen their deceased spouse.

Considering the Continuing Bonds research is helpful here. The idea is a reversal of the model of detachment in grief therapy towards the opposite in order to maintain or build a new relationship with the deceased. This model grew out of observation of clients who were having anomolous experiences including sightings of the deceased, vivid dreams and sensations, the experiences of which were incredibly 'real' (similar to what led to M. Knight's account toward positive grief adaptation and resolution).

As we try to break this down to build a case for a literal interpretation of the dead, Cameron herself reflects on the stages of phenomenological awareness in explanation of how she contextualised her experience. Helpful too is anthropologist Jack Hunter's idea of 'ontological flooding' or an 'opening to the experience itself' as a necessary addition to the reductionist, social facts and phenomenological bracketing of current models of understanding anomalous experiences. Hunter argues that the reductionist approach sees anomalous experiences with the deceased as pathological or hallucinatory. Social facts approaches these experiences 'in which questions about reality are sidestepped in favour of exploring the social value and function of paranormal *beliefs*'.[15] And phenomenological bracketing (Husserl) sets aside the question of reality and turns to 'how the paranormal is experienced and interpreted by the experiencer'.[16] Hunter sees that the models themselves keep the exploration of such experiences 'bound' and unable to be explored apart from these frameworks and suggests that 'ontological flooding' provides a space for potential 'towards greater participation with the anomalous, and a more *empathetic* understanding of the experiential life-worlds of . . . informants'.[17] Hunter stresses:

The literal and the symbolic **15**

'we must be open to the possibility that what they tell us is true and real'.[18] His reasoning behind introducing this fourth approach is that

> [it] encourages us to take the complexity of such experiences seriously and to consider multiple perspectives simultaneously, rather than attempting an explanation in terms of a single . . . framework. For example, continuing bonds may very well perform vital psychological functions for the bereaved, they might very well rely on innate cognitive processes to be experienced and interpreted, and they are certainly socially real, but might they not also relate to some form of independent ontological reality – might there not be 'something more' going on?[19]

Ontological flooding therefore is an openness to the experience itself and Hunter relays how anthropologist Edith Turner's observation of the *Ihamba* healing ritual of the Ndembu in Zambia over many years was significantly surpassed by her actual experience of it:

> Suddenly Meru raised her arms, stretched out in liberation and I *saw* with my own eyes a giant thing emerging out of the flesh of her back. . .I was amazed – delighted. I still laugh with glee at the realization of having seen it.[20]

Turner's 'experiential understanding' prompted her to encourage other anthropologists to 'see what the Natives see'.[21] This type of empathetic understanding goes beyond giving the experient the benefit of the doubt but rather calls for therapists and practitioners to be open enough to their clients' experiences to move with them to integration and meaning-making.

Cameron and Hunter's approach assists in our project in that focus on what the dead are and how they could possibly appear misplaces and displaces the value of their appearance and its meaning in the first instance. Cameron explains that setting aside the 'scientific attitude' allowed her not to interpret her client as her symptoms alone, she sidelined questions of 'what is real' and finally in terms of 'psychological reduction' she 'did not try to explain why [she] was seeing a jellybean wriggling through the air – [she] just described what [she] saw/felt/perceived'.[22] This phenomenological approach enabled her to focus temporally on what was unfolding and to respond with consideration of the jelly bean. In a sense, Cameron engaged in ontological flooding such that a type of resolution to the experience resulted. In this respect, I see Cameron's interpretation of the jelly bean to have been a literal one.

Returning to her encounter for a moment, it is useful to see how she reflected on her own perception of the event.

> If I asked myself which sense I used in order to sense the disappointment conveyed by the jellybean, I would have to say that I don't know, but that I somehow sensed it with my whole body – or perhaps with an outwardly attuned sensitivity that nestles behind the flesh of my torso. And

16 Defining the terrain

> the jellybean itself? I saw that – sort of. I did not see it in quite the same way as I saw Mary, but nor was it purely a mental picture. It seemed to inhabit a space between the physical and the imaginative.[23]

This description is really very useful in that Cameron breaks down the dynamic of sense perception used by therapists perhaps as an unintentional modus operandi and perhaps one would say even unconsciously. That is, perhaps this is a type of intuition that she engaged in as a result of sharing the psychic field with her client. As she describes, due to 'our physical proximity, almost as if she extended into space around her and that I extended into that space'.[24] This suggests that Jung's ability to see the dead might be a varied perceptive process resulting from the encounter with the unconscious.

For Cameron, the literal or the phenomenological moment guided her to the appropriate response and in some respect to resolution. If she had responded with thoughts such as 'why am I seeing this?' or 'what does this mean?' her cognitive distraction would have prevented her from grasping her client's disappointment (the jelly bean).

Cameron's ability to be literal and not move on to a symbolic application is a necessary and important step for our concerns. Von Franz reminds us that, 'Impatience to get to the meaning as quickly as possible must be checked by patient attention to the formal aspect' because Jung warned about trying to 'snatch the meaning out of a few hints too quickly and miss[ing] those contents that might have come to light in a genuine confrontation'.[25] Therefore, although the wont of Jungian psychology is to understand and even mine material for meaning, rushing to this step can miss some crucial if not immediate gems of understanding from the original encounter.

Yet, symbolic interpretation assisted Jung with making public and academic such experiences from his intimately personal material. By interpreting the dead as symbolic, Jung was able to create distance between what might have been embarrassing public admissions and even vocal doubt by his professional circles. A process of going back and forth between literal and objective would be a hallmark of Jung's psychological exposition.

As is evidenced in *The Red Book*, Jung's ego and narrative voice were both decidedly and unwaveringly centred, and this allowed him a method to explore, then to manage his discoveries and eventually interpret them for a professional audience. This later interpretation never dismissed his original encounters. In fact, Jung's commitment to a literal experience guided him to an understanding of how we live alongside our dead, and on behalf of our dead, but also with our unconscious selves.

The tension that has existed between the literal and symbolic interpretation of the dead also has hovered over the distinction between normal vs paranormal. Paranormal and occult are terms that feel worn by years of rejection of experience that is now given a bit more air and space to be considered. I feel we are in an age when 'paranormal' must be replaced by a more contemporary and in

The literal and the symbolic **17**

turn responsive term. To speak to the average person it is difficult to find anyone who has not had a non-ordinary experience that they had difficulty explaining: 'at least one in three people have reported experiencing an [after death communication] sometime in their lives'.[26] The terms 'non-ordinary' or even 'exceptional' or 'anomalous experience' might fit the need for an expression for a visionary experience outside of traditional sight. These terms also sit outside the controversial history of spiritualism. What Jung experienced before and during his *Red Book* period was so much more than paranormal or occult. In fact non-ordinary as a category of experience also falls short in terms of the depth and breadth of how he visioned in unconscious spaces. I suggest it is time we move on from the 'paranormal' to describe anomalous, exceptional or even transrational as integral terms.[27]

How does the literal approach to the dead assist?

When Jung stressed to Aniela Jaffé that it was important when finding one's myth that 'one was together with one's dead', Jung allocated to the dead a function that clearly directed attention to the psyche.[28] The dead assist with orientation and reconciliation of the past and present. As a result of such work a future emerges in which one is more fully aware of the unconscious or paradoxically toward an aware unconscious. Such awareness has a rounding effect, an ability to sense the psyche as part of the conscious/unconscious dynamic. This in turn highlights the guiding forces that influence daily decisions. It was this faculty and Jung's visioning that allowed him to understand the dead in the *Sermones*, who had not had such experiences and therefore carried with them a deficit to their psyches when they passed. When Ezechiel stresses to Jung that he can't join the dead on their way to Jerusalem because he has a body, lack of a physical body was not the deficit that those journeyers suffered. Rather, they carried over from their incarnate lives a deficit in understanding a sense of life after death, or the continuation of life. Their deficit was a psyche that had not grown and developed around the idea of an aware unconscious.

Von Franz had an interest in precognitive death dreams and those that pointed to impending death.[29] She makes the point:

[T]he unconscious pays very little attention to the abrupt end of bodily life and behaves as if the psychic life of the individual, that is the individuation process, will simply continue . . . The unconscious 'believes' quite obviously in a life after death.[30]

Further, von Franz tells a revealing anecdote:

A friend of mine had an experience, in which her dead mother told her, in a dream, that she should work on becoming more conscious, as much as she could, because in the beyond nothing could change any more . . . could they themselves not acquire knowledge any longer? It seems to be a paradox.[31]

18 Defining the terrain

If we take the function of the dead literally then we are able to metabolise the experience personally, starting from the significant moment that speaks to each one of us. It requires us to engage with and answer the dead, where and how they are. If we start with a symbolic understanding, this risks diluting the moment to a meaning that might partially address the reasons for the visitation or sighting, but might not encompass the experience in its totality, it might just fall short. Yet, if we move on to the symbolic *from* the literal, we have the deep satisfaction of having assimilated the encounter's literal meaning in whatever direction it leads, and then the symbolic might just guide us to a broadening of understanding of our unconscious selves.[32]

The point here is that to default to a symbolic position without first acknowledging the dead's literal presence disallows and disengages the steps needed to integrate the experience of seeing them and determining why they have come in the first instance. It is not only a disservice to dismiss the dead *in se* as a psychological if not a metaphysical encounter, but it is unethical.

People often wonder, 'Why do the dead return?' There are as many reasons for this as there are people who are asking the question, they come for the very specific reason that the experient has encountered them and this is different for everyone. A literal approach to the dead allows for meaning-making to happen, which is specific, intimate and evolutionary to each person, for that time and that place.

For Jung it was to guide and teach him about the unconscious and to make him a veritable specialist in visioning; to make him a specialist in their language of symbolic communication. For others, it might be a message to locate them physically in the unconscious, to grow their perception, and still for others to have those unanswered questions resolved: 'You are not alone', 'I will always love you' and even, 'The insurance papers are in the bottom drawer of the desk'.

Notes

1   *MDR*, p. 217.
2   Nick Totton, 'Funny You Should Say That: Paranormality, at the Margins and the Centre of Psychotherapy', *European Journal of Psychotherapy & Counselling* 9, no. 4 (1 December 2007): 390.
3   Sarah Blalock and Janice Holden, 'Preparing Students to Counsel Clients with Potentially Spiritually Transformative Experiences', *Counselling and Values* 63 (April 2018): 33.
4   Elizabeth. C. Roxburgh and Rachel E. Evenden, '"Most People Think You're a Fruit-Loop": Clients' Experiences of Seeking Support for Anomalous Experiences', *Counselling and Psychotherapy Research* 16 (2016): 211–221.
5   Martina Belz, 'Clinical Psychology for People with Exceptional Experiences in Practice', in *Exceptional Experiences in Health: Essays on Mind, Body and Human Potential*, ed. Christine Simmonds-Moore (Jefferson, NC: McFarland, 2012), p. 224.
6   E. Baeur, M. Belz, W. Fach, R. Fangmeier, C. Schuppe-Ihle and A. Wiedemer, 'Counselling at the IGPP-an Overview', in *Perspectives of Clinical Parapsychology An Introductory Reader*, eds. W. H. Kramer, E. Baeur and G. H. Hövelmann (The Netherlands: Stichting Het Johan Borgman Fonds, 2012), p. 154.
7   Michele Knight, *Ways of Being: The Alchemy of Bereavement and Communiqué* (Unpublished doctoral thesis, University of Sydney, 2013), pp. 54–55, https://ses.library.usyd.edu.au/handle/2123/13764 (accessed 16 May 2008).

The literal and the symbolic **19**

8 Elizabeth C. Roxburgh and Rachel E. Evenden, '"They Daren't Tell People":Therapists' Experiences of Working with Clients Who Report Anomalous Experiences'. *European Journal of Psychotherapy & Counselling* 18, no. 2: 123–141.

9 Rose Cameron, 'The Paranormal as an Unhelpful Concept in Psychotherapy and Counselling Research', *European Journal of Psychotherapy & Counselling* 18, no. 2 (2012): 142.

10 Ibid. I suspect this approach is the reason there has been continued academic discussion in the discipline of counselling due to this position regarding both clients' experiences as well as counsellors' reports of the uncanny during sessions.

11 S. M. Dannenbaum and R. T. Kinnier, 'Imaginal Relationships with the Dead: Applications for Psychotherapy', *Journal of Humanistic Psychology* 49, no. 1 (2007): 111.

12 Cameron, 'The Paranormal', p. 45.

13 Ibid., p. 149.

14 Ibid., p. 146.

15 Jack Hunter, 'Ontological Flooding and Continuing Bonds', in *Continuing Bonds in Bereavement: New Directions for Research and Practice*, eds. Dennis Klass and Edith Maria Steffen (London: Routledge, 2017), p. 195.

16 Ibid., p. 191.

17 Ibid., p. 197.

18 Ibid.

19 Ibid, p. 198

20 Edith Turner, *Experiencing Ritual: A New Approach to African Healing* (Philadelphia: University of Pennsylvania Press, 1998), p. 149, cited in Hunter, 'Ontological Flooding', p. 197.

21 Edith Turner, 'The Reality of Spirits: A Tabooed or Permitted Field of Study?' *Anthropology of Consciousness* 4, no. 1 (1993): 9–12.

22 Cameron, 'The Paranormal', p. 151.

23 Ibid., p. 152.

24 Ibid. Pillard has successfully described a dynamic definition of intuition. The idea of the 'under-conscious' looks to trace the space between consciousness and the unconscious and is defined and mediated by what Pillard identifies as intuition. Here intuition is somewhat like the tool for the space that assists with the concept of movement and formulation of meaning from the unconscious to consciousness.

25 Marie-Louise von Franz, *C. G. Jung: His Myth in Our Time* (Toronto: Inner City Books, 1998), p. 112.

26 Jenny Streit-Horn, 'A Systematic Review of Research on After-Death Communication (ADC)' (Unpublished doctoral dissertation, University of North Texas, Denton, 2011), p. 73, https://digital.library.unt.edu/ark:/67531/metadc84284/m1/1.

27 Jerome Bernstein introduced the idea of transrational reality in *Living in the Borderland: The Evolution of Consciousness and the Challenge of Healing Trauma*. (Hove, UK: Routledge, 2005, p. xv).

28 Shamdasani, 'The Boundless Expanse', pp. 26–27.

29 She also saw in dreams instances of 'the end of bodily life … which always also contain statements … that point to an afterlife'. It is this reason that Jung, she suggests, encouraged aging people to explore death. Von Franz, *On Dreams & Death*, p. x.

30 Ibid., p. ix.

31 Marie-Louise von Franz, 'Archetypes Surrounding Death', *Quadrant* 12, no. 1 (Summer 1979): 18.

32 Pilard's idea of an under-conscious sits interactively between the unconscious and consciousness. She describes: 'Jung's under-conscious is a state in between the unconscious and consciousness, where symbolical and literal are equivalent – the very moment, for instance when someone has a vision.' Nathalie Pilard, *Jung and Intuition: On the Centrality and Variety of Forms of Intuition in Jung and Post-Jungians* (London: Karnac, 2015), p. 57. I am proposing that instead of taking these moments as 'equivalent' that starting with the literal will give the experient more opportunity for integration of meaning.

3

JUNG'S WAYS OF SEEING

To call Jung a visionary may be to misplace attention and to underestimate his actual skills. There is evidence of a wide variety of visionary experiences in Jung's personal material including: active imagination, lucid dreaming, waking dreams (metachoric visions[1]), prescient visions, channelling, remote viewing, near-death experience (NDE), out-of-body experience, interpsychic rapport[2] and the ability to discern figures in their various states within an unconscious dynamic. The stories relayed by his first circle of analysts, that Jung could interpret a client's dream without hearing it, would fit comfortably within his skill set.

The reason for surveying Jung's visioning is not simply to exemplify how deft he was, but to confirm his ability to discern various types of material in unconscious spaces. This process assisted him in being able to devise psychological theories about the relationship between the unconscious, its workings and consciousness. Thus, when referring to 'the dead' we can assume that Jung was able to discern nuanced visual content, which for him appeared differently to other figures of the unconscious.

In a sense, Jung became his own adept or 'was his own medium'.[3] As he continued, his experiences reinforced a first-hand encounter with the multiplicity and multidimensional nature of his psyche and in turn assisted with his understanding and incorporation of it. Pilard's discussion of C. Maillard makes the point that 'what is to come' is a process of creating a future from the present: 'it starts now, in the present of its enunciation'.[4] I might add that Jung's ability to use what he learned while learning it, allowed him to understand the timeless and multifaceted present, that is the presence of the psyche, or the psyche in the present. Pilard calls this his 'present practice, or, rather, present testing of the method within himself'.[5] By incorporating more understanding into his movement within active imagination, he became more conscious and in turn more centred in a psychic perspective, which expanded his visionary faculty and visionary knowing. This process became Jung's individuation.

Inextricably linked to his visionary experiences are those of the dead, who in fact introduced Jung to his visioning. In many (if not perhaps all) instances his first visionary occasions were linked to the dead, death, ensuing death and mass death: 'It is not simply that we see our dead loved ones in visions after they have left us, the dearly departed are the seat of the visioning faculty itself.'[6]

Apparitions, ghosts and spectres were the players and the unconscious the location. The fact that he not only recounted these aspects of visionary skill and contextualised these experiences for a psychology that hosted an unconscious dynamic inclusive of the dead, is a testament to his dedication to his own process. Although obviously frustrated at times, and feeling decidedly misunderstood, his descriptions of varied states of visioning have expanded our understanding of the unconscious within a psychological framework.

The breadth of Jung's ways of seeing

By way of example, two of Jung's experiences, the garden party dream and his NDE exemplify his extensive visioning skill. Each highlights his ability to discern content within context. Although both experiences occurred much later than *The Red Book* material, they are useful to examine because they demonstrate the breadth, depth and faculty that Jung developed, I would propose, as a result of his early encounters with the dead before and during his confrontation. Each example reveals Jung's discernment of the experience and his description as he understood it to have unfolded. It is worth noting that although each episode is quite different in terms of locale, feeling tone and method, each reveals the multifaceted nature and process of the unconscious as it includes the dead.

Where the garden party scene comes from the depths of dreaming, Jung's near-death visions occurred within an expanded sense of space and time and describe an ecstatic experience. In each example he clearly identifies the dead as well as impending death, in both instances prescient, and we assume this is due to a nuanced discernment of the unconscious field he has entered.

The garden party dream

In the garden party dream (post 1935), Jung was surprised to see his sister as she had died some years previously.[7] Here Jung is able not only to identify the players in the dream, but more specifically to observe and detail their relationship to the unconscious. He recounts the people in attendance were, 'A deceased friend . . . people who were still alive . . . [and] my sister was accompanied by a lady I knew well. Even in the dream I [concluded] the lady was going to die. "She is marked."'[8] Jung's ability to distinguish in a dream context those living (attendees), those dead (his sister and his friend) and those about to die (the lady) is notable. The dream holds an added quality of being prescient as well as verified. Jung tells us that although upon waking he could not remember who the lady was, and only remembered weeks later when a friend died in an accident, he recalled that it was her he had seen in the dream. The ability

22 Defining the terrain

to discern such qualitative differences within the same unconscious space is skilled and suggests a refinement on Jung's part when reading unconscious material. Jung identified the status of each character in the dream context because he confirms that it was during the dream that this knowledge became clear.[9] The assumption here is that the dead appear different next to those who are still alive within an unconscious (dream) context and those transitioning. Perhaps they appear not as dense as those who are still living and in the same dream space. The alternative possibility is that Jung simply knows each person in context and this knowledge is facilitated by his visioning of the dream. It is difficult to discern if he learns the status of each player through what he is seeing or if he simply knows. Or still again if it is a linking of the visionary information along with his cognitive assessment and these two pieces of information together facilitate his designation of each player in the dream.

In Jung's telling we see that the unconscious terrain is host to the incarnate, the discarnate and a place where veridical details related to consciousness coexist. His discernment of competing psychic material assured him what he was seeing and his knowing was to be confirmed enough times that he trusted what the psyche was showing him. His ability to recognise these various players and their ontological designation reveals Jung's increased acceptance of his visionary ability.

A further example of his prescient sense occurred when he was on a train and experienced a vision of someone drowning.[10] Again, the vision had to do with a potential death. When he arrived home, he learned that his grandson, who did not know how to swim, had fallen into the water and was saved by his brother. He attributed the image to a memory of an incident that occurred when he was stationed in the military. Yet this happened while he was on the train. In this respect his visioning had been distracted by a memory that aligned with what was happening simultaneously. His psyche provided simultaneous cues to an event of import, and although he does not allude to the vision being of his grandson drowning, the memory recalled served as a proxy to the knowledge of the event occurring at the same time. His metachoric visioning replaced his physical location on the train to a time/place of significance.[11] Or the imposition into his mental field was caused by the intensity of a family trauma. Jung referred to such occasions as 'spontaneous foreknowledge'[12] and of course has qualities of synchronicity. Main explains:

> Such incidents raise the question of how a person's mind can register images of things that are simultaneously happening a great distance away or, even more radically, have not yet happened but will do so in the future . . . it seems that the way in which time and space normally operate to allow for the transmission of information between events and images has been bypassed. There seems to be an immediate connection between the events and the images regardless of their separation in space and time . . . [this] led Jung to hypothesise that in the unconscious psyche the categories of space and time do not operate in the same way as they do in the world of conscious experience. [Jung] speaks of the 'relativisation' and even of the 'abolition' of time and space in the unconscious.[13]

Jung's near-death and out-of-body experience

The specificity of Jung's visioning appears also during what is known as his out-of-body experience after his heart attack in 1944, the second example. In fact, Jung's experience here serves as a textbook case of an NDE where he explains being on death's door. This proved to be significant for him, at some points lasting well over an hour and over a period of three weeks. Whereas his previous active imaginations accounted for in *The Red Book* dealt with plunging to the depths, these visions related to expansiveness, heights and might be described as peak experiences.

NDE: breaking it down

Cardiologist Pim van Lommel has researched near death and out-of-body experiences prompted by his patients' experiences. He defines NDE as, 'The reported memory of a range of impressions during a special state of consciousness, [and] is usually transformational, causing enhanced intuitive sensibility, profound changes of life insight, and the loss of the fear of death.'[14]

Many of these qualities Jung experienced and proved significant as he moved towards integrating its meaning. Specifically, the range of details in Jung's experience coincide neatly with psychiatrist Bruce Greyson's scale of NDE traits.[15] It is worth considering not that Jung had an NDE accompanied by out-of-body details, but that considering his skills at visioning this had not happened sooner. Someone as comfortable with his unconscious by that time might have had such an experience much earlier in his life.

Table 3.1 highlights Greyson's NDE attributes specific to Jung's description of the experience as it is relayed in *Memories, Dreams, Reflections*. Although Greyson discusses more categories in the scale, Table 3.1 signifies how many of the attributes Jung experienced and how typical his NDE proved to be.

TABLE 3.1 Greyson's NDE attributes specific to Jung's description as detailed in *Memories, Dreams, Reflections*

Did you feel separated from your body?	'I was high up in space' (p. 321) 'I floated' (p. 323)
Unnaturally brilliant light	'I saw . . . earth, bathed in a gloriously blue light' (p. 320)
Life review/ego loss	'I had the feeling that everything was being sloughed away . . . the whole . . . earthly existence, fell away . . . I now carried along with me everything I had ever experienced or done' (p. 321)
A mystical or unearthly being?	'A black Hindu sat silently in lotus posture . . . I knew that he expected me' (p. 321)

(continued)

24 Defining the terrain

TABLE 3.1 *(continued)*

Thoughts unusually vivid	'I consisted of my own history, and I felt with great certainty: this is what I am. I am this bundle of what has been' (p. 322)
	'My life seemed to have been snipped out of a long chain of events and many questions had remained unanswered' (p. 322)
Sudden understanding	'I knew at once: "Aha, this is my doctor of course . . . he is coming in his primal form"' (p. 322)
Border or point of no return	'I had reached the outermost limit' (p. 320)
	'[T]here was a protest . . . I had no right to leave the earth and must return. The moment I heard that the vision ceased' (p. 323)
Feeling of peace Feeling of joy	'It was as if I were in ecstasy . . . filled with the highest possible feeling of happiness. "This is eternal bliss . . . This cannot be described; it is far too wonderful!"' (pp. 324–325)

A recent survey of Americans found that 4 per cent, almost 9 million people, have experienced an NDE.[16] Greyson describes the NDE as: 'The paradoxical occurrence of a heightened, lucid awareness and logical thought processed during a period of impaired cerebral perfusions raises particular perplexing questions for our current understanding of consciousness and its relation to brain function.'[17] The perennial question is if the NDE is actually occurring and therefore what people report in terms of out-of-body sensations is really happening or due to the brain's traumatic changes these experiences are a physical by-product of decreased neurological capacity.

Current research found some intriguing discoveries about the brain during recall of NDEs:

> A recent electroencephalographic study showed that, at neural functioning level, NDE recall more closely resembles remembrances of real-life events than of imagined life events. NDE memories are stored as episodic memories of events that have occurred in an atypical state of consciousness (Palmieri et al., 2014). This means that people who have had a NDE have memories of something that they actually experienced, and examining the features of these memories should help us to understand why such experiences are perceived as so profound and upsetting.[18]

This might explain Jung's response and later conclusions about his experience: he knew that he was dying and convinced that he was at least a thousand miles high in

Jung's ways of seeing **25**

space and able to perceive both countries and bodies of water from that vantage. With such expanded awareness he knew he was experiencing himself 'in an objective form' and concluded most likely this is why he was able to see his doctor in his.[19]

This recognition occurred in 'unconsciousness', and highlights the paradox of metachoric visions, which replace the physical setting of the experient with an entirely different scene. Since this included not simply visionary impressions but sensory as well, Jung demonstrated his ability to be lucid and participatory, while grasping the distinction between what he was seeing as visions and the hospital room where he lay.[20] This is particularly evident as he had these intense experiences on and off over a three-week period.

The quality of floating and the type of detail he shares make this convincingly an out-of-body experience as well, similar to that of an ex-static experience:

> In ex-stasis either a part or all of the subject's consciousness principle, usually conceptualised as the 'soul' or 'spirit' separates from the physical body and it is this disembodied soul-substance or spirit-substance that is reputed to be the agency that performs deeds or perceives things that are otherwise impossible while one is in the ordinary waking state subject to the normal limitations of the physical body.[21]

This *ex-static* condition looks to be what Jung experienced. An out-of-body awareness with expanded sensations resulted in his ability to perceive his doctor in his 'primal form'. Jung concludes that had he not been experiencing his own objective state at that time, perhaps he would not have seen this same quality in his doctor. This appearance signalled to Jung that the doctor would be dying soon.[22] Of course, the purpose of the doctor's appearance was to tell Jung that the doctor had been directed to inform Jung to return to his earthly life, which Jung did begrudgingly.[23] Their communication with one another unsurprisingly took the form of exchanging thoughts and from this again Jung gleaned that the doctor would be passing soon thereafter.

The most significant effect of his out-of-body experience is that Jung described it as ecstasy. And although he identified qualities of endless expansiveness and even vast emptiness, he felt he had experienced 'eternal bliss'.[24]

Religious scholar Jesse Hollenback describes:

> Ecstasy . . . refer[s] to [a] state . . . of such intensity that the mystic loses awareness of both his or her physical environment and body . . . [it] implies an even more radical process of abstraction from the body and the physical world . . . that sensation . . . of literally seeming to stand outside of themselves . . . from a vantage point exterior to it.[25]

This peak experience stands in obvious contrast with the difficulties Jung faced throughout his earlier material. *The Red Book* shows the womb of the universe in a much different light, including the dead, death and dissolution as a part of

26 Defining the terrain

life's cycle. Here Jung experienced an all-encompassing bliss where he grasped creation in its various forms, perhaps a quality he might recognise during his own death.[26]

Jung wrote to Kristine Mann about his illness, 'On the whole my illness proved to be a most valuable experience, which gave me the inestimable opportunity of a glimpse behind the veil . . . I was free, completely free and whole, as I never felt before.'[27] Thus, he emerged profoundly moved by what he saw and entered into a new stage of productivity, buoyed by his visions of the end. Thus it is not surprising that Jung would describe what he gleaned from the experience as such,

> I am absolutely convinced of personal survival, but I do not know how long it persists. I have an idea that it is (. . .) or (. . .) months – I get this idea from dreams . . . I am absolutely convinced of the survival of the personality – for a time, + of the marvellous experience of being dead. I absolutely hated coming back, I did not want to come. It was much better to die – just marvellous and far surpassing any experience I have ever had.[28]

Jung's descriptions in his chapter 'Visions' reveal his perception and understanding of the transition between incarnate and discarnate realities of soul, including the sensation of being separated from the physical body. In a letter to Cary Baynes about the visions, Jung describes:

> The soul seems to detach from the body pretty early and there seems to be almost no realisation of death. What follows is well nigh incredible. It seems to be an adventure greater and more expected than anything one could dream of.[29]

Where he experienced *The Red Book* material as an incarnate, firmly planted in physical space with a centred narrative voice, this experience saw Jung detaching his soul from his body resulting in expansive perceptions. Jung experiences what the dead, who received the *Sermones*, were trying to grasp, but too late.

His descriptions of the images of the sacred weddings (*mysterium coniunctionis*) suggest being released from his incarnate state to be united with the vastness of the unconscious also experienced by the collective dead.[30] But, his descriptions go even further than his journeys through *The Red Book*. The difference here is that he experiences these images as one who has pondered the conditions of being discarnate, of being a soul on his way to a full discarnate state while fully cognisant of the spiritual knowing he grasped about the dead throughout *The Red Book*. He encountered these visions as someone who had been working on and in the unconscious for many years and was already knowledgeable about the psyche. This experience provided for him the depth of soul knowing that he had been lacking.[31]

Jung's ability to experience this blissful ecstasy perhaps is in part as a result of his service to the dead and his understanding of the suffering of the collective dead to accept their discarnate states. As he processed his *Red Book* experiences to begin

Jung's ways of seeing **27**

to grasp the capacities of the unconscious, all of this *prima materia* enabled him to vision with such expansiveness and acceptance, thus the reason he describes the experience so positively. He had a lifetime of honing his visionary capacities in unconscious contexts culminating with this fully expansive visioning. Certainly his statement of grasping all days simultaneously is a profound perspective of the unconscious and a moment of individuation if not an opportunity to glimpse briefly at his own evolution towards death.

Notes

1 Metachoric visions are those 'in which the normal perceptual environment is entirely replaced by an hallucinatory one, which may on occasion be a convincing replica of the world of normal perception'. Celia Green and Charles McCreery, *Lucid Dreaming: The Paradox of Consciousness During Sleep* (London: Routledge, 1994, p. 56). I feel considering that *C. G. Jung and the Dead* has as a principle the nuances of the visionary experience, a term like hallucination sits outside the discussions here. In this type of vision, Jung's external environment is replaced by a vision that in some instances is veridical and therefore the term does not capture what occurred. Green and McCreery's explanation is worth considering here. 'Metachoric' is composed of the Greek word for change and the word for place: 'The word in its literal connotation is perhaps most appropriate in the case of out-of-the-body experiences and some waking dreams, in which there is an apparent displacement of the subject's point of view; reasonably appropriate in the case of lucid dreams and false awakening ... and least appropriate in the case of apparitional experiences, in which the subject usually continues to "see" the world from the normal point of view. However it proved difficult to find roots which more exactly corresponded to the rather abstract idea of "replacing the entire perceptual field with a hallucinatory one".' Green and McCreery, *Lucid Dreaming*, p. 170 n. 2.
2 This term I suggest includes the intentional focus and engagement of active imagination without the final stage of the transcendent function, which I contend does not work with the dead *in se*. Stephens, 'Active Imagination and the Dead'.
3 C. G. Jung, '"S.W." and C. G. Jung: Mediumship, Psychiatry and Serial Exemplarity', *History of Psychiatry* 26, no. 3 (2015): 288–302, at 297.
4 Pilard, *Jung and Intuition*, p. 91.
5 Ibid.
6 Mogenson, *Greeting the Angels*, p. 8.
7 *MDR*, p. 334. It is interesting that the only other mention of his sister is in regards to her birth and death. Jung mentions feeling distrustful of his sister's birth (*MDR*, p. 41) and this could have been due to Emilie's previous miscarriages. Deirdre Bair, *Jung: A Biography* (New York: Back Bay Books, 2003), p. 18. About his sister's death, Jung mentions how moved he was to discover that she, after going in for a routine operation did not survive, but had put her affairs in order beforehand (*MDR*, p. 133).
8 *MDR*, p. 334.
9 Ibid.
10 *MDR*, p. 333.
11 Green and McCreery, *Lucid Dreaming*, p. 56.
12 *MDR*, p. 335.
13 Main, *The Rupture of Time*, p. 26. This is not unlike the telling of Swedenborg's vision of the fire. C. G. Jung, 'Synchronicity: An Acausal Connecting Principle', in *CW* 8 (1955), pp. 481 and 483.
14 Pim van Lommel, 'Near-Death Experiences: The Experience of the Self as Real and Not as an Illusion', *Annals of the New York Academy of Sciences* 1234, no. 1 (2011): 19.
15 Bruce Greyson, 'Congruence Between Near-Death and Mystical Experience', *International Journal for the Psychology of Religion* 24, no. 4 (2014): 298–310. Although

28 Defining the terrain

Jung's account of being stripped of himself falls into the ego-loss category, entering the temple to speak to the Hindu looked more like the life-review category, which he was not to complete.

16 Bruce Greyson. 'Getting comfortable with near death experiences. An overview of near-death experiences'. *Missouri Medicine*, 110, no. 6 (2013): 475–481.

17 Ibid., p. 22.

18 Simone Bianco, Marco Sambin and Arianna Palmieri, 'Meaning Making After a Near-Death Experience: The Relevance of Intrapsychic and Interpersonal Dynamics', *Death Studies* 41, no. 9 (2017): 562–573.

19 *MDR*, p. 322. Jung compares this experience to his encounter with his deceased wife in which he saw her in total objectivity. This appears partly as a quality that comes with discarnates or perhaps is credited to Jung's increased clarity during encounters with discarnates.

20 In the hospital episode in *The Red Book*, Jung experienced a vision within a vision. This is not the same as a vision that replaces a current active imagination. In this instance, Jung is not replacing one active imagination for another, or one scene for another, rather he was experiencing himself quite physically in the hospital within an active imagination, then experiencing a further distraction with physical attributes that pulled him deeper into the unconscious, as indicated with his feeling of being on a ship (*RB*, p. 298a).

21 Jess Hollenback, *Mysticism: Experience, Response, Empowerment* (University Park, PA: Penn State University Press, 1996), pp. 136–137.

22 *MDR*, p. 324. This state is resonant of 'the mark' Jung saw in his friend at the garden party, which foretold her impending death. Also, a similar perspective emerged when Jung saw Emma after she died exuding an objective presence that only could have been perceived by Jung in a state able to perceive it.

23 *MDR*, p. 323.

24 Ibid., p. 324. In reference to another quote: 'death with its cold embrace is the maternal womb'. C. G. Jung, *Symbols of Transformation*, in *The Collected Works*, eds. William McGuire, trans. R. F. C. Hull, Vol. 5 (Princeton, NJ: Princeton University Press, 1956), p. 218 (hereafter cited as *SOT*, *CW*, vol. 5).

25 Hollenback, *Mysticism*, pp. 136–137.

26 *MDR*, p. 326.

27 C. G. Jung, *Letters: 1906–1950*, Vol. 1 (Princeton, NJ: Princeton University Press, 1992), pp. 357–359, as cited in Shamdasani, 'The Boundless Expanse', p. 23.

28 Ibid.

29 Ibid., p. 24.

30 Jung describes several unions and weddings (*MDR*, p. 325). That he attributes these celebrations occurring 'in the afterlife' holds obvious significance and points to the soul preparing to sever from the body to return to its source. He made note of a similar experience upon hearing of his mother's death that although he felt grief he could hear music and laughter (*MDR*, p. 345).

31 Brazilian psychologist L. A. Gasparatto claims that 'there are many people suffering from illnesses that have their origins in the spirit world … a little recognized yet essential aspect of healing is for the living to learn how to die peacefully and honourably and the dying to learn to enter consciously into the spirit world … the awareness of the continuity of life after death is an essential part of the healing process.' Alberto Villoldo and Stanley Krippner, *Healing States: A Journey Into the World of Spiritual Healing and Shamanism* (New York: Fireside Books, 1986), p. 7.

4

JUNG'S PRIMARY ORIENTATION TO THE DEAD

It is well known that Jung experienced a curious identification with two tangible aspects of his personality, No. 1 and No. 2.[1] He described them as 'two different persons' and yet, he insisted, this was not about 'dissociation'.[2] In spite of Jung's attributions of each, some scholars have disregarded Jung's own assessment and concluded he was 'narcissistic (Homans, 1979) . . . schizophrenic (Winnicott, 1964)' and probably had, 'some form of dissociative disorder'.[3] Yet, even retrospectively Jung never identified anything pathological in the dynamic. His self-reflection and ability to define this quality indicates a solid ego and in turn a decidedly centred narrative voice throughout *The Red Book*.

Although the two often vied for influence, at other times they seemed to sit side by side.[4] No. 2 was seminal in importance and was like a spirit 'perpetually present'.[5] The fact that Jung related his No. 2 as being both dead and alive revealed that his self-perception was fundamentally linked and inherently tied to a presence of or an orientation to immortality. This discernment is indicative of having experienced, even as a child, the expansiveness of the psyche and an ability to locate in such expansiveness his self and his No. 2, perhaps a practice that would later assist him with visioning.

What is evidenced in *The Red Book* is that No. 2, or the spirit of the depths, was *foundational* in managing Jung's journey to and through the unconscious.[6] Not only does the spirit of the depths link Jung to the deepest reaches of his unconscious and to the dead, but he plays a seminal role in assisting him to locate and identify his soul as a singular entity.[7] The spirit of the depths then facilitates an initiation for Jung into his visual faculty.[8] Whereas the spirit of the depths 'possesses a greater power', the spirit of the times changes with generations.[9]

As Jung clearly considered No. 2 ever present, it is no wonder that during his university years he took up the topic of the existence of ghosts. This appears as an

30 Defining the terrain

attempt to legitimise the potent acknowledgment that this second personality was a reality he lived with daily and did so consciously.[10]

Elijah and Philemon

The relationship between the spirit of the depths and his No. 2 personality must be noted as similar again to both figures, Elijah and Philemon. Jung confirms how Philemon evolved from Elijah, while he also notes Philemon's relationship to No. 2 as 'the "ancient"' was always there and would survive into the future.[11]

This correspondence between the spirit of the depths as Jung's No. 2, Elijah and Philemon reveals the similar perspective that each figure shares, one oriented in the collective unconscious and one inherently positioned to assist Jung with his relationship to the dead. Given Philemon's role as 'teacher and friend of the dead', he serves as a convenor of the dead and a medium between their community and the living Jung. [12]

Notes

1 *MDR*, pp. 50, 51, 62, 84, 108, 252.
2 Ibid, p. 62.
3 Brian Skea, 'Trauma, Transference and Transformation: A Study of Jung's Treatment of His Cousin, Hélène, A Jungian Perspective on the Dissociability of the Self and on the Psychotherapy of the Dissociative Disorders', *The Jung Page* (3 February 1995) [online], www.cgjungpage.org/learn/articles/analytical-psychology/802-a-jungian-perspective-on-the-dissociability-of-the-self (accessed 10 May 2009).
4 *MDR*, p. 84.
5 Ibid.
6 Shamdasani equates the spirit of the times and the spirit of the depths with Jung's No. 1 and No. 2 respectively (*RB*, p. 208a).
7 *RB*, p. 232b.
8 Ibid., p. 235b.
9 Ibid., p. 229b.
10 This also seems to be Jung engaging to understand his encounter with his deceased father the same year. This is discussed in more detail in Chapter 5, 'The big dream'.
11 *MDR*, p. 252.
12 *RB*, p. 316b.

5

THE BIG DREAM

In 1896, Jung's father died. Jung was present and noted the process of deterioration but was intrigued.[1] This was Jung's first personal and significant death remembered with clarity even years later. Six weeks later his father appeared in a dream, which now can be considered an after-death communication (ADC).[2] He recalls his father suddenly appeared to say that he was back from a holiday and returning home, Jung responded feeling 'ashamed because [he] . . . imagined he was dead'.[3]

The way Jung presents the dream suggests that he experienced *seeing* his deceased father appear, rather than dreaming *about* him. This distinction differentiates a visitation dream, i.e. an ADC, from a dream experience in which his father was playing a symbolic role. Jung is surprised that the appearance of his father seemed exactly as if he were there: 'People often speak of a visitation dream as feeling "realer than real", and when the dreamers awaken these electrifying feelings carry over into waking awareness, remaining surprisingly strong and easy to recollect many years later.'[4] His shame results from imagining his father to be dead and this is significant because it reveals he has now allocated his father somewhere, to a place in the psyche.[5]

When Jung wonders, 'What does it mean that my father returns in dreams?'[6] he has posed a very different question than 'why' he is dreaming about his father. In a sense, Jung is really asking, 'What does it mean that my deceased father has returned and I am able to see him?' The assumption is that Jung's father has taken his place among the dead and returns to visit.[7]

The dream was 'unforgettable' and it prompted him to contemplate the possibility of after-death survival.[8] Jung certainly would have pondered this before the death of his father, especially considering his family background. But, it is the profound personal nature of the experience, which prompts him to look further into the possibility of life after death. Later that same year, Jung would explore this topic in the Zofingia lectures where he would advocate for the validity of an immortal soul.

32 Defining the terrain

This profoundly moving visitation dream can be viewed as, what Jung would call, a 'big' dream. The dream was powerfully emotional and prompts him to delve into a much larger question: after-death survival. I suggest that due to this dream, his profound interest in the dead would continue throughout *The Red Book* and would spur his intense speculation throughout his life about the unconscious as a place and process. In this respect, the content of the dream transcended his personal relationship with his father and became principally 'a universally human problem, which because it [had] been overlooked subjectively forces itself objectively upon the dreamer's consciousness'.[9] The telling of the dream retrospectively shows Jung to have considered it a major moment in his life. Its resonance and significance remained with him from the time it occurred to its telling in *Memories, Dreams, Reflections* many years later.

'Big dreams' also point to their perceived derivation. Jung asserted that the 'collective unconscious . . . lies at a deeper level and is further removed from consciousness than the personal unconscious . . . the big or "meaningful" dreams come from this deeper level'.[10] He designates a location for such dreams while also suggesting a type of psychological typography, which assists in laying the terrain of the unconscious in general. This is more vividly described in *The Red Book* where the collective unconscious is seen as deeper and existing in layers, seasons and times. When Jung dreams or rather falls asleep within an ongoing active imagination, this indicates his ability to access varied levels of the unconscious.[11]

In his chapter 'On Life After Death', Jung describes the relativity of psychic existence where the further away perspective is from consciousness the closer 'to an absolute condition of timelessness and spacelessness'.[12] From the examination of various dreams and visions, what becomes apparent is the perceived location of the dead in terms of Jung's conscious awareness *as an incarnate participant*. It is significant that his father might have come from a deeper place in the unconscious and, at the same time, to have felt so 'real'. This suggests the possibility that it is not necessarily the quality exuded by the deceased Paul Jung that locates him in the unconscious (although it could very well be), but perhaps it is Jung's ability to *perceive* this distance and in turn his deceased father that lends him this 'real' quality. Dream researcher Kelly Bulkeley suggests that visitation dreams or dreams in which deceased friends or family appear are often described as 'incredibly vivid and intense, so unlike "ordinary" dreams that . . . people wonder if they were even sleeping during the experience. The dead person, they say, was *really there* . . . it felt as real as anything in waking life.'[13]

More succinctly, it is the degree of consciousness that Jung brings to his visioning encounter that might influence the degree of clarity in how and what he sees. Throughout Jung's dreams and active imaginations, his incarnate perspective becomes more significant in defining what is occurring within his visioning.

Toni and Emma: where are they exactly?

During a conversation in 1957 between Jung and Aneila Jaffé, Jung discussed a dream he had of Toni Wolff coming back to life, 'there had been a type of misunderstanding that she had died, and she had returned to live a further part of her life'.[14] During the discussion Jung shared the impression

> that Toni Wolff was nearer the earth, that she could manifest herself better to him, whilst his wife was on another level where he couldn't reach her. He concluded that Toni Wolff was in the neighbourhood, that she was nearer the sphere of three dimensional existence, and hence had the chance to come into existence again.[15]

This description is an important one in that Jung was not dreaming *about* a deceased Toni Wolff, but that she, in her post-mortem form, appeared to him because she was 'closer to earth', closer to his personal unconscious and 'could manifest herself better'. The description again favours a literal interpretation as Jung does not frame the dream in terms of attachments or projections of a subjective psyche. Similar to the visitation dream of Jung's father, having returned from holiday prepared to take up his place again among the living, it might be plausible to suggest the two visitation dreams were derived from similar levels of the unconscious. Although Paul Jung's dream could be derived from a deeper level of the unconscious, on each occasion Jung mistakes them for being dead. Again, this might be due primarily to the level of conscious perception that Jung is applying within the unconscious dynamic, or the level he has dreamed into that permits him access to visitations.

Jung contrasts the type of dream encounter that he had with Toni with where he thinks Emma might be. That 'he couldn't reach her' seems to point to his attempt at trying to do so. Similarly, as Jung imagined his father to be dead, he has identified his deceased wife somewhere, and that somewhere is difficult to locate. The reason could very well have something to do with what Jung described in a letter to Erich Neumann, shortly after Emma Jung's death:

> [T]wo days before the death of my wife, I had what one can only call a great illumination which, like a flash of lightning, lit up a centuries-old secret that was embodied in her and had exerted an unfathomable influence on my life. I can only suppose that the illumination came from my wife, who was then mostly in a coma and that the tremendous lighting up and release of insight had a retroactive effect upon her, and was one reason why she could die such a painless and royal death . . . this experience [has] been a great comfort to me. But the stillness and the audible silence about me, the empty air and the infinite distance are hard to bear.[16]

The conditions surrounding Emma's passing seem to locate her in 'another level'. This could be likened to the difference between personal dreams and big dreams, the latter stemming from deeper in the unconscious. Here, we have an insinuation that the dead inhabit various levels of the unconscious either closer to consciousness or further away and perhaps dependent on their plans next. Toni, being closer indicated her ability to incarnate easier with the added benefit of appearing to Jung

34 Defining the terrain

more clearly. Whereas, the 'great illumination' that Jung experienced with Emma launched her further or deeper into another level of the unconscious, perhaps due to what might follow next in her life as a member of the deceased. Jung reflects on this: 'Certain souls . . . feel . . . three-dimensional existence to be more blissful than . . . Eternity . . . perhaps that depends upon how much of completeness or incompleteness they have taken across with them.'[17] Not only does this indicate how Jung thought about such conditions experienced by the deceased, but also speculates as to the various types of conditions that might influence and hold meaning in the next stage in death. Here, Jung confirms von Franz's assertion that 'the unconscious acts as if it continues after life' and into death. Emma's passing seemed to be influenced by a level and degree of consciousness she embodied while alive.

Jung refers to one of his most meaningful dreams in the chapter, 'On Life After Death', which occurred in 1956, close to a year after Emma's death, at a time when he *was* able to make contact with her. Jung relays how he awoke one night knowing for certain that he had been with Emma in the south of France and was touched that she was still working on her Grail scholarship. Jung felt the dream revealed the potential for the soul's growth after death.[18] Yet, even after such a moving account, he admitted that such thinking was 'inaccurate and give[s] a wrong picture'. In one paragraph he moved from the subjective encounter when he was certain he was with Emma, to an objective shift in which he discusses dimensions and whole numbers. As if he can recount salient moving details about his time with Emma, but then feels obligated to dismiss the manner of account for an academic professional interpretation. Interestingly, his details in one paragraph are more touching than his attempt at justifying them by metaphor in the next.

Jung acknowledged that a symbolic interpretation fell so short of what he had experienced as their time together, thus a visitation with the deceased Emma is how he interpreted the encounter. In this instance they appeared together in the unconscious where the dreaming and dead mingle. From this deeply moving reunion, Jung understood what Jungian analyst Greg Mogenson would call the 'life of the dead'.[19] The reassurance that Jung had from learning of Emma's continued study might have been due to the specific focus on the Grail vessel itself. The Grail was a symbol of a grave, more specifically 'the grave of Christ . . . is [where] . . . the mysterious transition from death to life, the resurrection, took place'.[20] Thus to have been with Emma seems to have enacted the very same Grail research that she had been pursuing in her 'life of the dead'.[21]

There is one further instance important for this discussion, when Jung 'saw' Emma in a dream/vision.[22] He describes her as 'objectively wise' and having in her expression the entirety of their relationship.[23] The vision was so moving for Jung that he defined it as purely objective and indicative of 'a completed individuation with all projections and emotional ties removed'.[24] This is Emma's completed individuation. Yet, there remains a sense that in order to grasp her in such objectivity, a refined visioning was necessary on Jung's part, that is Jung's own projections and ties needed to be withdrawn and only then would he be able to 'reach her'.[25]

The big dream **35**

Analyst P. Kugler discusses this dream, pointing out that Jung shifts his interpretation of the dream from a subjective to the objective level because his approach 'had become tired, worn out, and monotonous' and that in his older age spirits became 'experientially real' for him.[26] He suggests this shift assisted Jung 'to keep the meaningfulness of the dream alive'.[27] Does this perspective help support the 'meaningfulness' of Jung's connection to the now discarnate Emma? I think not. The significance of Emma's objective presence is not considered, while Kugler's interest is in Jung's shift in interpretation. He does not do the encounter justice when he states 'What we view metaphorically at one point in the human life cycle, may appear increasingly literal at another moment . . . During the process of aging, *the quality of Jung's sense of time changed, and that transformation exerted a significant influence on his understanding of the role of the dead in psychic life*'.[28] Yet, we know from both *The Red Book* and now a reconsideration of passages in *Memories, Dreams, Reflections* as a result, that Jung's experience of the dead *in se* did not necessarily change, he just spoke publicly, relativising the dead into symbolic and psychic perspectives while encountering the dead personally as a literal experience. Kugler's explanation feels like an awkward accommodation for Jung's relationship status. The statement could very well be true, but it does not feel like a substantial explanation of an experience with such numinous effect.

This discussion helps sketch a working idea of the terrain in which the dead occupy the unconscious and highlights the nuances that Jung himself identified. These visitation dreams prompted him to look deeper at the issue of life after death as well as to discern the difference between psychological projections and actual visits from the deceased. As von Franz pointed out, although Jung's wont was to explain these occurrences in terms of the psychological disposition, there were occasions when this approach was insufficient in scope and the role of the objective presence of the dead was necessary to consider.

THE PSYCHOID AND THE DEAD

Analyst Jeffrey Raff designates encounters with spirits and the dead to the psychoid realm, which can be defined as an objective unconscious with transpersonal elements. He attributes the experience of visions to two types of figures:

> The first type originates in the inner, unconscious world and personifies archetypes and complexes. These figures may also embody the self with its power and wisdom. The other type derives from the psychoid world, from an imaginal world that is real unto itself and that transcends the psychic world of human beings. Figures of the second type may incarnate from this other reality in the psyche of the human being.[29]

(continued)

36 Defining the terrain

> (continued)
>
> This is an important consideration when examining the possible source of visions and their experience. Raff confirms the possibility that the objective psyche originates externally, transcendent to the psyche. The dead therefore possibly enter the psyche of the individual from the psychoid realm and prompt a visionary experience.[30] He goes on to confirm the position Marie-Louise von Franz shared with Jung:
>
> > If they [i.e. the dead] enter the dream of a person, that dream has a different feel to it than if the person is dreaming about a part of their own psyche projected onto the dead. So on death I think we move into the psychoid realm.[31]
>
> According to Raff, the psychoid allows the dead to encounter incarnates in both dreams and visions and lends a different quality entirely.[32] In Emma Jung's case, there appeared a distinction about her death that qualified her for a refined placement in the unconscious, one more difficult for Jung to locate later. Yet, when he was able to find her, it appeared they shared a dream space together, which relied on Jung meeting her in that space i.e. the south of France. These differences in placement or designation are specific to the discussion of the dead in Jung's work and become more important as Jung becomes more adept in the spaces of the unconscious.

How and where are the dead?

Marie-Louise von Franz and Jung discussed the appearance of the dead not simply as symbolic or subjective content, but objective presences in the psyche. Such discussions assisted not only a therapeutic context, but allowed for an alternative explanation to exist where a subjective interpretation did not appear viable. Von Franz relays how Jung 'usually interpreted such images on the subjective level, that is to say, as symbols of psychic contents to be found in the dreamer himself. Yet, she discusses an instance when the only possible interpretation was indeed that there occurred a visit from the dead *in se*:

> I . . . was once asked by a woman analyst to study the dreams of a patient of hers, a young girl who had lost her fiancé, a pilot, in an airplane accident. She dreamed of the pilot almost every night, and the analyst and I at first interpreted the dream figure as the image of her own animus, which she had projected onto the fiancé. The unconscious seemed to be suggesting that she withdraw this projection and, by so doing, cure herself gradually of the 'loss of soul' suffered through the fiancé's death – that she detaches herself from her tie with the dead. But there were six dreams, which somehow I could not interpret in this manner. Therefore I told the

The big dream **37**

analyst that in those dreams the appearance of the pilot was probably the dead man himself.[33]

The most interesting part about this case is that the analyst, disagreeing with von Franz's conclusion, took the dreams to Jung who, without knowing von Franz's conclusion, not only chose the same six dreams out of the sequence as different to the others, but concluded, as von Franz did, that these particular dreams needed the objective perspective to be understood. She qualifies this by stating, 'It seems to me that one can "feel" whether the figure of a dead person in a dream is being used as a symbol for some inner reality or whether it "really" represents the dead.'[34] Jung appears not to have shied away from the explanation of such a possibility.

Although this case occurred after Jung's confrontation with the unconscious, it is revealing in that an intuitive discernment of the dream material was able to reveal no other conclusion than the deceased pilot had been in contact. Why is this important? Jung's analytical skills (as well as von Franz's) included an ability to perceive a difference in unconscious content, to discern, evaluate and designate a difference between a projection and the dead *in se* appearing in dream material.[35] This nuance is similar to Cameron's jelly bean episode, the ability of a practitioner to distinguish between subtle differences of phenomena suggests that not all phenomena are created equal. In Cameron's case her perceptive translation was piqued due to another party, she knew the jelly bean was not 'hers'. And with von Franz and Jung a quality of independent and non-projected presentation of the pilot designated him into the literal category of the deceased.

On occasions, when Jung identifies the dead, it would seem to be due to a degree of perceptive clarity that 'sees' the unconscious as well as, and this is alluded to a few times in Jung's material, a quality that the deceased might exude themselves within the unconscious dynamic that makes them visibly accessible. Perhaps Jung's father embodied this quality, which the dead have when they appear either in dreams or visions, that makes one question the fundamental nature of the experience. Perhaps the dead have a presence that significantly affects the dreamer and maybe that feeling or quality is a numinous one. Von Franz admits that the subjective level too can often yield a numinous quality and stresses the difficulty in ascertaining 'universally valid criteria' for this feeling.[36] I propose that Jung also felt that these two types of visions, one called the dead and the other figures of the unconscious, defied 'universally valid criteria' for discerning them apart. I also suggest that this was the reason that it took Jung almost forty-two years to publish his essay, 'The Transcendent Function', written after emerging from his confrontation in 1916, principally because these two types of figures were so very difficult to discriminate.

Notes

1   *MDR*, p. 117.
2   Streit-Horn's metastudy of thirty-five researchers and teams revealed 'ADC's occur in every state of consciousness, although they may occur most frequently during sleep but feel qualitatively different – more real and more vividly memorable – than dreams.'

38 Defining the terrain

Blalock and Holden, 'Preparing Students to Counsel Clients', p. 35. Jungian work on bereavement is almost solely focused on bereavement dreams in which the deceased appear to the mourning dreamer. The literature has not addressed the dead who appear in active imagination as Jung experiences in *The Red Book*.

3 *MDR*, p. 117.

4 Kelly Bulkeley and Patricia Bulkeley, *Dreaming Beyond Death: A Guide to Pre-Death Dreams and Visions* (Boston, MA: Beacon Press, 2005), p. 18.

5 Jung's father was temporarily away on holiday and is now returning home. In English the word 'holiday' is composed of Holy and Day, which can refer to the eight holy days of the Christian calendar. The last of these days, the Last Great Day is meant to celebrate the Lord's raising of the dead (Ezekiel 37:1–10, Revelation 20:11–15). Therefore it puts the time of the dream sometime in the second week of March, two weeks before Easter that year, on 5 April. Framed in this way, Paul Jung returned from his Holy Day of resurrection from the dead with the intention of making an appearance to the living Jung. A 'good recovery' is a successful resurrection at being recognised by the living, dreaming Jung.

6 *MDR*, p. 117.

7 Analyst Susan Olson considers this dream from another perspective, describing its central problem as 'a conflict between two different perceptions of reality – that of the dream-father and that of the dream-ego'. She continues to explain Jung's issue with the dream: 'Our loved ones can be both dead in the outer world and "alive" in our imaginal world, but we may not quite "get" this yet.' Olson, *By Grief Transformed*, pp. 68–69. Although this perspective is of interest to archetypal psychologists and analysts it is actually unhelpful to this study, as it does not acknowledge Jung's objective experience of his dead. Olson's explanation does not contribute to the direction the dead were assisting Jung to understand, that is the nature of the unconscious in relation to the dead.

8 *MDR*, p. 117. The sightings recounted in his 'First Years' chapter in *Memories, Dreams, Reflections* could also be considered in this category of experience. Jung describes an occasion when he sees figures with floating detached heads (*MDR*, p. 33). These could be considered sightings of the dead, although Jung does not appear to know them personally.

9 C. G. Jung, 'On the Nature of Dreams', in *The Structure and Dynamics of the Psyche*, trans. R. F. C. Hull, *The Collected Works*, Vol. 8 (Princeton, NJ: Princeton University Press, 1956), §555 (hereafter cited as *CW*, vol. 8).

10 Ibid. See Jung's discussion of relative distance in relation to rebirth, discussed with Jaffé and noted in Shamdasani, 'The Boundless Expanse', p. 25.

11 *RB*, p. 302. The feature film *Inception* (2010) is a well-rendered example of the dynamic that Jung experienced in parts of *The Red Book* where he moves between levels of experiences within the unconscious.

12 *MDR*, p. 336.

13 Kelly Bulkeley, *Spiritual Dreaming* (New York: Paulist Press, 1995), p. 7.

14 'Protokoll der Sitzung', Jung papers, ETH–Archive (known as the Jung–Jaffé protocols), p. 138, in Shamdasani, 'The Boundless Expanse', p. 25.

15 Ibid.

16 Jung, *Letters: 1951–1961*, pp. 145–146. Letter to Erich Neumann dated 15 December 1955.

17 *MDR*, p. 353.

18 Ibid., p. 341.

19 Mogenson, *Greeting the Angels*, p. 105.

20 Emma Jung and Marie-Louise von Franz, *The Grail Legend* (Princeton, NJ: Princeton University Press, 1970), pp. 7 and 128.

21 The same double meaning is apparent with Jung's dream of his deceased neighbour, discussed in Chapter 15.

22 It is unclear how Jung perceived the difference between the two. If the effect of the encounter was so real that it was more like a vision and thus he felt he had more interplay or if it was dream-like and thus he had less influence and conscious engagement. That he

The big dream **39**

included the detail of seeing her might indicate that it was more like a vision as opposed to him dreaming *about* her.

23 *MDR*, p. 327.
24 Ibid., p. 328.
25 Shamdasani, 'The Boundless Expanse', p. 25.
26 Kugler, *Raids on The Unthinkable*, pp. 125 and 122.
27 Ibid., p. 125.
28 Ibid. Italics in original.
29 Jeffrey Raff, *Jung and The Alchemical Imagination* (York Beach, ME: Nicolas-Hays, 2000), p. 31.
30 Personal correspondence, 25 January 2009.
31 Ibid.
32 Raff defines the difference in quality between these experiences: 'If [the] entity belongs to the unconscious, the nature of the encounter, however profound it may be, is psychic and imaginal ... If the entity is of the psychoid realm, the encounter not only includes this inner, imaginal sense but has psychoidal affects as well. Such affects might include a major shift of consciousness into an altered state ... In such cases, the inner image creates a sense or feel of another that appears to be outside you, outside your own inner world.' Jeffrey Raff, *Healing the Wounded God* (York Beach, ME: Nicolas-Hays, 2002), p. 121.
33 Von Franz, *On Dreams & Death*, p. xv.
34 Ibid.
35 Hillman notes: 'What [Jung] sought and achieved, already in his doctoral dissertation, was the integration of the parapsychological within a broadened psychological theory.' James Hillman, 'Some Early Background to Jung's Ideas: Notes on C.G. Jung's Medium by Stefanie Zumstein Preiswerk', *Spring* (1976): 126.
36 Von Franz, *On Dreams and Death*, p. xv.

6

DEATH DREAMS

Jung experienced four death dreams between 1911 and 1912, which anticipated his confrontation with the unconscious in 1913. These, in addition to the pivotal dream of his deceased father in 1896, served as a preparatory phase that would point to what Jung was to experience in *The Red Book*. The dead in each of these dreams appeared prominently to guide Jung into the varied experiences offered by the unconscious. Here, they point to themselves as a psychic reality and seem to anchor and focus Jung's attention within an unconscious landscape. Further, they demonstrate that the unconscious was a dynamic venue of transformation, in which appeared levels of action and activity, assisted by Jung's presence.

It is clear in the following death dreams that Jung thought and wrote intimately about the experiences and that they appear more literal in presentation and experience than symbolic. This partly allows Jung to come to realisations about the unconscious as a result. It is possible to see the dead as Jung did and to trace their influence on him and his understanding of how the unconscious works with consciousness.

Ancestral spirits dream

After the dream of his deceased father in 1896, Jung's next death dream occurred in 1911, which years later Jung concludes was about a deceased ancestor.[1] In his dream, several wigged spirits posed a difficult question to Jung in Latin, whose answer he could not remember. In the dream he recalls understanding the spirit but not being able to answer him. Feeling 'profoundly humiliated', he then woke.[2]

Where Jung's father prompted him to reflect on the universal problem of after-death survival, these ancestors want something else from Jung that he is unable to

Death dreams **41**

give. During the dream of his father, Jung feels 'ashamed' when he assumed his father was dead. Both of these encounters weigh heavily on Jung, in particular, their expectations of him.[3] In the face of the immensity of the unconscious, both conceptually and experientially, Jung feels daunted that with the psychological unknowns, his scientific approach does little to assist. This dynamic is confirmed at the beginning of *Liber Primus*, when the spirit of the times struggles to hold firm his position alongside the spirit of the depths.[4]

He understands what this 'spirit of the dead' is asking, but his difficulty lies in not knowing the answer. He did not have enough command of Latin (a 'dead' language or here the language used to speak with the dead) to respond. He does not have enough experience with the language of the unconscious to bridge the temporal and psychological communication gap to make himself understood by the spirits. Considering that he was then working on his book *Psychology of the Unconscious*, which was a study on the relationship to the unconscious, he was engaged in researching the symbolic language of the unconscious itself. Therefore, it is not a surprise that the ancestor posed him a question, which also he did not know *how* to answer.

Jung's engagement with these spirits puts demands on him in two respects. He acknowledges and validates them as a psychic reality. Then he communicates with them. These ancestors are asking for a collaboration, and by acknowledging their questions, Jung is functioning in their context. Since this triggers an immediate response by ending his holiday and returning to work on the book, the spirits incite Jung to action in the conscious world. This encounter has already proved to be different to his experience with his father or to the previous visitation dreams with Toni Wolff or Emma. It was after this dream that Jung concluded the dead need the living more than the living need them and that they seem eager and ready to see what decisions the living will make.[5] Responding to the ancestral spirits by returning to work, Jung felt he was formulating an answer to the question he was unable to answer in his dream.[6]

Jung felt that the dead were inherently linked to the living by the living's efforts and pursuits to continue learning and expanding consciousness. This position is different from spiritualist circles of the time that maintained the dead were able to offer specific knowledge inaccessible to the living.[7] Here Jung identifies himself with 'spiritual forefathers' as if he considers himself connected not only to these particular ancestral spirits, but also to ones who shared his proclivities and particular questions. In this way Jung linked himself to an ancestral tradition to which he identified as an integral member and who not only has something to discover on their behalf, but also to contribute. Jung alone is capable of answering this particular question for this particular ancestry. Shamdasani asserts that this dream is *the* dream that connects Jung to a theology of the dead alongside Jung's own about his myth.[8] Jung discussed this idea with Aniela Jaffé on 13 June 1958 and 'noted that one could only find one's myth if one was together with one's dead'.[9]

42 Defining the terrain

JUNG'S MYTH AND HIS DEAD

Several scholars mention the association of Jung's myth to his dead, 'a mythology informed by his own dreams as well as those of his patients, hypothesizes that life continues after death in an imaginal form'.[10] Murray Stein attributes to the *Sermones*: 'This work contains what I believe one can consider a central piece of Jung's myth for the second half of his life.'[11] Charet stressed 'the myth that was ordering his life seemed to be associated with the dead'.[12] Evans Lansing Smith points out that in Jung's commentary of *The Tibetan Book of the Dead*, 'the initiatory revelation occurring at the moment of death corresponds to "the transformation of the unconscious that occurs under analysis" (523), thus suggesting that the descent to the underworld was the central myth of his psychotherapy'.[13]

In this dream, Jung's level of conscious involvement facilitated action in his conscious world. That this book, *Psychology of the Unconscious*, would be instrumental in the break with Freud, seems to provide an adjustment to Jung's conscious attitude as well as validating the experience of encountering the dead in a dream setting. His visioning in such a dream expanded his conception of how the unconscious accommodates ancestral lineage related to him personally.

What the dead know

By including the ancestral spirits dream in the chapter 'On Life After Death', Jung meant to use it as an example of an occasion when the dead were seeking out the living for knowledge and answers. How did Jung come to the understanding that it was necessary to instruct the figures of the unconscious and the dead? Details in this chapter compiled much later than the first set of death dreams reveal what he meant by this. The content here is fundamental in establishing an understanding of what Jung thought about the dead in relation to the nature of the unconscious. In fact the entire chapter is affirmation that Jung considered the dead a separate category of psychic experience. His in-depth examination of *what* the dead know and *how* they know in fact confirms that these interactions served as a 'prelude' to what he eventually wanted to articulate about the unconscious.[14]

He discusses in detail the opinion that 'souls . . . "know" only what they knew at the moment of death'.[15] Using examples from his own death dreams as well as those of his patients and students, Jung reveals how he thought thoroughly about the psychological possibilities of after–death survival and more specifically how this might appear to the living and the dead alike. He raised doubts that the dead were 'possessors of great knowledge' in order to explain how his own experiences at times seemed to prove otherwise.[16]

Jung makes statements about the kinds of knowledge that exists: 'unlimited knowledge . . . but . . . comprehended by consciousness' and only at the perfect time.[17] Jung thought that the unconscious contained 'better sources of information' due to 'its spatio-temporal' relativity.[18] And most importantly, the unconscious holds more knowledge than consciousness but it is 'knowledge in eternity, usually without reference' to the present.[19] Thus Jung designates qualities to the unconscious that are vast and omniscient while at the same time limited from the viewpoint of a conscious perspective. It is unclear if the qualities of the unconscious appear to dictate the qualities embodied by the dead, or if such qualities emerge from being dead.

He recounts a dream of one of his students who expressed a fear about dying. She said that in the afterlife the newly arrived summarised their whole lives 'just as if . . . experiences . . . in space and time, were the decisive ones'.[20] Jung notes carefully that the dead are interested in the psychological understandings of a life lived and particularly that part which the recently deceased are able to carry over with them into the unconscious landscape.[21] Although the region called the unconscious seems endowed in an eternity of knowledge, the deceased appear intrigued by the psychology of the living condition or how the living come to know and use what they have learned to improve themselves and their lives. Thus the importance is the degree of consciousness that the psychological perspective of the living invites. The ability to self-reflect and grow perception increases consciousness as well as the orientation to the Self. In this respect, Jung perceived the dead interested in how and what the living have learned about themselves, about being human and specifically about being incarnate.

What becomes important in Jung's encounters in *The Red Book* is his orientation as an incarnate in contrast to the dead as discarnates. Jung's experience of the unconscious is influenced by encountering the dead and other figures as *those who have a body* and therefore have an ability to process information differently to figures that do not.[22] Similarly, as with the ancestral spirit dream, the dead are waiting on the living to answer them, to give *them* information. In Jung's opinion 'omniconsciousness' needs the living, but also needs change in order to be useful. Change allows for the evolution of knowledge and its applicability in the world. Without the living's ability to respond, change and evolve, unlimited knowledge is useless. The technicality inferred here seems to suggest that 'omniscience . . . could flow only into the psyche of the living, into a soul bound to a body'.[23] Such a dynamic permits the dead an opportunity to make their eternity of knowing applicable and perhaps increase consciousness for them both. For Jung, this was a critical aspect of the relationship between the incarnate and the dead because human beings have 'the capacity for . . . decisive cognitions'.[24]

Jung concludes it is the living mind in a living body that is the best container by which to receive information from the dead. The dead still maintain a faculty that might be similar to mind, but it is not able to cogitate as a living mind does and this he sees as specific to human, embodied consciousness. Thus, what appeared to be a discarnate advantage in terms of access to unlimited information from the unconscious becomes useless if there is not a conscious context to accommodate it.

44 Defining the terrain

Yet, Jung presents some problematic reasoning, 'The maximum awareness . . . attained anywhere forms . . . the upper limit of knowledge to which the dead can attain.'[25] This is quite a complex statement as it reinforces that the dead do in fact change, and appears to contradict his earlier suggestion that the dead only know what they know at death. He points to this ability to attain knowledge at the highest degree of accumulated knowledge, either in consciousness or the unconscious. By considering that knowledge resides in both places or conditions, this gives the dead the *ability* to strive to understand and acquire knowledge in either the conscious or the unconscious as long as the knowledge exists somewhere. Perhaps as with the living, who have varied knowledge bases and vastly different attainments, the dead possibly have an equally varied degree of knowledge and possibility. The important point inferred here is that when examining the prospect of knowledge, the dead, in their continued existence, have the conditions possible to attain further knowledge, in a similar manner as Emma Jung continuing with her Grail studies as well as the dead coming back from Jerusalem wanting to be taught.

The implications of this addresses analyst Susan Olson's question if the dead individuate?[26] This seems to indicate that yes, they do. In part this would necessitate a degree of conscious awareness of both parties and in particular a knowing on the part of human consciousness that the dead as unconscious agents are a dynamic involved with the living. To understand this, Jung knew was valuable, thus he shared with Jaffé the importance of understanding the demands of one's dead.

But how might the dead's individuation occur? When Jung turns attention to the discussion of increasing consciousness, he stresses that the conditions that must be present are the tension of opposites, which allow for an increase in consciousness.[27] Emphasising that raising consciousness can only contribute to the collective consciousness via the living seems to contradict many of the examples he has set out in this same chapter (and in the *Sermones*), which show the dead aware of what they lack. Even with such efforts to understand the dead and their condition, he maintains a conscious-centric perspective, which sees earthly life as most important and the dead and figures of the unconscious the support team for the experience of living. As an aside he suggests that this is why the living condition is of such importance, and it is with this that Jung seems to disinherit the dead of their discarnate advantage of being omniscient.[28]

What is clear are Jung's examples, which support the idea that the dead want to address what they had not while alive.[29] This can be applied both to Emma Jung's pursuit of her Grail studies, which she had not yet completed upon her death, as well as von Franz's account of her father, who appeared in a visitation dream carrying a violin case. He was a gifted musician who had ignored this during his lifetime and now 'he [was] working on what he had neglected in life'.[30] These examples point to the dead being able to individuate based on the living's attention and intention. It must be said, similar to von Franz's position, that the dead are 'living in such utterly different conditions' and this makes it difficult to understand them as inhabitants of an ever-dynamic unconscious from the conscious, incarnate perspective.

The most pertinent point in Jung's own conclusion to the chapter 'On Life After Death', is 'just as the unconscious affects us . . . the increase in our consciousness affects the unconscious'.[31] Jung finally considers integrating more unconscious material that will have bearing in an integral way not only on the unconscious, but on the dead. So how does this statement apply to them? The examination of *The Red Book* material now indicates how thoroughly Jung considered his encounters with the dead and his commentary in 'Nox Secunda' suggests that it is possible to vacate the unconscious of the dead if one acknowledges and tends to their needs.[32]

By being conscious of the dead, he became in service to them and proved to balance their effects with his conscious life. In this way he integrated an understanding of them.[33] As a result, he concludes, 'The immortal in me was saved'.[34] That is, as a result of such efforts, a consciousness as aware as possible of the psyche and its attributes confers a type of timeless and spaceless quality to the present.

If the dead assist the living they are in a sense endeavouring to assist themselves. The term 'unfinished business' can look like the yearning of the deceased but might also be a reflection of that same issue with the living, that the dead and living work together to heal one another.[35]

It is in such a cyclical manner that evolution of consciousness as well as 'maximum awareness' is able to increase. Jung accommodates for the possibility that the dead can improve their knowledge by virtue of what the living do with their lives as a result of the information that the dead pass on to them. In this way, Jung arrives at his role of instructor of both the dead and figures of the unconscious.[36] The incarnate Jung, aware of the discarnate state, engages with the dead and thus assists with the augmentation of their knowledge.[37] Jung arrives at the idea of serving the dead and in turn himself as a result of his interaction with the ancestral spirits in this dream.

In the chapter, 'On Life After Death', we see Jung not only grappling with the idea of an unconscious that accommodates the presence of the dead, but we see him contemplating their role in the psychological development of the human being. His ruminations reveal his depth of visioning and ability to hold the purpose of the dead's' appearance and their role in the living Self. His penetrative exploration attempts to conceive benefits to a relationship with the dead.

Austrian customs official/knight dream

In 1912 while still working on *Psychology of the Unconscious*, Jung had another death dream, claiming it to be one of his most seminal and that augured his split with Freud.[38] Considering the mounting tension between Jung and Freud, it is not surprising that the dead would appear again. In the preceding dreams, Jung's father as well as the ancestral spirits sought out Jung, here, it appears as if Jung has entered the dream space in the evening. He encounters an Austrian customs official who he describes as 'stooped', 'peevish', 'vexed'.[39] Others in the dream tell Jung that the man 'was not really there but was the ghost of a customs official who had died years ago [and] 'couldn't die properly'.[40]

46 Defining the terrain

The significant point to the death dream is that Jung sees what is not physically present, i.e. he is able to see in the unconscious. The customs official appears as a ghost to both Jung as well as to these dream figures. What quality of the unconscious presents a ghost to figures already in the unconscious as well as to the dreaming psyche of Jung's personal unconscious? Could it be that the others present are a part of the collective unconscious and Jung has dreamed deeply out of the personal? Is it reasonable to suggest that this is a further example of the various levels of the personal and collective unconscious into and out of which events and figures occur, levels similar to where Paul and Emma Jung reside?

Each party meets in the dream space from different vantages and experiences the ghost. It is others in the dream who designate the official with qualities of not really being there and who cannot truly die. Given the officer's appearance, this may indicate that he earned his ghostly status because he is stuck between death and being fully dead or between death and perhaps the state Jung's father attained, fully integrated in what death entails and resurrected from death to exhibit live qualities for the dreaming Jung. There appears something of the earthbound in the custom official's presentation, while the luminous quality typical of ghosts is noticeably absent.

The next part of the dream describes a knight fully regaled, walking in a town square. When Jung relates this dream to his lecture audience in 1925, he details the setting and time of the dream (noon), then inserts 'which as you know is the hour when spirits are abroad in southern countries'.[41] This is delivered with such ease and in such a factual manner one wonders what the reaction of the audience was at that time. Could Jung have been referring to the fact that daytime in the northern hemisphere equates with night in the southern when most people are sleeping? Or could he simply have been referring to Mediterranean countries, whose inhabitants might be predisposed to believe in spirits? Or, is Jung inferring that spirits could appear as the result of out-of-body experiences for those who are asleep? The statement implies that the unconscious serves as a holding place, or transitional space for *all* spirits. If Jung found the knight walking around in the same dreamscape as the prosaic customs official, is it possible that all ghosts and spirits inhabit the same unconscious space along with other competing visionary expressions? These issues are important to consider when sketching a working definition of the unconscious and those who reside there.

Jung determines the knight to be a crusader and identifies with the medieval connection as his own, far apart from Freud.[42] As a father figure, Freud's influence was dissipating for Jung. While the world that was temporally closest to Jung was fading in importance, the world furthest away or deepest was more alive and more accessible. Jung began to move away from Freud's ideas to shift toward a 'crusade' for a psychology with its seminal idea being a multifarious unconscious.[43]

Jung finds remarkable the fact that no one appears to see the knight except him. In fact during the dream he describes reflecting on the appearance of the ghost and the knight and it seemed as though someone responded that the apparition was a normal occurrence. This inflection demonstrates an aspect of lucid dreaming. By maintaining a degree of consciousness in the dream setting: 'The lucid dreamer . . . characteristically does reflect on his or her experience while it is happening; indeed such reflections are one of the most characteristic features of lucid dreams.'[44] In the 1925 seminars Jung attributed the answer to his question to his shadow, here the shadow points out that no one besides Jung sees the knight and this causes Jung 'bewilderment'.[45] In 1925 Jung admits: 'I realized the antagonism between the figure of the Crusader and that of Freud . . . They were different and yet both were dead and could not die properly.'[46] Whereas Jung describes the customs official as shadowy and prosaic, the knight 'was full of life and completely real . . . this was numinous'.[47] This detailed discernment on Jung's part qualifies the figures in the unconscious not only to be exhibiting varying energic qualities, but also varying degrees of being dead. One might very well assume that the ghost, since it is temporally closer, would be easier to perceive, and the knight more difficult. Yet again, the quality of their presentation and effect is what is noticeable to Jung. The knight, with its inherent numinosity, seems similar to Emma in her last vision to Jung. And although Toni Wolff died before Emma, Wolff appears closer to 'three-dimensional existence'. In terms of the presentation of the dead themselves, these dreams confirm the unconscious to be an area not bound by time and space as these dead confirm. And how Jung perceives each has more to do with him as an incarnate presence in the same unconscious space, than any uniformity that all ghosts and the dead might be thought to exhibit.

The symbolic meaning of the expressions 'fading apparition' vs 'completely real'[48] seems appropriate given Jung's waning relationship with Freud alongside his own shift to the concept of an unconscious as a more active principle in his psychological model.[49] These descriptions remain relevant as details about the dead themselves. Such an apparition with 'shadowy' countenance points to a denser spirit, whereas the knight might come from deeper within the unconscious, similar to Emma Jung. It could be possible that Jung is doing the real moving around the unconscious in order to grasp these figures and not necessarily they to him.[50]

The loggia dream

In December of 1912, Jung had the loggia dream.[51] The most dynamic dream in the sequence has transformation as its theme, revealing the living contents of the unconscious. It builds on the qualitative differences offered by figures in the unconscious as seen in the previous dream.[52]

The setting of the dream was in an Italian loggia with Jung seated in a gold Renaissance chair (renaissance meaning rebirth), at an emerald green table.[53] The chair enables access to secrets not only about rebirth but also about the inherent transformational qualities of the unconscious. The gold points to a sense of arrival in the alchemical tradition with gold being the end product of the alchemical operation.[54] In both the 1925 seminars and *Memories, Dreams, Reflections*, Jung confirms that the green table reminded him of the story of the alchemical tablet of Hermes Trismegistus, the Tabula Smaragdina, on which all alchemical wisdom was written.[55]

48 Defining the terrain

The Tabula Smaragdina was associated with Hermes, the psychopompic god, one of whose jobs was to escort souls from earth to the underworld.[56] This task has Hermes returning the newly deceased to their pre-life form as souls, thus the descent to the underworld in itself is seen as a rebirth or birth into the realm of death. The setting of the dream indicates a purpose and context that points to transformation of the soul as the goal of alchemy.

The dream continued with a white bird landing on the table and changing into a blonde little girl, who ran off to play. This amused Jung and when she returned she hugged him, then turned again into a dove and said that early at night, 'I transform myself into a human being, while the male dove is busy with the twelve dead.' She then flew away and Jung woke.[57]

The second part of this dream acts out the transformative process hinted at by the emerald table. The transmogrification of the bird to girl to bird again alludes to the connection between human being and human spirit, with the dove often associated with the Holy Spirit and love.[58] The dream presents Jung with the opportunity to locate spirit or the soul in the unconscious. The idea of the human spirit located in the unconscious points to immortality.[59] Perhaps, the unconscious itself, due to its nature, enables metamorphosis and highlights the spiritual or otherwise hidden facet of the human being. The unconscious, in addition to hosting the dead, or that part which survives death, also houses the spirit, that connection and fluidity between the conscious and the unconscious. Jung noted in *Mysterium Coniuntionis*, 'As the "Tabula Smaragdina" shows, the purpose of the ascent and descent is to unite the powers of Above and Below.'[60] This harmonises the conscious and unconscious. The inscription on the Tabula Smaragdina in Latin reads:

Visita Interiora Terrae Rectificando Invenies Occultum Lapidem

[Visit the Interior of the Earth and Rectify What You Find There and You Will Discover the Hidden Stone][61]

In other words travel inward and reconcile what you find so that you might discover the true self. By engaging with the unconscious, this looks at Jung's attempt at understanding his dead. The entire dream anticipates Jung's encounters in *The Red Book*.

Von Franz discusses that one of the goals of the alchemist was 'the making of the philosopher's stone [which] was linked with the idea of death'.[62] The pursuit of the stone becomes comparable to grasping the spiritual or immortal self and 'was conceived as the "immortal body" of the dead'.[63] Such searching for the soul and immortality makes more conscious what has been unconscious. From the dream, Jung defines the concept of transformation not only in terms of rebirth, but specifically with respect to the dead.

That the bird is able to change into a human while the male is busy might suggest that the female embodies the spiritual in order to become human, while the male principal is busy bringing the alchemical realities to fruition by enacting the twelve steps of the emerald tablet.[64] Yet, after contemplating the meaning of the dream, Jung felt unsure about the reference to the dead. He surmised that the dream was pointing to 'unusual activation of the unconscious'.[65] It was then he noticed the repetitive theme of something dead present while still alive. This quality and feeling tone would repeat throughout the first series of death dreams and was in part the paradox, which prompted him to examine further how the unconscious related to the presence of the dead. This dynamic appears to have been present as far back as the dream of his father's return. This material would come to resolution in the row of tombs dream.

Row of tombs dream

The dream began with Jung walking along a laneway with tombs adorned with effigies. He stopped to contemplate one of them when suddenly, the stone figure 'came to life' yet Jung concludes it was due to his focus and attention on him.[66]

This dream pointed to the conception of the archetype, but also expands on Jung's experience with the recognition of the dead in the dream space. Once again what appears dead is really alive. The operative concept here is, 'because I was looking at him', suggesting that where Jung placed his attention and focus there followed a resurrection of life,[67] and in these instances a discovery of life in death. Jung's participation in the dream scene facilitates this resurrection; he brings the dead to life or rather the significance of the dead's presence is made due to his acknowledgement. This dynamic exemplifies the idea of *betrachten*, meaning to make pregnant. Jung explains:

> [L]ooking psychologically, brings about the activation of the object: it is as if something were emanating from one's spiritual eye that evokes or activates the object of one's vision . . . That is the case with any fantasy image; one concentrates upon it, and then finds that one has great difficulty in keeping the thing quiet, it gets restless, it shifts, something is added, or it multiplies itself; one fills it with living power and it becomes pregnant.[68]

The encounter with the dead appears here as an activation of contents. Again, Jung has 'an extremely unpleasant feeling' when faced with what should be dead and yet has life. This recalls the insecurity and extreme reactions he experienced when he faced his father and the ancestral spirits.

The time periods that Jung visits point to the layers of the collective unconscious of the psyche, and even to its inherent vitality. His concentrated attention in the dream space simultaneously elicits change while witnessing that same change. This detail becomes important later when considering the development of active imagination and its use in *The Red Book*.

Jung mentions a curious detail that the knights were not stone but rather mummified. The term refers to a state of preservation, that is what has been preserved is life in death.[69] The archaic descriptions do not refer to memories or dream details,

50 Defining the terrain

but rather a lively part of Jung's psyche. The dead, represented by mummified figures thought to be carved from stone, are not dead at all.

Jung speaks about feeling disturbed by these images, being unable to interpret them and using play therapy as a way to access their meaning. As the dead became more active in his dreams, this was mirrored in activities such as play in order that he might activate in consciousness what might have been occurring beneath it. He responded similarly with his return to work on his book after his conversation with the ancestral spirits. He answered the activity in his dreams by addressing their meaning in his daily life, addressing the alchemical wisdom 'as above, so below' shown in the loggia dream.

These dreams point to the allocation of the dead in unconscious spaces as well as the live qualities they displayed. Taken together they point to Jung's attempt to make sense of the dead alongside other figures of the unconscious who appeared in the same spaces. The literal approach has the dead assisting Jung in defining themselves and their habitual function. That they could serve as symbolic material might very well be the case, yet the dreams especially of Emma, Toni, Paul Jung and the ancestors appear as visitation dreams.

Most importantly, these preparatory experiences with the dead and themes of death highlight Jung's faculty of visioning before his discovery of active imagination. By this time in late 1912/1913 he was dreaming through layers of the unconscious and recognising them as such. This allowed him to understand the depth of the unconscious and its players. He found nothing stagnant here, particularly with respect to the visitation dreams, which he interpreted as being the dead returning, not a symbol of what his deceased father, wife and lover represented.

Notes

1 *MDR*, p. 338. This dream does not appear chronologically in *Memories, Dreams, Reflections*, but is included in the chapter titled 'On Life After Death' in which Jung discusses what spirits learn from the living. By including the dream here, Jung explains that spirits appear when they require something from the living. Shamdasani dates this dream in 1910. Shamdasani, 'The Boundless Expanse', p. 16.
2 *MDR*, p. 338. Jung includes here that the feeling tone of the dream reminded him of the same during his vision of 'the black rock temple' in 1944 (ibid.).
3 Ibid.
4 *RB*, pp. 229b–230a.
5 *MDR*, pp. 337, 339; Mogenson, *Greeting the Angels*, pp. 31, 114. This is discussed in depth in the commentaries of the most extended section about the dead in *The Red Book*, 'Nox Secunda'. Here Jung speaks clearly about the dead, their needs and the community that he feels he serves (*RB*, pp. 295–298 and 340 respectively).
6 *MDR*, p. 338–339. Shamdasani convincingly links the ancestral question to Jung's attempt to understand his myth. Shamdasani, 'The Boundless Expanse', pp. 17–18.
7 Shamdasani, 'The Boundless Expanse', pp. 26–27.
8 Ibid., pp. 18–19.
9 Ibid., pp. 26–27. Also Mogenson, *Greeting the Angels*; Charet, *Spiritualism*; Murray Stein, 'Individuation: Inner Work', *Journal of Jungian Theory and Practice* 7, no. 2 (2005): 2; Evans Lansing Smith *Descent to the Underworld in Literature, Painting, and Film 1895–1950: The Modernist Nekyia* (London: Edwin Mellen Press, 2001), p. 11.

Death dreams **51**

10 Mogenson, *Greeting the Angels*, p. 108.
11 Stein, 'Individuation: Inner Work', p. 2.
12 Charet, *Spiritualism*, pp. 239–240.
13 Smith, *Descent to the Underworld*, p.11.
14 *MDR*, p. 217.
15 Ibid., p. 339.
16 Ibid.
17 Ibid.
18 Ibid., p. 335.
19 Ibid., p. 343.
20 Ibid., p. 336.
21 The example of Jung's dream of a deceased friend who had lived with an unfortunate 'unreflecting attitude'. When Jung found him, his daughter was explaining psychology to him and he was so fascinated he showed no interest in Jung. Jung's conclusion was that it was necessary for him to understand his psychic life, which he had not managed during his lifetime (*MDR*, pp. 340–341).
22 Similar to the poisoner episode in *Liber Secundus* (*RB*, p. 322a).
23 *MDR*, p. 339.
24 Ibid.
25 Ibid., p. 343.
26 Olson, *By Grief Transformed*, p. 6.
27 *MDR*, p. 343.
28 Ibid.
29 Ibid. This idea is taken up by Jung during his encounters with the tramp (*RB*, p. 265a).
30 Von Franz, 'Archetypes Surrounding Death', 18. And expressed in *MDR*, p. 340.
31 *MDR*, p. 358.
32 *RB*, p. 323a. The same dynamic of course appears with the arrival of the dead from Jerusalem clamouring for the *Sermones*.
33 Consider the previous discussion of the transcendent function, the dead themselves have not integrated into Jung's personality, they have shared the experience of Jung's incarnate life in the process of Jung serving them. As a result, they are sated and disappear into their lives as souls in the unconscious.
34 *RB*, pp. 323a and 230a.
35 Stephani Stephens, 'The Spectre and Its Movement: The Dynamic of Intra and Transgenerational Influence', *International Association of Jungian Studies Conference*, Cape Town, South Africa (2017).
36 *MDR*, p. 338.
37 Jung arrives at the idea of serving his dead by means of his interaction with the ancestral spirits in this dream. His further encounters with the dead also see him understanding the exact nature of his service to them and this is explored in his commentaries in *The Red Book* (pp. 295b–298a).
38 *MDR*, p. 186.
39 Ibid.
40 Ibid., p. 189.
41 C. G. Jung, *Analytical Psychology: Notes of the Seminar Given in 1925*, ed. William McGuire, Bollingen Series XCIX (Princeton, NJ: Princeton University Press, 1989), p. 39 (hereafter cited as *AP*).
42 *MDR*, pp. 188–189.
43 The break with Freud was attributed to conflicting opinions about libido: Freud insisted that the unconscious was a storehouse for repressed sexual libido and Jung advocated a more transformational nature inherent in the unconscious (*MDR*, p. 191). During this very time Jung became involved with a patient, Sabina Spielrein and it cannot be underestimated the pressure and influence that this relationship had on Jung. For an in-depth timeline of events involving Jung, Freud, Sabina and Emma see the excellently

52 Defining the terrain

researched *Sex and Survival: The Life and Ideas of Sabina Spielrein*. (New York: Overlook Press, 2017) by John Launer.

44 Green and McCreery, *Lucid Dreaming*, p. 12.

45 *AP*, p. 39.

46 Ibid.

47 *MDR*, p. 189.

48 Ibid.

49 Jung continues in 1925 from a psychological perspective: 'The meaning of the dream lies in the principle of the ancestral figure – not the Austrian officer – obviously he stood for the Freudian theory, but the other, the Crusader, is an archetypal Christian symbol that does not really live today, but on the other hand is not wholly dead either' (*AP*, p. 39). Jung's meaning of 'not wholly dead' might imply a lucidity of consciousness within the unconscious. If it is not alive, then it must be dead. Jung expressed a similar sentiment in the extended essay on Elijah and Salome appearing in Appendix B in *The Red Book*, where he states that they have always been present in the psyche of humanity (*RB*, p. 365b).

50 Of course this is obvious in *The Red Book* with his active imaginations that take the form of a journey from one place to another. There is one moment in *The Red Book* that shows Jung's unique perspective during the episode of 'The Anchorite', when he visits a holy man in the desert. At the end of their conversation the Anchorite becomes agitated and lunges for Jung, who confirms that he is safely grounded 'in the twentieth century' (*RB*, p. 272b). Although Jung is clear about returning to his daily life after each active imagination, this is one of the only instances in *The Red Book* that sees Jung decidedly aware of his transition from the unconscious back to consciousness.

51 The loggia dream and the next death dream in the series, the row of tombs dream, are both included in Jung's *Memories, Dreams, Reflections* in a chapter titled 'Confrontation with the Unconscious'. Thematically they are well positioned next to the other dreams experienced during the year before *The Red Book* material begins. Jung's loggia dream occurred in December of 1912 and the row of tombs dream sometime before his visions of massive flooding in October of 1913. Jung's last correspondence with Freud was in September of 1913 and he resigned from the *Jarbuch* editorship on 27 October 1913. Although the ancestors dream occurred in either 1910 or 1911, it too sits appropriately alongside the two dreams above and anticipates the material in *The Red Book*. In addition to a substantial section of *Liber Primus* not appearing in either *Memories, Dreams, Reflections* or *Analytical Psychology*, *The Red Book* material includes Jung's visions of October 1913, his first active imagination, the Siegfried episode and a much-extended interaction with Elijah and Salome.

52 Shamdasani reveals that in *Black Book 2*, Jung noted that it was this dream that convinced him to take up a relationship with Toni Wolff (*RB*, p. 198b).

53 Peter Homans interprets the dream as such: 'It is possible that the aristocratic opulence and the quiet, regal grandeur of this dream embodied a theme of narcissistic reinstatement whereby Jung, the former "crown prince", reendowed himself, in imagination, with the valued self-esteem he had lost through the breakdown of his relationship with Freud. If this is true, the dream can be understood as initiating in the unconscious a process of restitution whereby Jung began the long task of bringing coherence to the self that had been so injured by the loss of connection with Freud and the analytic movement.' Peter Homans, *Jung in Context* (Chicago, IL: University of Chicago Press, 1995), p. 77. Homans is the only scholar to attribute the transformative dynamic of this dream to Jung's regeneration of self in relation to his personal history with Freud.

54 'The physical goal of alchemy was gold, the panacea, the elixir of life; the spiritual one was the rebirth of the (spiritual) light from the darkness of Physis: healing self-knowledge and the deliverance of the pneumatic body from the corruption of the flesh.' C. G. Jung, *Mysterium Coniuntionis*, ed. William McGuire, trans. R. F. C. Hull, in *The Collected Works*, Vol. 14 (Princeton, NJ: Princeton University Press, 1963), p. 90, §104 (hereafter cited as *CW*, vol. 14).

55 *MDR*, p. 196.

Death dreams **53**

56 Jenny March, *Cassell's Dictionary of Classical Mythology* (London: Cassell, 1998), pp. 390–391.
57 *MDR*, p. 195.
58 *SOT, CW*, vol. 5, §198. Jung mentions the association of soul to birds and how he 'attributes serious physical diseases to loss of soul. There are innumerable rites for calling the "soul-bird" back into the sick person.' 'The Psychological Foundation of Belief in Spirits', *CW*, vol. 8, §586. In Greek mythology there exists a tradition of birds associated with transformation as a result of grieving over the dead. Alcyon, is changed into a kingfisher after the loss of her husband, Ceyx and the sisters Procne and Philomela are transformed in grief into a nightingale and swallow respectively. March, *Cassell's Dictionary*, pp. 76 and 732–734.
59 Jung associates the spiritual world with the world of his No. 2 personality, known as the spirit of the depths, as well as the world of his own soul (*RB*, pp. 208a and 236a respectively).
60 *CW*, vol. 14, §288.
61 The Rosicrucian Archive [online]. Rosicrucian Library, last modified 7 September 2003, www.crcsite.org/Tabula.htm; and Thom Cavalli, *Alchemical Psychology* (New York: Tarcher/Putnam, 2002), p. 197.
62 Von Franz, 'Archetypes Surrounding Death', p. 6.
63 Ibid., p. 7.
64 The significance of the twelve dead might point to the possibility that the instructions of the Tabula Smaragdina, according to the Rosicrucians, appear in twelve steps. See www.crcsite.org/Tabula.htm.
65 *MDR*, p. 196.
66 Ibid.
67 Compare this to Jung's first recorded dream from his childhood of a phallus. The same anticipation seems present here very early on, his fear that animation might occur that it might awaken and move toward him (*MDR*, p. 27).
68 Joan Chodorow quotes from Mary Foote's private mimeographed seminar notes Lecture I, 4 May 1932. Chodorow, *Jung on Active Imagination*, p. 7. Also noted in his commentary in *Liber Secundus* that if you pursue your curiosity into the unconscious, this alone will cause it to transmute (*RB*, p. 263a).
69 Jung used the term mummified on several occasions in *Memories, Dreams, Reflections*: here (p. 196); in reference to the dwarf in his first active imagination (p. 203); and in a conversation with Freud of some significance, also discussed in Chapter 9 (p. 180).

PART II
Liber Primus

7

THE RED BOOK

The Red Book contains substantial material about the dead and the question was to determine if the narrative thread of the recurring references to the dead so prevalent in Memories Dreams Reflections, was enhanced and perhaps elucidated here. My goal was to look at episodes in which the dead featured prominently in order to gain a clearer idea as to their specific role in Jung's confrontation and to what effect. Therefore, it is hoped that the reader examines discussions in the following chapters as part of the larger narrative of The Red Book and sees this contribution as just one theme to the work as a whole.

Predecessors to The Red Book

Jung is not alone in being an intellectually inquisitive seeker who encountered non-ordinary, exceptional or transrational experiences. Literature is replete with accounts of other-world adventures, which suggest a psychological component to the literal and symbolic journey. Helen Luke, author of a Jungian study of Dante's Divine Comedy stresses that such journeys are for a purpose:

> [W]e must never forget that our final concern is with . . . the living man, who will return to ordinary human consciousness, and for whom . . . the darkness of the pit, the clarity and hard work of purgation and the intuitions of bliss are simultaneously present conscious or unconsciously.[1]

She further emphasises: 'the theme of the whole poem [is] the conscious return of a man . . . to the Center . . . by the hard road of individuation'.[2] These three elements also apply to Jung's enterprise in The Red Book. It is by way of struggle through his visionary material that he emerges more conscious and with a blueprint for a future psychological model of the unconscious. Yet the style of the work as

58 *Liber Primus*

a whole reflects literary predecessors whom Jung knew well. What helps implicate the text is that now it sits alongside literary works that describe details of visionary journeys and specifically those to the underworld.[3] *Gilgamesh*, *The Odyssey*, Virgil's *Aeneid*, Dante's *Inferno* and Swedenborg's *Heaven and Hell* are obvious antecedents. However, *The Red Book* contrasts notably. When Odysseus makes a sacrificial fire, he does so *in order* to speak to his deceased mother. Aeneas journeys to the underworld for the *expressed purpose* of speaking to his deceased father. These episodes differ significantly to Jung's project in *The Red Book*.[4] Although Jung experienced death dreams before his confrontation, which could be seen as a harbinger for that seminal time, his descents, as far as can be understood, were not for the intended purpose of meeting the dead. Rather, these encounters were the by-product of attempting to manage the psychic pressures of the moment through the method of descent. Such a distinction makes Jung's encounters with the dead not just spontaneous in terms of timing and content, but more authentic in that as far as we know there was no preconceived notion on Jung's part that he would meet the dead. This, of course, would have differed distinctly during the many séances that he attended.[5]

Thus, *The Red Book* can be viewed as an account of a visionary tale in which his discovery of the dead *in addition* to other figures of the unconscious contributed to an adjustment of Jung's conscious attitude. In this instance, Jung shares the same journey as any hero who comes to the end of his physical and emotional reserves and simply must try a different way in order to adjust to the hardships of life. With Odysseus and Aeneas, their journeys came to a literal halt and they appealed to the wisdom of the deceased to obtain a vision of the future and of themselves. Gilgamesh descends to gain immortality and a relief from the burdens of grief. Similarly, Dante's vision of Hell assists him with a literary landscape in which he can place the moral and spiritual challenges of his day.[6] As Roger Woolger points out, addressing the same literary precedents to *The Red Book*: 'Jung is painfully aware he is following a well-trodden path.'[7]

Swedenborg also must be included here, more specifically because his visions include a type of spiritual cosmology in which revelations about the dead and their lives as discarnates are specifically detailed. Swedenborg's angels, he believed, 'were the souls of departed human beings once alive, who live in Heaven in the form of their old bodies, and consociate with those whom they have most loved on earth but who now dwell in heavenly societies'.[8] His impressions of the afterlife and some of Jung's own conclusions contain similarities. Swedenborg sees stages in the afterlife in which the newly deceased come into realisations: 'The first state . . . resembles his state in the world.'[9] This resonates with what Jung discusses in the *Sermones* as the degree of awareness that the living have of the dead, which they appear to carry over into the afterlife.[10] Swedenborg's second state or 'state of deeper interests' is so named because 'we are given access to the deeper reaches of our minds, or of our intentions and thoughts, while the more outward interests that engaged us . . . become dormant'.[11]

This of course sounds similar to Jung's opinion that the dead can only take over into death the psychological growth made during their lifetime and it is this that the dead are intently interested in learning from the recently deceased.[12] This corresponds to Swedenborg's third state, which was one of instruction or 'preparation for heaven'.[13] This final state is similar to Jung's role as instructor to the recently deceased in the *Sermones*, in which this part of the text now appears specifically tailored for the recently deceased and their new life as discarnates.

Swedenborg's writings came as a result of trance states in which 'inward visions [occurred] while awake, but with eyes closed'.[14] He further described being '"inspirited" that is, through his soul in connection to the Divine'.[15] Similarly Jung describes:

> It would be going perhaps too far to speak of an affinity; but at all events the soul must contain in itself the faculty of relationship to God, i.e. a correspondence otherwise a connection could never come about . . . It enables the soul to be an eye destined to see the light, for 'As the eye to the sun, so the soul corresponds to God'.[16]

Thus the relationship both men had to their visions served to help orient and define an inward faculty of visioning.

Like Jung, Swedenborg was wholly changed by his visionary experiences and where Swedenborg built a theology from his visions of heaven and hell, Jung gleaned a psychological map, one assisted by the literal dead. What still must be considered to have influenced Jung's conception of the episodes in *The Red Book* is the method that he used to access these depths, active imagination and more specifically with the dead, *interpsychic* rapport. This remained just as fundamental to his psychological model as did the content he found there.

In this respect, William Blake, also a follower of Swedenborg for a brief time, holds some similarities.[17] It was known that Blake attended his brother while dying and is said to have witnessed: 'At the last solemn moment, the visionary eyes beheld the released spirit ascend heavenward through the matter-of-fact ceiling "clapping its hands for joy."'[18] He also claimed that he spent consistent periods of time in communion with his deceased brother[19] and it was in one of these visions that he acquired an idea that changed the way he approached the production of his printed engravings: 'his brother Robert stood before him in one of his visionary imaginations, and so decidedly directed him in the way in which he ought to proceed, that he immediately followed his advice'.[20] This enabled him 'a method of creating words and images in a single operation', 'a wholly new kind of art that proclaimed the unity of human vision'.[21]

Even without the knowledge of such influence from the deceased, Blake's art looks so singularly influenced by his visions that details of these conversations are not necessary to know that depictions of angelic beings might have derived from his actual visions.[22] It is Peter Ackroyd's concise statement, 'He *saw* what he imagined', that is so apt for Jung.[23] They both were prompted to action as a result of these exceptional experiences: for Jung kept a visual and narrated account composing *The Red Book* and Blake did the same with his art and poetry.

60 *Liber Primus*

Although Kant and Schopenhauer's contributions on spirits are readily detected in Jung's early work, Jung was not interested in proof of an afterlife philosophically or otherwise, but rather more interested in the benefits of and the need for a conception of an afterlife.[24] For him, this was a way of strengthening one's psyche towards the inevitable and to be able to meet death in the conceptual work done beforehand.

He visited the topic even much later after his confrontation. And yet, because Jung emerges from *The Red Book* with a more certain understanding as to the interplay between the unconscious and conscious, the work just might need to be discussed in terms of the same method and content he uncovered in the form of the visioning in active imagination. His real commitment was in experience and that true knowledge was based on empirical data. Therefore, he deemed the psychological implication of a relationship with the dead more important than the need to prove the dead's existence. Any metaphysical truth was less important than the psychological truth of those experiences.[25]

What is wholly unique and must be evaluated far apart from the literary precedents of such visionary works is what Jung eventually does with his discoveries. He develops an architecture of the psyche and emerges from his underworld exploits with an understanding of it as a psychological terrain. Miller puts it well:

> The descent into the underworld of souls (psychai, animae) is a descent into a soul perspective or depth-perspective . . . One might say that the descent into hell is actually the ascent of soul . . . it gives the human ego a perspective from a soulful point of view. The descent is itself a resurrection.[26]

That is, as a result of his explorations, Jung discovers structural aspects of his Self amidst a personal and collective unconscious and uses the content to inform the process of the unconscious dynamic. Whereas these literary precedents used the descent to revision their own lives and gain clarity and perspective as a result, Jung emerged with a plan for others, a map that would allow others to take their own journey and emerge hopefully with confirmation of similar results.

Notes

1   Helen Luke, *Dark Wood to White Rose: Journey and Transformation in Dante's Divine Comedy* (New York: Parabola Books, 2003), p. xv.
2   Ibid., p. xviii.
3   *The Red Book* can also be considered a part of a genre of visionary literature that would include visions such as St Augustine's conversion, Boethius' *Consolation of Philosophy*, and the visions of Perpetua, but for this study it is the works with visions of the dead that are comparatively the most useful.
4   This research project began as a Jungian analysis of Book VI of the Aeneid. I was struck by the parallels particularly with Anchises, Aeneas' father, appearing to him as a ghost and requesting that he come to the underworld to show Aeneas his future in founding the settlement and people that would become the great city of Rome. I found Jung's dream of Paul Jung a profound moment in Jung's attempt to understand the dead in his personal

The Red Book **61**

material. Each father uses his appearance in deceased form to guide his son to his future, Aeneas to carry on his journey, and Jung to pursue the psychological questions of the dead.

5 Jung was to attend séances as late as 1931. Charet, *Spiritualism*, pp. 282–283 n. 230.
6 Luke, *Dark Wood*, p. xvii.
7 Woolger also links the work to T. S. Eliot's *Waste Land*, Egyptian sacred texts, Gnostic texts and the 'Walpurgisnacht' in Goethe's *Faust*. Roger Woolger, 'Understanding C.G Jung's *Red Book*, Part 1', *Network Review* (Summer, 2011): 1–5, at 5.
8 Taylor further compares the backgrounds of both: 'For Jung, Swedenborg's ideas also represented a teleological and mythopoetic iconography of personal transformation ... Both had come from intensely religious families. Both had first turned to science and then ended in religion. Both had made the transition after an extended struggle with the unconscious that led to [life-] transforming experiences. Both evolved a mythic vision of the interior world that had great pragmatic usefulness in their respective careers. Jung thus used Swedenborg in a number of ways to corroborate aspects of his own psychology of the unconscious.' Taylor is referring to Jung's reference of Swedenborg in his Zofingia lectures and early professional writings. Eugene Taylor, 'Jung and His Intellectual Context: The Swedenborgian Connection', *Studia Swedenborgiana* 7, no. 2 (June 1991): 7.
9 Emanuel Swedenborg, *Heaven and Hell* (West Chester, PA: Swedenborg Foundation, 2010), p. 294, §493.
10 This is what emerges in the teachings of the *Sermones*.
11 Swedenborg, *Heaven and Hell*, p. 294, §493.
12 *MDR*, p. 339.
13 Swedenborg, *Heaven and Hell*, p. 305, §512. Similar to the dream of one of Jung's patients who recalled giving a lecture to the deceased on what it was like to be in the hereafter (*MDR*, p. 336).
14 Bergquist, Lars, *Swedenborg's Dream Diary* (West Chester, PA: Swedenborg Foundation, 2013), p. 44.
15 Ibid., p. 45.
16 C. G. Jung, 'Psychology and Religion: West and East', trans. R. F. C. Hull, in *The Collected Works*, Vol. 11 (Princeton, NJ: Princeton University Press, 1970), §11 (hereafter cited as *CW*, vol. 11).
17 Peter Ackroyd, *Blake, A Biography* (New York: Ballantine Books, 1995), p. 101.
18 Ibid.
19 Ibid. 'With his spirit I converse daily & hourly in the Spirit ... & See him in my remembrance in the regions of my Imagination. I hear his advice & even now write from his Dictate' (p. 101). Ackroyd continues: '[Blake] stated this some thirteen years after the experience of Robert's death and there is a suggestion here, highly significant to the biographer, that to contemplate the dead is also to hold communion with them' (ibid.)
20 Ibid., p. 111.
21 Ibid., pp. 112, 115 respectively.
22 See conversation of Blake and the Arch Angel Gabriel with details of ensuing vision. p. 195.
23 Ackroyd, *Blake*, p. 82
24 *MDR*, p. 333.
25 Main, *Jung on Synchonicity*; Shamdasani, 'The Boundless Expanse'.
26 David Miller, *Hells & Holy Ghosts: A Theopoetics of Christian Belief* (New Orleans, LA: Spring, 2004), pp. 36–37.

8

INTRODUCTION TO *LIBER PRIMUS*

Where the preceding years dealt with personal dream material, it must be remembered that the content that makes up *The Red Book* is composed almost exclusively of material gleaned from Jung's experimental approach of active imagination.[1] Shamdasani's footnotes and editorial annotations assist in tracking the differences between the original material taken from Jung's *Black Book* entries and the commentary and reflections on those original visions added later. Often Jung's commentary is quite helpful in terms of contextualising the vision alongside his own analysis of the symbolism and I have used this and the copious content in Shamdasani's footnotes to assist in creating a clearer picture of the significance of the dead amidst other competing material that Jung discovers in the unconscious.

Liber Primus serves as a rich introduction to Jung's confrontation.[2] It presents several key episodes, the importance of which rests in demonstrating how Jung came to identify the dead as such. In addition, what was previously understood to be Jung's No. 2 personality, as presented in *Memories, Dreams, Reflections*, is now fully conceived here in the exchanges with his spirit of the depths. Here, Jung's conception of his No. 2 proves to be *foundational* in terms of his orientation to his unconscious, his dead and his journey through the material composing *The Red Book*.

The role played by the spirit of the depths is specific; to assist Jung in awakening the dead.[3] Once the spirit of the depths orients Jung's focus inward, he initiates Jung not only into the deepest regions of the unconscious, but also into its very exploration using active imagination.[4] Barbara Hannah describes that due to his mother's No. 1 and No. 2, Jung understood 'the idea of an eternal and a temporal figure in each of us, which, many years later, he named the Self and ego'.[5] Jung was able to identify this presence or orientation in other people.

Jung's principle struggle and achievement in *Liber Primus* is moving toward discernment of all the figures while visioning within both a place (the very tangible parts of the unconscious) and a process (active imagination).

Introduction to *Liber Primus* **63**

In summary, the narrative action of the book focuses on the spirit of the depths and his initiation of Jung into his unconscious.[6] He meets other figures of the unconscious who inhabit the same personal and collective unconscious as the dead. While he struggles with the demands of the spirit of the depths, Jung's soul emerges as a separate and distinct entity adding yet another dimension to Jung's challenge in discerning such varied figures.[7] The arrival of his soul in the dialogue lays the foundation for Jung's first active imagination, the murder of Siegfried and finally meeting Elijah and Salome, which Jung calls the 'Mysterium Encounter'.

The theme of initiation is important throughout *Liber Primus* and is resonant of the ancient Mithraic mysteries, which Jung discussed in his 1925 seminars:[8] 'Awe surrounds the mysteries, particularly the mystery of deification. This was one of the most important of the mysteries; it gave the immortal value to the individual – it gave certainty of immortality.'[9]

The 'certainty of immortality' does not specifically point to deification, rather it is an orientation in the unconscious that sees the 'immortal value' or the quality of life in death, which Jung would continue to discover. He did not emerge from this initiation imbued with the sense of having become a god, but rather that he had overcome a fear of death, which in turn enabled him to forge a life-long relationship with the community of the dead.[10] Principally, the spirit of the depths assists Jung with 'healing the immortal' within.[11]

'The way of what is to come'

Liber Primus opens with the discussion of the two conflicting perspectives of Jung's personalities, No. 1 and No. 2. His No. 1 personality, known as the spirit of the times, assisted Jung the doctor to orient in the physical world. Personality No. 2, the spirit of the depths, called to Jung from a deeper more enigmatic place that the course of *The Red Book* explores in detail. He plays a much more central role in Jung's discoveries of the unconscious than previously gleaned from references in *Memories, Dreams, Reflections*, here assuming the roles of initiator, psychopomp and representative of the community of the dead.[12] In fact, the spirit of the depths is the principal entity through whom Jung identifies and orients his innerscape. His influence and importance cannot be underestimated. The spirit of the depths was not simply a psychological distraction, but served as the principal motivating agent for Jung's discovery of all figures of the unconscious, including the dead. Jung can be seen here working to understand the role and influence held by each of his No. 1 and No. 2 personalities and how these played into his understanding of the unconscious as both place and process.

The spirit of the depths proves his role foundational by orienting Jung inward, by defining him in terms of an image of eternity, and by attributing himself as a source of prophetic vision.[13] The claim that the spirit of the depths is stronger than the spirit of the times, who appears differently at each generation, implies a constant both in presence and perspective.[14] The spirit of the depths deposes the influence of the spirit of the times, forcing Jung to question not only his perspective as a scientist, but also his

64 *Liber Primus*

very livelihood. With his first words to Jung his perspective of immortality becomes clear: 'You are an image of the unending world, all the last mysteries of becoming and passing away live in you.'[15] By awakening Jung to his depths and awakening in him the notion of perpetual life, the spirit of the depths connects Jung to his own immortality and lays the way for his discovery of the unconscious, the underworld and his dead. Thus, Jung's very entrée into the realm of the dead is by way of the spirit of the depths or his personality No. 2. And so here we discover at the beginning of *Liber Primus* the real importance of No. 2.

Jung's soul and meaning-making

Part of the spirit of the depths' project is to prepare Jung for solitude, which allows him to perceive images as the method of communication, a start to his visioning faculty. He begins the process of trusting the spirit of the depths and describes a type of healing mercy that made him difficult to resist. What was missing for Jung during this state of total immersion was a semblance of truth, he needed 'a visible sign' that would reveal the veracity of the spirit of the depths' influence.[16] Such a request for a sign indicates the need for control in order to ascertain the truth of what was unfolding in him. Although the images were confronting and overwhelming, his cognisant self was asking the spirit of the depths to help confirm a link between his personal material and the 'outside' world. He received his answer in the form of the visions of flooding.[17]

It is important to note here that this vision came on spontaneously while Jung was on a train journey, and lasted for an hour.[18] The form the vision took looks to be a waking dream or a metachoric experience, one in which one's physical surroundings is replaced with a vision of a whole scene: here, the percipient 'temporarily loses his awareness of his normal environment, and seems to be perceiving a different one'.[19] Metachoric visions differ from daydreams or even from passive thinking, in which one's mind wanders into spaces and thoughts that might include visual content. Metachoric experiences appear to *emerge into* one's consciousness and distract with the perception of an altogether different and encompassing environment. We do not know during that hour if Jung was entirely engaged with the vision of the floods and blood, or whether this was occasionally broken by his reengagement with sitting on the train. Yet, we understand that the two experiences were occurring simultaneously.[20]

The significance here rests with Jung having posed a question to the spirit of the depths, within an active imagination, and receiving an answer 'in broad daylight'. This is an important developmental moment for Jung, that his attempt to make meaning of his experiences with the spirit of the depths was confirmed by outward events (i.e. the war broke out in August of the next year). In one respect this link between his inner and outer realities was confirmed, even though at the time Jung couldn't understand the significance of the visions. Nevertheless, a centring occurred around the veracity and confirmation of what unfolded for him. This was no less unsettling, but such a confirmation would have brought some relief as

Introduction to *Liber Primus* **65**

to the extreme doubts he was experiencing due to the wave of material emerging from the unconscious at the time. The depth from which the visions arose signalled to Jung that they were from the spirit of the depths, and felt deeply significant.

With this series of events, the precise intersection between Jung's spirit of the depths, his own soul and his narrative voice, reveal an extraordinary capacity for discernment. The shock of the visions of the flood, prompts Jung to call out for a seemingly absent soul. The 'unbearable longing' he experiences is the distance he feels from the spirit of the times, his life and equally his soul. He begins to realise how immersed he has become in the spirit of the depths and this region of the unconscious.

Shamdasani suggests this vision was linked to Jung's break with Freud and his resignation from the editorship of the *Jarbuch für Psychoanalytische und Pscyhopathologische Forschungen*.[21] There is a gap of sixteen days between 27 October 1913 when Jung resigned, signifying his break with Freud, and when he calls out to his soul on 12 November 1913. The vision was totally immersive, lasting two hours and was prescient by several months. I suggest that Jung's request to confirm the veracity of his encounters was the impetus for the visions and yet exacerbated by the events in his daily life.

Jung recounts that the spirit of the depths was pressuring him to acknowledge his soul as an independent entity. Bewildered, he hadn't realised his soul had been missing. That is, the service to his daily life had been lived without meaning and he needed a revisioning approach to his life with his soul: 'through whom I existed'.[22] At this point neither the spirit of the depths nor Jung's soul is visible. The discourse in this exchange unfolded with no apparent visual details about either one.

Jung grants that all the human trappings of influence, affluence and status were the result of living with a focus on the spirit of the times.[23] Yet, his desire diminished and he found himself yearning, a time he would later identify as the second half of life when one's focus turns inward.[24] This was the case with Jung, thus he needed to meet this challenge of death head on.[25]

On the service of the soul

15 November 1913

The real relationship between the spirit of the depths and Jung becomes clear during Jung's descent. The spirit of the depths says: 'Look into your depths, pray to your depths, waken the dead.'[26] It is precisely in this instruction that the importance of the spirit of the depths becomes clear; he initiates Jung into his own unconscious and into the very faculty that will assist him in discerning the dead.[27] The directive to look inward, to pray and to awaken the dead, orients Jung to seek the same region where the spirit of the depths himself resides and to prompt Jung to uncover his own relationship to it. This scene sets the course for Jung's further descents and of course his eventual discovery of the dead. Although Jung encountered the dead in his dreams the previous year, here the spirit of the depths indicates not only *that* he can find the dead, but *where* they can be found.

66 *Liber Primus*

At first, Jung doesn't seem to understand exactly what the spirit of the depths is demanding and when he looks inward, all he finds is memories of previous dreams, i.e. the spirit of the times. This shows Jung to be traversing regions of the unconscious specific to each of his No. 1 and No. 2 personalities. Jung's introspection has only brought him to a certain level of his personal unconscious, not the deeper, more collective level the spirit of the depths is asking him to reach.

The desert and its greening

Up to this point the narrative was comprised principally of discourse. As a result of the initiation, Jung begins to describe terrains and marks the first of many detailed descriptions of physical settings. The introduction of colour in particular is a notable addition and is due to the spirit of the depths' insistence that Jung return to his inner world to find the dead. He delves deeper, thus enabling visioning. As a result this scene is the first, which points to the unconscious being both place and process.

Jung wonders why he is finding his self in desert conditions, was it due to how he had lived up to this point?[28] And he admits to attending only to his spirit of the times at the cost of his soul and the spirit of the depths.[29] Not only does the visual setting correspond to Jung's inner orientation, but there appears a shared inner terrain inhabited by both the spirit of the depths and his soul. His inner landscape was arid and barren revealing neglect of them both. The greening of the desert is a direct result of his efforts to grow closer to the realm of the spirit of the depths and in turn his soul. The colour is a by-product of the process of inner focus and shows the facility of the unconscious to respond to concentrated libido.[30] Similar to the row of tombs dream, the idea of *betrachtan* is at play here. Jung shows his ability to observe changes while engaged in the visioning process.

It took twenty-five nights for Jung's soul to emerge from the shadows into a 'free-standing being'.[31] She grew not only closer to Jung, but Jung's perception of her became clearer. His focus and effort to interpret his visioning gave way to his soul's ability to reveal herself as a clear entity distinct and separate from the spirit of the depths. This project of discernment can also be credited with assisting Jung with the more involved encounter of his first active imagination.

Notes

1 One notable exception to consider is the case with the Siegfried episode presented as a dream in *Memories, Dreams, Reflections*, but the episode in *The Red Book* details it to be a 'dream vision' (*RB*, p. 241 n. 112).
2 The death dreams discussed bring the material up to the autumn of 1913, with the loggia dream not appearing in *The Red Book*. But, his first active imagination and the Siegfried dream do (December 1913).
3 *RB*, p. 235b.
4 Shamdasani and Paul Bishop connect the spirit of the times to the same expression used by Goethe in *Faust* (*RB*, p. 229 n. 5); Paul Bishop, '*The Red Book* in Relationship to German Classicism', lecture at Jung's *Red Book* Conference, San Francisco Jung Club (4–6 June 2010).

Introduction to *Liber Primus* **67**

5 Barabara Hannah, *Jung His Life and Work* (New York: G. P. Putnam's Sons, 1973), p. 70.

6 *RB*, p. 235b.

7 Ibid., p. 232a.

8 *AP*, pp. 97–98. Murray Stein points to initiation as the function of the spirit of the depths, but he uses the sense of the term to mean the region/era as opposed to Jung's personified sense of the term. See *The Red Book* (p. 238b), where Jung clearly refers to the spirit of the depths as 'he'. Murray Stein, 'Critical Notice, Jung, C.G., *The Red Book: Liber Novus*', *Journal of Analytical Psychology* 55 (2010): 423–434, at 426.

9 *AP*, p. 97.

10 Richard Noll, *The Jung Cult* (New York: Simon & Schuster, 1994), pp. 214–215. Shamdasani, in his book *Cult Fictions: C.G. Jung and the Founding of Analytical Psychology* (London: Routledge, 1998), takes up Noll's assumption that Jung 'formed a cult based on his self-deification' (p. 12). Shamdasani explains that Noll's claim is based solely on Jung's vision in which he experienced assuming the Christ figure during crucifixion. Noll's explanation regarding the symbolic encounters being similar to a mystery initiation now look to be accurate in light of the version published in *The Red Book*. Yet, I disagree with Noll's conclusion because he fails to address the psychological significance that the encounter prompts, i.e. that initiates into the mysteries participate in rites whose end result allows them to experience themselves in transformation. Thus, by concluding that Jung's experience can be reduced to self-deification with cult status seems to ignore the psychological dynamic of not only the transcendent function, but the psychological effects of initiations in general.

11 *RB*, p. 230a.

12 Ibid., pp. 207b; *MDR*, pp. 50, 51, 62, 84, 108.

13 *RB*, pp. 229b–230a.

14 Ibid., p. 229b.

15 Ibid., p. 230a. This was similarly expressed in Jung's chapter 'The Tower': 'There I live in my second personality, and see life . . . as something forever coming into being and passing on' (*MDR*, p. 265).

16 *RB*, p. 230b.

17 This vision occurred spontaneously during a train journey in October 1913, during the day. He includes the detail of the sea turning to blood as well as his visions the next summer of the cold snap sweeping Europe (*RB*, p. 231a and *MDR*, p. 199).

18 *MDR*, p. 199.

19 Green and McCreery, *Lucid Dreaming*, p. 2.

20 This incident is wholly similar to Swedenborg's vision of the fire in Stockholm in 1753. Swedenborg was 300 miles away in Gothenburg when he became distracted and began to relay details of a huge fire occurring simultaneously. The visionary dynamic is similar in terms of being metachoric, but Jung's was also prescient and he would see the details come true several months later. *CW*, vol. 8, pp. 481, 483.

21 *RB*, p. 232 n. 33.

22 Ibid., p. 232b.

23 Ibid., pp. 231b–232a.

24 Ibid., p. 232 n. 32. Shamdasani notes Jung discussed this in an ETH lecture he gave on 14 June 1935.

25 Not only was Jung intrigued with the Nekyia episode of the Odyssey, but he was also reading Dante during this time. Sonu Shamdasani, 'Carl Gustav Jung and *The Red Book* (part 1)', *Library of Congress Webcasts* [online], 19 June, 2010, www.loc.gov/today/cyberlc/feature_wdesc.php?rec=4909 (accessed 6 June 2011).

26 *RB*, p. 235b.

27 A note on terminology: The terms land of the dead, the underworld and the beyond, are all terms Jung uses, and here I use them interchangeably to refer to that part of the unconscious in which the dead reside. What is clear is that although a theoretical association has been made between these terms and the unconscious, through Jung's dreams and then extensive active imaginations, Jung proves the literal designation that these terms represent.

68 *Liber Primus*

28 *RB*, p. 235b.
29 Ibid., p. 236a.
30 This again is an example of *betrachten*. This can also be interpreted as the transcendent function where his focused dialogue affects his environment. See a similar dynamic with the Red One in *Liber Secundus*.
31 *RB*, p. 237a. Shamdasani notes that it took twenty-five nights for Jung to understand the spirit of the depths, and it would appear to have taken the same twenty-five nights to grasp his soul.

9

DESCENT INTO HELL IN THE FUTURE

Jung's first active imagination

12 December 1913

The spirit of the depths' overpowering perspective has already been associated with prophecy specifically with respect to visions of World War I.[1] By travelling to these perspectives, Jung reaches a level of the unconscious that either contains knowledge of future events or reveals the spirit of the depths' ability to access such.

Active imagination

Jung's first extended exposure to contents of the unconscious otherwise known as active imagination was described by Barbara Hannah:

> [T]he whole of what he discovered at this time can be seen in the term 'active imagination', because in it the ego plays an active role – it makes a conscious decision to drop down into the fantasy and then plays an active role in the subsequent development. Before Jung made this experiment in December, 1913, he was just an observer of 'passive imagination' that is, he watched fantasy after fantasy, as helpless to have any influence on it as a spectator in a cinema. But once he learned to take an active role in it himself, he found that he could have an influence on its development and that he was no longer a passive spectator at an unending flood of fantasies.[2]

Up to this point conversations with both the spirit of the depths and his soul, although considered active imagination, were dialogue driven and lacked the element of a physical orientation. In this first active imagination, Jung moves through his vision actively exploring terrain, differing significantly from his previous experiences of observation. His first active imagination (recounted in *The Red Book*) begins when the spirit of the depths introduced

70 *Liber Primus*

Jung to the inner world of his soul.[3] He credits the spirit of the depths, his No. 2, with his ability to see in the unconscious. Jung finds himself perceiving further and developing his inner vision. He would note in *Symbols of Transformation*: 'The visionary phenomenon produced by the first stage of introversion can be classed among the well-known symptoms of hypnagogic vision. They provide the basis for the actual visions or "self-perceptions" of the libido in the form of symbols.'[4] Here the visionary experience is a process of inner focus and visual discovery that amounts to an extended psychic interoception of the Self. The discovery of visual forms are a self expression of libido. In part, this process is the initial calculation of perception.

Visionary experiences have been associated with both the descent and initiatory rites. Joseph Henderson describes how the descent prompts a 'visionary primordial experience' and associates this with a 'rite of vision', indicating the response is universal.[5] Classicist Walter Burkert's notes about ancient mystery initiations:

> Quite common and in fact one of the main characteristics of mysteries is the *makarismos*, the praise of the blessed status of those who have 'seen' the mysteries. As the initiate is accepted and hailed by a chorus of those who have gone through the same . . . his feelings of relief will rise to the heights of exultation. Yet the texts insist that the true state of blessedness is not in this emotional resonance but in the act of 'seeing' what is divine.[6]

From Burkert's perspective, it is Jung's ability to 'see' what he is experiencing that defines the successful initiation.[7] Thus the spirit of the depths continues to drive Jung's discovery of the content of his own unconscious as well as the method he uses to discover that content. His body of knowledge about the process and what he 'sees' while engaged moves him toward an understanding of how the unconscious works.

The vision

This well-known scene, appearing first in *Memories, Dreams, Reflections*, yet more fully recounted in *The Red Book*, is Jung's first conscious descent, his first active imagination.[8] The richness in visual imagery and symbolism marks a turning point in unconscious material. He explains how the spirit of the depths usurped perspective and power from the spirit of the times, partly due to his ongoing conversation with his soul the preceding twenty-five nights.[9] With this orientation, Jung positions his soul as the new representative of his personal unconscious with his spirit of the depths representing his link to the collective. And what is certainly to become a much-quoted line, Jung states: 'Your soul is your own self in the spiritual world.'[10] Included in a footnote, he adds an intriguing detail that it was a dwarf who represented the spirit of the times and who stood in Jung's way of entering the deepest reaches of the 'innermost'. Described as 'clever . . . made of leather . . . sere and lifeless', the dwarf has been likened to Freud.[11] Here it is the spirit of the times reduced in size to a little man, with equally little

Descent into hell in the future **71**

influence in the unconscious world. From the vantage point of the unconscious, the spirit of the times has literally lost traction and influence with no ability to prevent Jung from descending to the underworld.

As Jung allows himself to drop into a cave with dark water, the vision begins with shrieking in the background. He removes a bright red stone from an opening in the rock face to see a bloody body floating followed by a large black scarab in the water. The scene ends with a red sun emerging from under the water as serpents shadow it and a profusion of blood.

In the seminars of 1925 Jung claims that the approach as a method worked well, but he hadn't understood all of what he had seen.[12] He felt that the image of an opening was perfect for initiating a descent, and by concentrating on going deeper Jung explains:

> I was using an archetype of considerable power in stimulating the unconscious, for the mystery attaching to caves comes down from immemorial times, one thinks at once of the Mithraic cult, of the catacombs etc. . . . the more I worked on the fantasy hole the more I seemed to descend.[13]

The cave indicates a clear orientation to the undiscovered parts of his unconscious: 'The cave . . . belongs to the dark territory of the underworld', it is 'a dwelling as well as a tomb . . . the vessel of death'.[14] Jung himself associated the cave with a grave showing that such an underground orientation holds symbolic association with not just the unconscious but with death itself.[15]

In *Symbols of Transformation*, Jung describes:

> [M]an at death comes to the waters of the Styx, and there embarks on the 'night sea journey'. Those black waters of death are the water of life, for death with its cold embrace is the maternal womb, just as the sea devours the sun but brings it forth again. Life knows no death.[16]

This quote not only ties together several thematic ideas present in Jung's first active imagination, but also reveals the inherent transformative quality of the unconscious that Jung begins to discover during the process of these descents. He expresses the same idea, with additional elements in *Psychology of the Transference*: 'a kind of *descensus ad inferos* – a descent into Hades and a journey to the land of ghosts somewhere beyond this world, beyond consciousness, hence an immersion in the unconscious'.[17]

This vision begins the journey motif, which is explored in great detail throughout the rest of *The Red Book*. Jung considered the episode to be one of death and rebirth.[18] In the *Memories, Dreams, Reflections* version, the physical descriptions point to themes of death, but discernibly of birth as well. Descriptors such as 'soft, sticky' and 'squeezed . . . through the narrow entrance' indicate birth motifs as he is being introduced into the deepest reaches of his psyche as well as into the very method of its exploration.[19] This scene is the first in *The Red Book* that links the unconscious

72 *Liber Primus*

with both death and rebirth. Although the scene lacks dialogue, Jung's inner focus and desire to follow the experiment where it leads, prompts not only the rich visual details, but lays the way for figures of the unconscious to emerge along with the conversational component in later attempts.

Mummification

On three occasions Jung uses this term mummification when recounting dreams or visions: his first active imagination, in the row of tombs dream and in a conversation in 1909 with Freud of some significance.

Mummification is a process of preservation for/from death or in Jung's case preparation to meet it: 'In Egyptian belief the preservation of the corpse was crucial to the continuation of life after death.'[20] What remains becomes a relic of an historic time and a marker of symbolic significance. Mummification was used to insure a successful passage into the afterlife. Von Franz explains how this 'sacred art of mummification was a symbolic performance whose goal it was to produce the resurrection body or "eternal body" of the dead'.[21] That Jung uses this word three times in his writings to identify certain images is not in itself notable, but rather the context reveals why he used this particular word. Mummified images prepare Jung in the first instance to orient his focus where alchemical work occurs in the unconscious. Then to discover both the lively contents as it is related to the dead and how it serves as the location of the transformation towards immortality. Mummification, as the recurrent image on these occasions, points back to the loggia dream, when Jung witnessed the potential for transmogrification of the girl shifting into a bird, which mummification as a process also attempts.

Although *The Red Book* makes clear that Jung experiences the spirit of the times as a dwarf, in the *Memories, Dreams, Reflections* version of the episode Jung squeezes past the dwarf who is just as much guardian of the entrance into the deeper level of the psyche as witness. The dwarf represents both the shadow and perhaps even the mummified or preserved feelings that Jung holds for Freud.[22] Whereas Jung passes the dwarf and willingly continues deeper into his vision, the dwarf remains on the previous level, worn, leathery and, most importantly, as if mummified.

In 1909 Freud and Jung travelled to the United States together to give talks at Clark University. He and Freud had a conversation when they met up in Germany, where Jung began discussing the bog men of Bremen. He describes confusing them with mummies and this agitated Freud, who pressed Jung about this fascination, he then fainted.[23] Jung differentiated the bog men corpses from the mummies, perhaps due to his interest in their 'natural mummification' and accessible visibility.[24] He had been thinking about a sort of preservation not only of the past, but of the dead. And his apparent slip clearly points to his preoccupation with depth, layers and preserved activity, specifically of the dead.

During the same trip, Jung and Freud spoke at length about their dreams and one in particular of a house with many levels. Jung identified Roman walls, a cave, other cultures and skulls.[25] In his retelling of the dream, he is much more intrigued with the significance of the levels of the house and the symbolism of the skulls. With Freud's insistence that the skulls represented a death wish, Jung remained frustrated yet knowingly lied to Freud to see how he would respond. Freud was pleased with Jung's assignation that the skulls could be associated with a death wish towards his wife and sister and not himself.[26] Skulls for Jung symbolised a level of the unconscious accessible by a descent, a type of way marker. Again, a symbol associated with death, for Jung meant old and also accessible. According to Freud, Jung's seeming preoccupation with death, or rather the dead in death, was enough to rattle him, his fainting revealed perhaps his feeling overwhelmed at being confronted by his anointed son.[27]

The conflicts between Jung and Freud can be analysed from many angles, but here the struggle over libido surfaces. The mummification theme obviously looks toward the preservation of the past in the psyche but also looks at the issue of immortality as an extension to what Jung discovered in his death dreams. The connection between mummification, immortality and the dead must be spelled out. Mummification points to life, and the Egyptian idea of preparing for immortality or a continued life in death seems to be how it fits into Jung's interpretation. That mummification and immortality both are interested in how the dead remain alive is what Jung explores throughout *The Red Book* and in particular in the *Sermones*. For he could find the past in himself via the descent, simply by looking. Mummification serves as a holding place for the concept of *betrachten*. That is when Jung looks and sees, the preserved intention of immortality becomes operational.

The colour red

The whole of the active imagination is framed at the beginning and end by the colour red: at the beginning with the 'luminous' crystal, covering the hole 'like a ruby' and the end with the luminous', 'red' and 'newborn' sun.[28] These images, framing the movement of the vision, represent the feeling function: 'The growing redness (rubedo) . . . denotes an increase of warmth and light coming from the sun, consciousness. This corresponds to the increasing participation of consciousness, which now begins to react emotionally to the contents produced by the unconscious.'[29] The colour anticipates the loosening of Jung's superior or thinking function and its sacrifice makes available 'the libido necessary to activate the inferior functions'.[30] There occurs a warming of his previous mental approaches to the world with the appearance of the newborn sun serving as confirmation that consciousness is responding.

The rubedo or red stage in alchemy represents the colour and stage of transmutation and is considered the completion of the philosopher's stone. Von Franz states, 'the philosopher's stone of the alchemists was conceived as the "immortal body" of the dead. Its completion happened in the stage of the rubedo-redness'.[31] In this third stage, 'consciousness discovers the divine world'.[32] This alchemical process indicates that within the unconscious is all that is needed to forge a relationship to the immortal self.

74 *Liber Primus*

In Jung's own commentary of the vision, he explains that the scarab represented death as of course did the body of the slain hero. And just as the sun warms the earth for new growth, the midnight sun, or sun of the depths, emerges to 'quicken' or awaken the dead in the unconscious.[33] It also awakens dormant content, not just the dead. But, as the project of the spirit of the depths is to assist Jung in meeting the depths, awakening the dead and initiating the visual faculty to discern what he discovers there, it appears that the new sun augurs Jung's future relationship with the unconscious and all that he discovers there.

Classics scholar Peter Kingsley explains:

> Right at the roots of western as well as eastern mythology there's the idea that the sun comes out of the underworld and goes back to the underworld every night. It belongs in the underworld . . . The source of light is at home in the darkness . . . [Pythagoreans] saw volcanic fire as the light in the depths of darkness . . . For them the light of the sun and moon and stars were just reflections, offshoots of the invisible fire inside the underworld. And they understood that there's no going up without going down, no heaven without going through hell. To them the fire in the underworld was purifying, transforming, immortalizing.[34]

What meets Jung is a vivid display of death and regeneration. The blonde youth[35] is fatally wounded in the head indicating that the thinking function upon which Jung relied up to this point has been sacrificed or belaboured to excess (the theme is confirmed with the murder of Siegfried a week later). By abandoning the spirit of the times and following the instructions of the spirit of the depths, Jung descends to and wades through the dark waters of the underworld. He discovers the murdered youth and the location of death. His ability to abandon the spirit of the times quite possibly was the defining move that facilitated this vision. Now, it appears from the vision and what we know about the Siegfried murder, that the libido resulting from the sacrifice of his spirit of the times results in Jung's capacity to continue his explorations of the unconscious and his ability to vision the dead. This possibility seems positive as the youth, although dead, appears floating on a current of water, indicating continued movement and ready access to the feeling function.

In 1925 Jung includes another important detail to the vision about the outpouring of blood, 'I withdrew from the hole and the blood came gushing from it as from a severed artery . . . the blood kept gushing up and would not stop. I had the feeling of being absolutely powerless.'[36] Although he expresses confusion about its meaning, he attributes it to his visions of blood to augur both death and life.[37]

In later scenes of *Liber Secundus*, blood takes on a particular significance with regard to the dead. The connection between blood and necromancy or the ancient practice of speaking to the dead deserves attention. It is well known that shortly after the break with Freud, Jung went on a cruise on Lake Zurich with friends, one of whom was Jung's oldest friend, Albert Oeri. Several times Oeri read aloud the Nekyia scene from Homer's *Odyssey*, the episode when Odysseus journeys to the land of the dead.[38]

ODYSSEUS AND THE DEAD

Odysseus did not actually travel to the Underworld in the same or as detailed a manner as Aeneas in Book 6 of Virgil's *Aeneid*. Odysseus sees and speaks with his deceased mother only after a blood sacrifice. In fact, Homer writes that after the animal sacrifice is made in the sacrificial pit 'the souls gathered . . . From every side they came and sought the pit with rustling cries . . . Meanwhile [Odysseus] crouched with [his] drawn sword to keep the surging phantoms from the bloody pit'.[39] This indicates that the souls approach Odysseus, as opposed to Odysseus travelling *to* them. More accurately, Jenny March describes how 'Odysseus travelled to the edge of the Underworld'.[40] There is no journey imagery here as there is in *The Aeneid*. Classicist Daniel Ogden distinguishes the difference: 'Aeneas accomplished his necromancy by descent rather than by the raising of ghosts'.[41] Perhaps Jung was intrigued that due to its very brief description the Odyssey passage lent itself to a further and perhaps freer psychological interpretation than Virgil's most detailed account.

That Jung wanted to hear this passage several times is important because he was at the brink of engaging in his own descent almost as if hearing the tale would help him anticipate his need to do so. In 1935 in his essay on Picasso, Jung explains:

> The Nekyia is no aimless and purely destructive fall into the abyss, but a meaningful *katabasis eis antron*, a descent into the cave of initiation and secret knowledge. The journey through the psychic history of mankind has as its object the restoration of the whole man, by awakening the memories in the blood.[42]

From this perspective, it seems possible that his first active imagination presents an initiation rite into his ability to see the dead and anticipates his eventual ability to engage. The idea of memories in the blood is helpful when considering how urgent the dead's requests for blood are in episodes of *The Red Book*. Perhaps their need stems from a faint memory of their incarnate life and access to these memories can only be facilitated by a physical gesture. To the dead, blood might sing with memories of what they can recall about the living and awaken them to the possibility of connecting to the living still again. Or perhaps for them blood is the symbol of incarnate life. Either consideration allows the dead to draw nearer to the living.[43]

Serpents

Towards the end of the vision as Jung catches sight of the new sun shining from the watery depths, he describes terror at the sight of 'small serpents . . . a thousand

76 *Liber Primus*

serpents . . . veiling the sun'.[44] The serpent is also a libido symbol and one that reappears several times in *The Red Book*.[45] The image here clearly explains what was all too briefly described in Jung's 1925 seminars and brings clarity to that discussion.[46] The snake is both a libido symbol and a symbol of rebirth because; 'The dead heroes transform into serpents in the underworld.'[47] That is, the libido of the highest ideal, the hero, is transformed into the snake or serpent. At the end of his active imagination, after seeing the dead youth, Jung witnesses the collective libido available to him for further exploration of the unconscious and this is indicated to him in the form of the thousands of snakes covering the sun.

Jungian analysts Henderson and Oakes in the work, *The Wisdom of the Serpent*, discuss the symbolism of the serpents:

> Most snakes representing death also represent the souls of the dead, and they are only dead to this life; they live a heightened and more important life in the other world to which they have retreated. As such, they are the ghosts or ancestral figures, or mythical, primal titanic men who walked the earth in former times. Although impersonating death in its ghostly aspect, they are also the harbingers of that life which springs anew from the original source of all things.[48]

From Oakes' perspective this makes the shift from dead matter to serpents quite fluid. What is populating the underworld as serpents could possibly be the representatives of the spirits of the dead. In *Scrutinies*, Jung associates the two: 'The serpent is an earthly . . . spirit . . . akin to the spirits of the dead.'[49] Not only does Jung experience the possibility of rebirth with the appearance of the new sun, but with the assistance of the spirit of the depths he has awakened his dead in the form of snakes representing the community of heroic ancestors. The significance of the snakes veiling the sun could look to the prominence of the ancestors' power to influence Jung in the unconscious setting and could anticipate the role the dead will play in his future active imaginations. Where the symbolism of the sun appeared so prominent in the solar hero myth in *Psychology of the Unconscious*, Jung's experience here looks to rebalance the myth by considering the role of the dead.

Jung's first active imagination is important to include because it proves the effect of the spirit of the depths' commitment to encourage Jung to his furthest depths. This occasion incited him to experience the first richly visual encounter absent of dialogue. What Jung senses is that he has reached the muddy waters where death resides. These waters point to a source within Jung that houses both the disintegration promised by death and the renewal of libido represented by the newborn sun and serpents.

A week later, Jung would understand the significance of the vision when he had the Siegfried dream, which he considered to be an energetic continuation of the theme of death and rebirth first introduced here.[50] But truly the dynamic of active imagination would be fully inaugurated in the 'Mysterium Encounter' at the end of *Liber Primus*, when he meets Elijah and Salome. Thus, Jung experiences the shift

Descent into hell in the future **77**

from observer to explorer in this scene to a full-fledged participant in the Siegfried episode, then finally an active participant in discourse in the Mysterium. It is this latter seminal episode, which sees Jung engaged in active imagination proper.

Notes

1 *RB*, p. 231a.
2 Hannah, *Jung*, pp. 108–109. What we've seen up to this point is Jung struggling with discernment of the competing attentions of the spirit of the depths and his soul. Although there is struggle here, Jung does not come across in the first part of *Liber Primus* as a 'passive observer'. Hannah could be commenting on private conversations regarding personal material Jung shared or material included in the *Black Books* that is not included in *The Red Book*, to which she might have had access.
3 *RB*, p. 237b. A passage taken from the *Corrected Draft* indicates that with the help of the spirit of the depths, Jung reached 'the innermost' (*RB*, p. 238 n. 91).
4 *SOT, CW*, vol. 5, p. 175, §255.
5 Joseph Henderson, *Thresholds of Initiation* (Ashville, NC: Chiron, 2005), pp. 153–155.
6 Walter Burkert, *Greek Religion* (London: Wiley-Blackwell, 1987), p. 93. Similar is Kerenyi's association of the Eleusinian mysteries with the goal of 'visio beatifica' or seeing Persephone, the goddess of the underworld. Carl Kerenyi, *Eleusis: Archetypal Image of Mother and Daughter* (Princeton, NJ: Princeton, 1991), p. 95.
7 Although the question whether Jung is actually experiencing the divine is less important here, he does associate his encounters with the dead in terms of the divine (*RB*, p. 296b).
8 *MDR*, pp. 203–204; *AP*, pp. 47–48; *RB*, p. 238b.
9 *RB*, p. 238b.
10 Ibid., 288b.
11 Ibid., pp. 238–239 n. 91. Note, the dwarf does not appear in *The Red Book*, but does in *Memories, Dreams, Reflections*. Shamdasani includes the dwarf along with other details from the *Draft*. The dwarf in *Memories, Dreams, Reflections* is mummified and with 'leathery skin' but is not mentioned at all in *Analytical Psychology*.
12 *AP*, p. 48.
13 Ibid., p. 47. 'The catacombs were not originally places of concealment, but were chosen as symbolical of a descent into the underworld' (*AP*, p. 98). Jung also notes in *Symbols of Transformation*: 'The descent into the earth is a piece of womb symbolism and was widespread in the form of cave worship' (*SOT, CW*, vol. 5, p. 341). Both David Ulaney and Marvin Meyer locate the worship of Mithras as well as the site of the mysteries in 'subterranean sanctuaries' or caves, respectively. David Ulaney, *The Origins of the Mithraic Mysteries* (New York: Oxford University Press, 1989), p. 35; Marvin Meyer, *The Ancient Mysteries: A Sourcebook* (San Francisco, CA: Harper & Row, 1987), p. 199.
14 Erich Neumann, *The Great Mother* (Princeton, NJ: Princeton University Press, 1955), pp. 44 and 45 respectively. Jung, in his discussion of the Koran entitled 'The Cave', says: 'The cave is the place of rebirth, that secret cavity in which one is shut up in order to be incubated and renewed.' He calls this the 'rebirth mystery'. C. G. Jung, 'A Typical Set of Symbols Illustrating the Process of Transformation', in *The Archetypes and the Collective Unconscious*, trans. R. F. C. Hull, *The Collected Works*, Vol. 9 (Princeton, NJ: Princeton University Press, 1959), pp. 135, 240 (hereafter cited as *CW*, vol. 9).
15 *SOT, CW*, vol. 5, p. 338. In his *Draft* Jung added, 'To my astonishment I realized that my feet sank into the black muddy water of the river of death' [*Corrected Draft* adds: 'for that is where death is', p. 41] (*RB*, p. 239, n. 91). This detail suggests that Jung experienced travelling distances and arriving at a place that prompts the very real sensations of death. His description suggests not a metaphoric understanding of death's locale or even a symbolic representation of it, but rather a literal one. During the episode 'Death' in *Liber Secundus*, Jung observes the process of how all living things pass over into death. The scene gives the

78 *Liber Primus*

impression that Jung is experiencing the sensations of what death as a process entails (*RB*, pp. 273–275). Although in *Memories, Dreams, Reflections*, Jung links the unconscious to the 'mythic' land of the dead, his telling here reveals the physical sensations that he associates with it (*RB*, p. 216). The distancing from a literal interpretation of the underworld comes with Hillman's *The Dream and the Underworld*, in which he suggests that the unconscious is the underworld populated by images. These images, the foundation of the archetypal school, stand in contrast to the concrete manner in which Jung experiences his encounters in *The Red Book*. James Hillman, *The Dream and the Underworld* (New York: Harper Perennial, 1979).

16 *SOT, CW*, vol. 5, p. 218.

17 *CW*, vol. 16, §455.

18 *MDR*, p. 204; *Scrutinies, RB*, p. 339.

19 *MDR*, p. 203. *The Red Book* version reveals less birth imagery and instead stresses Jung's terror at the discovery of the dead youth. In 1925, Jung refers to the murder of the youth as 'secret' because: 'If you give up this thinking, this hero ideal, you commit a secret murder – that is, you give up your superior function' (*AP*, p. 48). This detail is not included in *The Red Book* or *Memories, Dreams, Reflections*.

20 David Silverman, ed. *Ancient Egypt* (Oxford: Oxford University Press, 2003), p. 138.

21 Von Franz, 'Archetypes', p. 6.

22 Steven Walker, *Jung and the Jungians on Myth* (London: Routledge, 2002), notes that the dwarf represents a shadow figure and specifically 'murderous energy' similar to the shadow/primitive in the Siegfried dream (p. 44). In contrast, von Franz accounts that dwarfs can also represent luck and good ideas. Betty Addelson, *The Lives of Dwarfs: Their Journey From Public Curiosity Towards Social Liberation* (New Brunswick, NJ: Rutgers University Press, 2005), p. 105.

23 *MDR*, p. 180.

24 Ibid., p. 179.

25 Ibid., p. 183.

26 Ibid.

27 Ibid., p. 181.

28 *AP*, p. 48.

29 *CW*, vol. 14, p. 307.

30 *AP*, p. 48.

31 Von Franz, 'Archetypes', 1979, p. 8.

32 Cavalli, *Alchemical Psychology*, p. 182.

33 *RB*, p. 239.

34 Peter Kingsley, *In the Dark Places of Wisdom* (Point Reyes, CA: Golden Sufi Center, 1999), pp. 68–69. Shamdasani notes a very worthwhile ETH lecture in 1935, where Jung discussed the sun as a universal symbol (Modern Psychology, p. 231) (*RB*, p. 239 n. 96).

35 There is no mention of the youth being blonde in this version of the episode, only in its commentary (*RB*, p. 239a, where he calls the youth 'the blonde hero') and Jung's painting of the scene in the calligraphic volume shows the floating body with blonde hair (folio IIIb). In *Analytical Psychology*, Jung calls him 'fair-haired' (p. 48).

36 *AP*, p. 48.

37 See *RB*, p. 239b. Shamdasani notes that Jung had the vision on his way to visit his mother-in-law for her birthday, which was on 17 October 1913 (*RB*, p. 231 n. 16).

38 Vincent Brome relays the story from an interview with Jolande Jacobi and says that this cruise occurred 'simultaneously' with the break with Freud. Vincent Brome, *Jung Man and Myth* (London: House of Stratus, 1978), p. 171. Deirdre Bair tells of times the two of them liked to sail together, 'taking turns reading passages aloud, particularly the "Nekyia"'. Bair, *Jung*, p. 263.

39 Homer, *The Odyssey*, trans. Robert Fitzgerald (New York: Anchor Books, 1963), Book 11. l, pp. 28–49.

40 March, *Cassell's Dictionary*, p. 343.

41 Daniel Ogden, *Greek and Roman Necromancy* (Princeton, NJ: Princeton University Press, 2001), p. 174.

42 | C. G. Jung, 'Picasso', in *The Spirit in Man, Art and Literature* (London: Routledge, 1966), pp. 139–140.

43 In discussion of 'blood memory' as it applies in Native American tradition: 'Blood memory, a memory though forgotten yet never lost, redefines Native American authenticity in terms of recollecting and remembering. The genetic constitution preserves memory in the body. H. Huang, 'Blood/Memory in N. Scott Momaday's *The Names: A Memoir* and Linda Hogan's *The Woman Who Watches Over the World: A Native Memoir*', *Concentric: Literary and Cultural Studies* 32, no. 1 (January 2006): 171–195, at 173.

44 *RB*, p. 237b.

45 Ibid., p. 353a.

46 'The serpents I thought might have been connected with Egyptian material' (*AP*, p. 48).

47 *AP*, p. 95; see also p. 89: 'many myths show the hero being worshipped as a snake, having been transformed into it after death'.

48 Joseph Henderson and Maud Oakes, *The Wisdom and the Serpent The Myths of Death, Rebirth, and Resurrection* (Princeton, NJ: Princeton University Press, 1963), p. 34. Jung also states in *Symbols of Transformation*; 'the snake symbolizes the dead, buried, chthonic hero' (*SOT, CW*, vol. 5, pp. 431, 671).

49 *RB*, p. 353a.

50 *AP*, p. 61.

10

SIEGFRIED AND THE MERRY GARDEN

Murder of the hero Siegfried

18 December 1913

Jung's first active imagination addressed a murdered hero, whereas the Siegfried episode, here described as a vision, sees the hero alive, but not for long. An intentional deed, a murder must occur in order for Jung to expunge 'all traces of the dead'.[1]

The dream here speaks to Jung lying in wait to destroy a symbol of strength, beauty and heroics. He confesses that before the scene, he was experiencing a conflict between an impulse to commit murder and the fear of impending death. In fact, his fear is fear of agency; his capacity to murder along with the guilt of knowing he is capable. Yet this is subsumed by a more prominent fear, that of death and this he feels viscerally.

Since Siegfried appears as an enemy, his threat is to Jung's mortal life, self-perception or spirit of the times, *not* to his immortal self or that which is unfolding due to the spirit of the depths. Therefore, the murder removes a threat to his ego consciousness and allows his spirit of the depths to make way for further exploration. The 'bones of the dead', which von Franz refers to and that makes Siegfried's entrance possible, certainly is facilitated by the dead themselves. He is a hero rushing to his own death via the destruction he himself has wrought.

In the seminars of 1925, Jung shares his own interpretation of the murder:

> It was a case of destroying the hero ideal of my efficiency. This has to be sacrificed in order that a new adaptation can be made; in short it is connected with the sacrifice of the superior function in order to get at the libido necessary to activate the inferior functions.[2]

SCHOLARS ON THE SIEGFRIED DREAM

Many interpretations have been written about this dream and its significance to the break with Freud.[3] Walker compares the dwarf in Jung's active imagination to the small dark-skinned hunter here, each having 'murderous energy as well as the insight, the shadow wisdom, needed to kill the hero and to transcend a youthful heroic attitude toward life'.[4] Burleson suggests a connection between the description of the Siegfried dream in *Memories, Dreams, Reflections* and Jung's description of seeing the black figure with the spear in Africa.[5] Siegfried is 'the heroic image that he himself projected onto Freud, and that the murder (and his subsequent guilt) is to be interpreted as a wilful act of parricide'.[6] Homans agrees; 'Siegfried, the German, wanted to impose his own will, have his own way, just as Jung felt that Freud was imposing his own theory on Jung's innovative efforts.' But, he insists that Jung 'did not simply project all the blame upon Freud'.[7]

Von Franz suggests the dream is:

a typical dream of middle life . . . now the hero, who is the midday sun, must die in order to avoid blocking the way for new life. Siegfried's chariot made of the bones of the dead shows . . . how many other possibilities of life have been sacrificed in the interest of what has so far been achieved by consciousness.[8]

Hannah expressed that in Africa:

Both [Jung's] No. 1 and No. 2 personalities were constellated and active at one and the same time. No. 1 felt the dark-skinned man as alien . . . but the timeless No. 2 reached right down through the layers of the unconscious to the primeval ancestors and naturally felt as if he already knew the man who was separated from him only by time.[9]

The death is transformative, unlike previous examples of the presence of the dead being both dead and alive. Jung's Self has killed the hero in the name of preservation with the result being a rechanneling of libido.

This dream had quite an effect on Jung upon waking. The intensity surrounding the need to understand its meaning increased to the point that Jung heard a voice demanding he shoot himself if he did not grasp the dream's meaning.[10] If he did not understand his shooting of the hero in the unconscious, then he had to do the same in waking life in order to grasp the meaning of the sacrifice. When Jung determined the dream's significance he felt the grief for destroying 'his ideal'.[11] With this action he removed the spirit of the times as an obstacle to his spirit of the depths.

The most significant result of the Siegfried dream/vision is that now Jung accesses personified contents in the unconscious. The episode marks the end of his initial

82 *Liber Primus*

struggle with understanding the dead in his dreams and visions. This step cannot be underestimated as it sees Jung active in response to his unconscious content, that is, he is managing what he finds and as a result has evolved into a new stage of autonomy. He is now agent to his own unconscious dynamic. This ushers a time that sees Jung actively engaged with unconscious content with intention, such as is seen with the shrinking of Izdubar.[12]

The reconciliation of the two parts of his psyche is noted by the rain, which washes away all indications of the presence of the dead.[13] The rain does not simply cleanse the act of murder but wipes away all that serves as an obstacle to his access of the deepest part of the unconscious. That is, the rain wiped out all that was 'sere and lifeless,' i.e. the dwarf's perspective or the spirit of the times, a perspective that has no place or influence in his explorations of his depths.[14]

Thus the problematic aspects of the presence of the dead in his dreams and his first active imagination have been resolved. This is not to say that the dead disappear, in fact the theme now flourishes throughout *The Red Book*. The focus now is on the dead themselves and precisely what they show Jung. In one sense, the dead are saying 'nothing in the unconscious is dead, not figures of the unconscious and certainly not us'. And now that Jung has deposed his superior function all that is alive can now be accessed. With this realisation Jung indicates the murder of the superior function made way for him to make peace with the great unconscious activity contributed by the dead up to this point and gives him permission to accept the dead as a psychological reality and what will be an entire host of figures of the unconscious.

The merry garden: a vision of the beyond

The Siegfried murder immediately gives way to a brief description of Jung's next vision, which could be described as a direct experience of the dead in the afterlife. Jung describes a 'merry garden, in which forms . . . clad in white silk [were] . . . covered in coloured light'.[15] Jung thought this to be 'a vision of the beyond', where figures were whole.[16] Jung claimed the vision helped him grasp that he was two things simultaneously.[17] This of course resonates with his No. 1 and No. 2 personalities, and equally points to the state of existing with conscious and unconscious perspectives simultaneously (in a similar perspective as Hannah would point out later regarding Jung's experiences in Africa).[18] Equally, this sees Jung accessing unimpeded the 'unknown' parts of his unconscious.

This scene describes a particular type of visioning, one that allowed for an orientation in two fields at once. What defines the efficiency of the vision is the degree of consciousness Jung applies to both fields and therefore the ability to define what is happening. Jung grasps man's physicality while at the same time recognising that he could see the unconscious stretching behind man 'like a saint's halo'.[19] What Jung sees as whole is man's body inclusive of his unconscious self, here physicalised in the form of light.[20] He also compares man's shadow to a 'light-coloured sphere'. The description is revealing in that now Jung has made visible or recognised visually psychological dimensions in a physical context. By attributing the halo to the unconscious and the shape likened to the 'shadow', Jung appears to have seen and understood the physicalising of psychological ideas in this vision of the dead. Thus, the unconscious at this stage in the narrative is not only a location of exploration but is discernible as an attribute of man (even while in the unconscious setting itself).[21]

This visioning resulted from the sacrifice of Jung's dominant function with the result of the Siegfried murder. The libido made available ushers in Jung's next major episode with Elijah and Salome.

In his commentary Jung goes on to describe the rain that washes and heals, yet he experiences a sense of mourning in himself for the dead.[22] Although there is relief in the presence of the rain, here he is pointing to a different kind of mourning process one that allows the dead to be celebrated and released to their new spiritual states. The libido, trapped in mourning, when released liberates the dead from their assumed lifeless termination to a renewed life.

Jung seems to be addressing the immense loss of life that will be the result of World War I, which begins within eight months of the Siegfried dream. Retrospectively, he sees grief on a collective scale. But, the mourning points to not just the dead who have appeared in his dreams the previous years, but his accustomed approach to life through his dominant function. It is this outmoded way of living that no longer accommodates his life, his visioning and the available perspective he now has due to the spirit of the depths. Jung can no longer deny what the spirit of the depths has initiated in him and in a sense the mourning of the dead is not simply the honouring of what is lost, but rather the tending to what emerges from the unconscious as a result of this renewed perspective.

Here we can see that once again the spirit of the depths is guiding Jung in how to discern *as* he visions. He is guiding Jung in seeing how such a murder can be framed within the context of the depths. This process becomes important when Jung himself assesses episodes in *Liber Secundus*.[23] Jung considered his participation in the murder and suffered, yet saw this as 'the first step to individuation'. The growth he has experienced spans from the guilt he felt at thinking his father dead, to an understanding of the dead in the unconscious.

This attribution to a newborn state suggests a new orientation to the unconscious with the dissolution of such a strong propensity towards the spirit of the times. With libido released, exhibited in the falling rain, this can now be used to compensate a previously held perspective. He has released the burden to mourn the dead, because as he has seen, death appears differently in the unconscious. The dead appear surrounded by light. In his newborn state he is able to continue his explorations of the unconscious with more available libido to engage in what will be his first in-depth attempt at active imagination with personifications: Elijah and Salome.

84 *Liber Primus*

Notes

1 *MDR*, p. 204.
2 *AP*, p. 48.
3 Walker links the two: 'The murder of the hero represents the need for a change, for a recalculation of earlier values at midlife. The shadow figures of the savage and the dwarf represent the murderous energy.' Walker also suggests unlike the murder of the blonde youth, which is followed by regeneration symbols, 'there is no expectation of renewal or resurrection, and given Jung's intense feelings of guilt the feeling tone of the dream is much less hopeful'. Walker, *Jung and the Jungians*, pp. 44 and 66.
4 Ibid., p. 44.
5 *MDR*, p. 283; Blake Burleson, *Jung in Africa* (London: Continuum, 2005), p. 61.
6 Anthony Stevens, *On Jung* (London: Taylor & Francis, 1990), p. 157.
7 Homans, *Jung in Context*, p. 78.
8 Von Franz, *C. G. Jung*, p. 109.
9 Hannah, *Jung*, p. 171.
10 *MDR*, p. 204.
11 Ibid., p. 205.
12 *RB*, p. 283a.
13 *MDR*, p. 204.
14 *RB*, pp. 238–239 n. 91.
15 Ibid., p. 242.
16 Ibid., n. 117.
17 Ibid.
18 Hannah, *Jung*, p. 171.
19 *RB*, p. 162 n. 117.
20 'The astral body of man to an initiate can be seen physically as 'an egg-shaped cloud . . . which not only surrounds the body but permeates it.' Rudolf Steiner, *Staying Connected, How to Continue Your Relationships with Those Who Have Died*, ed. C. Bamford (Great Barrington, MA: Anthroposophic Press, 1999), p. 24.
21 Aniela Jaffé quotes Paracelsus: 'thus there are in man two bodies, one compounded of the elements, the other of the stars; therefore these two must be clearly distinguished from each other. In death the elemental body goes to the grave together with its spirit, but the ethereal bodies are consumed in the firmament.' Jaffé expands: 'even after death man's "sidereal body", his "star body", walks and takes on the likeness of the dead'. Aniela Jaffé, *Apparitions: An Archetypal Approach to Death Dreams and Ghosts* (Irving, TX: Spring, 1979), p. 66.
22 *RB*, p. 242b. This refers to the growing seed that will become the new God in the form of Izdubar, in *Liber Secundus*.
23 In particular the episode 'Sacrificial Murder' sees Jung evaluating his role in humanity's crimes and suffering (*RB*, pp. 290–291).

11

MYSTERIUM ENCOUNTER

Elijah and Salome

22 December 1913

The last three episodes of *Liber Primus* complete Jung's initiation first begun with the spirit of the depths and his command for Jung to awaken his dead. The importance of the last three episodes of *Liber Primus* ('Mysterium Encounter', 'Instruction' and 'Resolution') rests in the complex nature of Jung's interaction with the blind Salome and the prophet Elijah. Here Jung participates in the most comprehensive and perhaps complex form of active imagination thus far. This includes a descriptive setting or 'composition of place' as appeared in his first active imagination, as well as in-depth dialogue, which did not.[1] Jung begins to experience the unconscious as both place and process, combining the previous efforts of the spirit of the depths, bringing Jung squarely into the land of the dead.[2] He meets the prophet Elijah who in his biographical story raised the dead just as Jung will continue to do throughout *Liber Secundus*.[3] Jung maintains a level of consciousness throughout the episodes, which is connected to his incarnate state. It is this perspective Salome calls on, the Jung able to journey this far into the unconscious with awareness.

Jung called this section the 'Mysterium' because of the intense interactions between himself, Salome and Elijah. The result of the ancient mysteries was initiation: 'Nothing about the Eleusian Mysteries was so striking as the initiates' awe of Demeter's gift, the grain, and their hope of life after death.'[4] Those in the Christian and Jewish faith could also gain entrance to the mysteries simply by explaining biblical and Talmudic passages discussing the raising of the dead.[5] Thus, the first part of Jung's initiation was an introduction into his visionary faculty and these encounters too will serve as an initiation into how he responds to what the unconscious offers him in terms of visioning.

86 *Liber Primus*

The setting and the players

Salome, I suggest, proves to be a figure of Jung's personal unconscious and Elijah, similar to the spirit of the depths, serves as representative of the community of the dead in his role as prophet.[6] Interactions with Salome are more subjective whereas Elijah maintains a more objective tone.[7] In his commentary, Jung refers to the prophet as a figure 'clear and complete', while suggesting Salome 'is my own soul'.[8]

Jung's visioning here highlights the unique perspective of being able to host figures from different levels of the unconscious while conducting in-depth conversations with both simultaneously. The complex nature of the exchange is similar to attempting to discern the difference between a figure who is dead and one acting like a projection within an active imagination.

Jung's greatest task in these final episodes of *Liber Primus* is to identify *where* he is, *why* Elijah and Salome are together and *how* he fits into their story. While each inhabits the same psychic space, *how* they participate in the space is instrumental in revealing Jung's relationship to each and contributes to the possibility that Elijah is a member of the dead, and therefore a part of the collective unconscious, and Salome a split-off part of Jung's personal unconscious. Jung is literally repulsed by Salome ('ambiguously erotic and sometimes sinister'[9]) yet reacts to Elijah in a far different manner. This points to the possibility that they might be different types of figures and serve differing roles to one another and to Jung.

Elijah appears during Jung's reflection on the 'essence of God' and this seems apt as Jung identifies him as 'the mouth of God'. Perhaps this assignation is why Elijah does not change or alter throughout Jung's conversations remaining wise, instructive and consistently emotionally ambivalent to Jung's struggles to comprehend the two of them as a pair.[10]

Jung travels further into the unconscious than previously, having arrived at 'a cosmic abyss'.[11] He proves that due to his incarnate presence, similarly as in the row of tombs dream, he effects change specifically by curing Salome's blindness. What was begun with Jung's participation in the murder of Siegfried is continued here with his ability to meet and respond to what the unconscious offers in terms of vision and narrative. His sense of autonomy and agency increases with the ever-growing demands that the content of his active imaginations presents. In this episode, Jung becomes an adept.

Elijah and Salome

Elijah identifies Salome as his daughter. They share a functional relationship because they are linked by his prophecy and her blindness; his ability to see the future and her inability to see at all. Yet, she is the wisdom that makes meaning of his ability to see, and thus perhaps this is her role for him and Jung as well.[12] As her blindness and his foresight have made them companions, this relationship of opposites has always worked for them.[13] Their connection is not simply father/daughter, or prophet/blind seer, but rather the eternity that they share is one by virtue of their location in the unconscious. They have been linked not by being similar in nature, or even opposite in nature, but rather due to their shared psychic field.

The relationship as it is described raises some pertinent questions. What exactly is Salome blind to? Her surroundings? Her function? Her self-worth? Or is she simply a literal product of her father's function as prophet of the future and a member of the dead? Jung indicates in his lengthy interpretation of the scene that 'she emanates from him'. Could this mean that Elijah and Jung share Salome as a projection?[14] Can Elijah as a representative of the dead have his own projections? His own split-off parts of the psyche? His own anima? And if so, does Salome serve that purpose for him? When Salome gains her sight will she see who and what she is, possibly a figure dependent on her surroundings for definition? Or as Jung's soul, is her autonomy limited to the scope of his willingness to see her?[15]

During Jung's initial exchange with Elijah, Salome remains silent, then her first utterance to Jung is, 'Do you love me?' In fact, the next utterances from Salome are: 'I love you' and 'You will love me'.[16] At the outset Salome suggests herself to be a figure of Jung's personal unconscious, as she relates to him in such an emotional manner.

Salome as anima figure

Jung resists everything about this encounter with Salome but looks to Elijah, who he esteems to help guide him. He tries to accept his steadfast confirmation of their relationship in the underworld yet, Jung can only see Salome as 'devilish'. He is tormented and equally shocked at Elijah's support of her.[17] Elijah's presentation throughout the three episodes remains consistent, measured and instructive, and this does not change, suggesting again his more objective relationship to Jung.

Salome's attempt to convince Jung of her father's gifts suggests that she is acting like a bridge spanning from Jung's personal unconscious to the collective, or the region of the spirit of the depths that Elijah represents. That she is drawing Jung's attention to Elijah sees her also drawing his attention to the very source of prophecy, forethought and to that timeless quality of the collective. Jung later would identify Salome as an anima figure:[18]

> the soul, the anima, established the relationship to the unconscious . . . for the unconscious corresponds to . . . the land of the ancestors . . . There [the soul] produces a mysterious animation and gives visible forms to the ancestral traces, the collective contents. Like a medium, it gives the dead a chance to manifest themselves.[19]

Not only is the relationship of the anima to the dead quite clear, but so is Jung's equivocation of the soul as anima and the manner in which the dead appear as a result of her efforts (like a medium). This is one of the clearest passages that indicates the autonomy of the dead to appear of their own volition, i.e. 'to manifest themselves' and not as personal projected material.

88 *Liber Primus*

Thus, Salome facilitates not only visioning for Jung but access to Elijah. As if her potential rests in instigating (in)sight, and access to the soul's world. Jung was becoming familiar with the images by this stage, but he had not yet recognised the collective level of the unconscious and for this Salome in her capacity serves as keeper of the threshold to Elijah. As a personification, she is the organising principle for the unconscious, otherwise its immersive quality would be unwieldy to process.

Yet, is it Salome who produces 'mysterious animations' or rather does she create the conditions in which Jung can see them? Does she open a door for Jung's access or is she herself the door? If as Jung defines the soul as the self in the unconscious, then she provides Jung access to its deepest reaches.[20] Thus the animated quality of the unconscious or *betrachten* is as result of the anima 'projected' or extended into the unconscious. It is both the anima's agency and the context of the unconscious that produces visioning conditions. As Jung became practised, he stated he no longer needed the anima as translator or bridge, he was able to access and interpret content without such mediation.[21]

Elijah maintains a consistent message regarding the reality of both himself and Salome by confirming several times that he and Salome are not symbols but rather real, as real as looking at man.[22]

If Jung were to consider what Elijah is saying, that perhaps they are not symbolically together in the unconscious, but rather literally so, then Jung could consider Elijah to be not the *symbol* of the prophet but *the discarnate* prophet sharing the same part of the unconscious as Jung's projection of the 'unholy' Salome. The Biblical account sees Elijah never having actually died, but rather having been raised to heaven by God (2 Kings 2:11). Thus his claim of being together with Salome for eternity works and again positions Elijah alongside the spirit of the depths with his archetypal qualities.

Instruction

22 December 1913

Jung returns again to the active imagination and to the same house, but he does not know why, explaining a 'longing' that drew him back again. Oddly, Jung confesses that he feels, 'more real here . . . yet I do not like being here'.[23]

The instruction that Elijah offers to Jung is a continuation of the previous teaching on symbols, here it is on the objectivity of thought. He encourages Jung to discern the difference between himself and his thoughts.[24] Such instruction helps Jung understand the objectivity of psyche but also he must have contextualised the literal dead for Jung.

This lesson is no sooner understood than Salome enters, embraces Jung and claims not only that they are siblings, but that Elijah is *his* father too. If Elijah is an elder figure in the same vein as Jung's No. 2, then this seems an appropriate designation. The important detail is that Salome suggests that Mary, the mother of 'our Saviour' is Jung's and Salome's mother. This throws Jung into such turmoil that he accuses them both of being symbols in an effort to create the distance he needs to understand what is occurring. Elijah is impervious to Jung's emotional responses, remaining matter of fact about himself, Salome and most importantly Jung's interactions with them both.

Christ

Yet, it is Salome who wishes to infer symbolic meaning by associating herself and Jung with the Christ story, a fitting validation for a figure of Jung's subjective unconscious as it forces him to question not only the significance of both figures, but prompts in him a reassessment of this particular narrative.[25] And, it must be remembered, not only Christ's raising of the dead but his three days of preaching to the dead in Hell. What Salome's suggestion does is to introduce the possibility that all three of them are related to the Christ story in order to prepare Jung for his role in curing Salome of her blindness. Salome asks Jung to assume a role in the Christ narrative in order to serve her, and by suggesting their mutual genealogy, she puts him on notice that he will share the attributes of Christ.[26]

Resolution

25 December 1913

This episode is both the culmination of the Elijah and Salome story as the final episode to *Liber Primus* and Jung's initiation. That this third and last night of the episode is also Christmas is significant in that the birth of Christ equally augurs for Jung the birth of a more comprehensive engagement with active imagination, which Jung will explore extensively throughout *Liber Secundus*.

Again, Jung returns to the active imagination in the house of Elijah and Salome, tormented by guilt and feeling still deeply compelled to return at the prospect of exploring still further the mysteries.[27] This longing seems an emotional response to his immersion in both his personal and collective unconscious. He approaches the entrance to the prophet's house, which appears to be at the bottom of the underworld.

Elijah commands Jung to gaze into a crystal and prepare himself in its light. This simulates a type of divination and looks to draw Jung into a still deeper level of the unconscious. He experiences a vision within an active imagination or a vision within a vision.[28] Divination partly attempts to access the future, or rather brings the future into the present and this is the effect it has on Jung.

The series of visions includes one of the Crucifixion of Christ. As Jung gazes into the crystal, he goes from observing the Crucifixion to assuming the same posture himself, driven by an 'incomprehensible power'.[29] Yet it is the sight of the serpent in the vision, which draws him from observer to participant. While he gazes at Christ on the cross: 'the black serpent coils itself . . . around my feet . . . I

90 *Liber Primus*

spread my arms wide . . . The serpent . . . wound itself around my body, and my countenance is that of a lion'.[30] This is an intriguing shift from watching the serpent in the vision to actually experiencing the serpent coiling around his own feet, as if the shift itself resurrects the necessary libido to complete the task before him. The act of the Crucifixion is one of suffering and sacrifice; Jung is sacrificing some autonomy to the unconscious process. And, if the serpent is a member of the dead, i.e. a deceased hero (and perhaps Salome's double in so far as they are both anima figures[31]), then it appears as if the incarnate Jung and the deceased hero as serpent mediate Salome's healing.

This visioning is unique in that by observation alone, Jung cannot effect the change needed, it was necessary to physically assume the Christ pose to effect the change. The physical re-enactment requires Jung to act unimpeded in the unconscious, as well as to respond consciously within the active imagination. So, in terms of the transcendent function, it takes both the unconscious and conscious perspective to shift Salome's blindness. Elijah cannot do this himself, he has not the ontological traction to effect change for her. Jung's engagement has now become not simply skilled but nuanced in response.

Jung is horrified that he is imitating the pose of the Crucifixion when Salome declares that Jung is Christ. What she means is that this is the Christ who heals, Jung is a Christ figure because he has died to his conscious limitations, sacrificed these limitations (as seen in both the cave and the murder of Siegfried) and has risen again in the land of the dead. One who is able to do this can cure Salome's blindness.

The serpent then squeezes Jung, blood streams from his body and then Salome wraps her hair around his feet and stays there. She suddenly shouts 'I see light!' as 'The serpent falls from [his] body'.[32]

By this series of actions, Salome's blindness has been cured. This initiatory experience is critically important for Jung's understanding of his own dynamic. Since an essential part of the ancient mysteries was immortality or rather the realisation of life after death, Jung grasped that what he had undertaken had been similar. Up to this point the spirit of the depths has guided Jung's initiations. Yet now, Jung has become the principal agent in his own unconscious dynamic by virtue of his conscious engagement (similar to his actions in the Siegfried episode). He has mastered the obligations posed by his unconscious that resulted in the movement of libido.

The result

Active imagination is fully operational here with its end result somewhat of a reversal of the transcendent function. That is, libido is not being incorporated back into Jung's personality, but rather Jung as agent has effected change. By way of blood pouring profusely, Salome lies at Jung's feet to receive the libido from both the blood and the serpent.[33]

If the serpent is meant to signify the deceased hero, then Jung's ability now to tend to the needs of the unconscious has been assisted by the dead (the serpent), a figure of the unconscious (Salome), Elijah (witness) and Jung, grounded in his incarnate perspective. The serpent is spent with the transference of libido and so lays still on the ground, having assumed the role of a current of energy, which facilitated the shift.[34] Thus, the transcendent function has worked in reverse, in which conscious energy and intention (by Jung) has been focused into and within the unconscious terrain to cure Salome. Jung's psyche does not absorb the libido represented by either the serpent or Salome. Rather, the serpent acts upon Jung to produce libido that shifts to Salome. Immediately after her sight is regained, they both attain a type of vision that sees Elijah in a resplendent form of blazing light, perhaps his true form in the collective unconscious. The process allows Salome to gain sight and Jung to gain vision. Once again Jung has been initiated, but this time fully into the collective unconscious.

By Jung healing his anima figure, he cleared the way for his own refined vision of both the personal and collective unconscious, thus giving way to the great amount of material that will follow in *Liber Secundus*. It could be argued that the transcendent function did not occur because the libido did not return to Jung, but rather to Salome. On the other hand, if Salome is Jung's anima and soul, it could be argued that by definition the process healed Jung. Thus Jung walks away with the knowledge of being an agent of change if not a healer in the unconscious.[35]

The Mysterium concludes

Elijah remains witness to the entire episode and confirms to Jung that he has completed the mysteries. Salome then drops to her knees 'wonderstruck' gazing into the light.[36] Upon leaving Jung describes feeling as if he is 'melting into air'. This idea indicates the dissolving reaction after holding the tension between himself and two different figures inhabiting both the personal and collective unconscious simultaneously.[37] It also points to the possible sensation of transitioning from an immersive active imagination back to consciousness and back into the room where he is sitting.[38]

Jung feels in awe as a result of what has occurred and kneels in front of Elijah. Elijah remains unmoved by the ceremony and suddenly appears as a 'flame of white light'.[39] His appearance as such results from both Jung's and Salome's refined sight.

As Biblical prophet, raiser of the dead and symbolic wise man in the land of the dead, Elijah can do nothing to cure Salome's blindness. Perhaps because they have been together so long, there is not enough oppositional tension or differentiation within the unconscious for him to be able to assist. So, Salome looks to Jung for a cure. Is it possible that only someone actually incarnate can effect change even in the unconscious and this is why Salome looks to Jung? Jung has not only healed his anima figure's vision but also his vision of his anima figure; gone is the repulsed reaction to her as she 'kneel[s] in devotion' to Elijah.[40]

The significance of the mystery for Jung here is not the attainment of immortality, but rather what Burkert identifies as recognition of the reality of what he sees

92 *Liber Primus*

and his ability to participate and alter it.[41] The importance of this episode cannot be underestimated. Once Jung arrives and encounters them he becomes part of their story and a player in their drama. He emphasised that these experiences were his: 'my mysteries . . . belong to me . . . You have your own'.[42]

Jung's initiation, journey and underworld are his. How the spirit of the depths appears to others is their task alone. Others need to find their own link to their depths as well as to find their own way in and through their unconscious both personal and collective, and most importantly must answer to their own dead.

Conclusion to *Liber Primus*

There is a sense to the narrative of *Liber Primus* that the sequence of encounters guides Jung toward the seminal scenes of the 'Mysterium Encounter'. In fact, all of the encounters in *Liber Primus*: Jung's identification of his spirit of the depths and spirit of the times; his discovery of his soul; his first active imagination; and the Siegfried murder, all look to prime Jung for the work he does here. Once the process of descent begins, and the orientation to his deepest unconscious is located, it is necessary for Jung to have available enough libido to continue further explorations. Therefore, the role of sacrifice and initiation are important thresholds that permit Jung access to libido necessary for further encounters. Jung's first active imagination looks to be an example of the unconscious as place whereas the Siegfried murder looks to reveal the unconscious as process, making libido available to enable Jung to engage in such a committed conversation with Elijah and Salome. Jung's curing of Salome reveals his effect on his unconscious process by way of his participation.

My suggestion is that Salome, in her more emotive and malleable relationship with Jung, is a projection of Jung's personal psyche and is subject to Jung's incarnate influence. This is why she is healed by his presence whereas the shift could not happen with Elijah's effort alone. Therefore I place the two in separate categories as a result of the way in which each interacts with Jung. There remains a consistent objective pose that Elijah exhibits throughout the discourse in *Liber Primus* and, in a sense, serves as a counterbalance to Jung's attempts to perceive an ever-changing and altering terrain.[43] I also suggest that Elijah with his archetypal qualities, while representing the region of the dead, could very well have assisted Jung with his eventual understanding of the concept of the archetype. In the very least the dead appeared to have played a role in Jung's formation of the idea by way of the spirit of the depths, Jung's No. 2 personality, Elijah and Philemon (who will become the teacher of the dead in *Scrutinies*). Whether Elijah represents the collective unconscious and Salome the personal, or whether they both share archetypal qualities and could be defined as anima/animus figures, might be less important than the fact that their very definition as such rests on the fact that Jung found them in the region of the dead, and was entirely insistent that he, in contrast, did not 'belong to the dead'.[44] In *Analytical Psychology*, he was to state quite clearly:

One word more on the theme of immortality. It is intimately linked up with the anima question. Through the relation to the anima one obtains the chance of greater consciousness. It leads to a realization of the self as the totality of the conscious and the unconscious functions. This realization brings with it a recognition of the inherited plus the new units that go to make up the self. That is to say, when we once grasp the meaning of the conscious and the unconscious together, we become aware of the ancestral lives that have gone into the making of our own lives . . . This feeling of the collective unconscious brings with it a sense of the renewal of life to which there is no end. It comes down from the dim dawn of the world and continues. So when we obtain a complete realization of self, there comes with it the feeling of immortality . . . It is the goal of individuation to reach the sense of the continuation of one's life through the ages. It gives one the feeling of eternity on this earth.[45]

Notes

1 Liz Greene, *The Astrological World of Jung's Novus Liber* (London: Routledge, 2018), p. 57. Episodes 'The Desert' and 'Experiences in the Desert' include detail about the desert as a setting. In the latter it is evident that the shift in terrain occurs as a result of Jung's attention. His first active imagination and then the 'Mysterium Encounter' relay richly detailed scenes that show a sense of progression alongside Jung's exploration.

2 *MDR*, p. 205; *RB*, p. 246a.

3 Jung's encounters with the dead in his dreams the previous year can be considered an example of raising his dead. Other biblical characters known to have raised the dead are Elisha: Kings 4:17–37; Peter: Acts 9:36–42; Paul: Acts 20:7–12; Jesus: John 11:38–44; and Elijah: Kings 17:17–24. Jung retells the raising of the dead child by Elijah in *Liber Secundus* (p. 304a).

4 Kerenyi, *Eleusis*, p. 106.

5 Ibid. pp. 106–107.

6 *RB*, p. 247a. Jung declared that it was important for Elijah and Salome, as personified Logos (Forethinking) and Eros (Pleasure) respectively, to let them be 'events and experiences' (*MDR*, p. 207).

7 Again the correspondence between Elijah, Philemon, his No. 2 personality and the spirit of the depths becomes more apparent. Jung equivocates Elijah with his No. 2 as well as emphasising that Philemon emerged from the Elijah figure (*RB*, p. 208 and *MDR*, pp. 252 and 207 respectively).

8 *RB*, pp. 366a and 241b. Although it is feasible to make the connection between Elijah and the spirit of the depths and Salome with Jung's soul, it is enough to keep the correspondence in mind (*RB*, pp. 248b and 249a respectively).

9 Greene, *The Astrological World*, p. 50.

10 *RB*, p. 246b.

11 *MDR*, p. 205.

12 Analyst and astrologer Liz Greene reminds us of the description of Waite's comparison of the Kabbalistic Shekinah to the High Priestess in the tarot alluding to what Greene would call 'an inner spiritual mediator': 'Mystically speaking, the Shekinah is the Spiritual Bride of the just man, and when he reads the Law she gives the Divine meaning. A valid consideration to the dynamic between Elijah and Salome.' Greene, *The Astrological World*, p. 56.

13 *AP*, p. 64; *MDR*, p. 206. In 1925, Jung relayed his shock in discovering that Elijah and Salome had always been together; 'I thought it was blasphemous for him to say this . . . Elijah and Salome are together because they are pairs of opposites' (*AP*, p. 93). Again Jung is surprised that Elijah a prophet of God would be together with what he calls an 'unholy woman' (*RB*, p. 246b).

94 *Liber Primus*

14 *RB*, p. 365b. The relationship indicates a subordination of Eros to Logos.

15 Jung comes to Salome with historical bias in place as a 'bloodthirsty woman' who was in love with John the Baptist, whom she murdered. He is horrified by Salome's expressions of love for him and wants no such relationship, especially from one responsible for the murder of a prophet. Yet, the love story belongs to a contemporary Salome, one found in Oscar Wilde and Strauss, it is this Salome who is besotted with John the Baptist, not the Biblical Salome who dances for her stepfather. The cultural significance of Salome is important: '[She] was ... *the* major fin-de-siècle icon of the femme fatale. She paraded through the art, literature, and music of the period from Moreau to Klimt and von Stuck ... and Strauss (even young Picasso drew her). Her popularity crossed the Atlantic and sparked a "Salome craze" that was in full swing when Jung visited in 1909.' Jay Sherry, 'Carl Gustav Jung, Avant-Garde Conservative' (Unpublished doctoral thesis, Freie Universität Berlin, 2008), p. 44.

16 *RB*, p. 246a.

17 Jung brings to this conversation a preconceived idea as to who Salome is, the temptress who danced for King Herod and asked for the head of John the Baptist (note who interestingly was Elijah returned).

18 *MDR*, p. 206; *AP*, p. 92.

19 *MDR*, p. 216. Jung's soul disappears just before the *Sermones*. Shamdasani notes this was 29 January 1916 (*RB*, p. 346b). Unknown from previous versions of the *Sermones* is that Jung's soul returns to announce the arrival of the dead from Jerusalem.

20 *RB*, p. 288b.

21 *MDR*, p. 213.

22 *RB*, pp. 246b and 249b respectively.

23 Ibid., p. 248b. When he first encountered Elijah, Jung claimed: 'I am a stranger here' (p. 245b).

24 *RB*, p. 249a. Jung discussed this passage in the 1925 seminars as being instrumental in his understanding of psychological objectivity. In *Memories, Dreams, Reflections* this passage is attributed specifically to Philemon 'and other figures' (p. 207) not Elijah as it is presented here. Shamdasani discusses the attribution as discussed in *Analytical Psychology* (p. 95), where Jung credits 'the old man' (*RB*, p. 249 n. 188).

25 *RB*, p. 368.

26 In Jung's in-depth discussion of the significance of Elijah and Salome as Logos and Eros, he includes analysis of Mary as the mother, Elijah as father and he and Salome as siblings, calling it the 'Christian solution' and indicating it to be 'undeniably cathartic' (*RB*, p. 368a).

27 *RB*, p. 251a.

28 This happens also in *Liber Secundus* from the episode 'Divine Folly' through to 'Nox Quarta' indicating a shift in the level of the unconscious from which Jung perceives information.

29 *RB*, p. 252b. This is a similar dynamic as when the spirit of the depths 'forced' Jung back into himself. What is implied in these instances is that Jung appears to be at the mercy of the unconscious' effect on him. This differs to his more proactive and confident demeanour in *Liber Secundus*, when he offers his assistance to the girl in the castle who is a figure of his unconscious.

30 *RB*, pp. 252a–b. This is the only mention of a lion in this vision, making Jung's claim in 1925 regarding Mithraic symbolism almost unfounded: 'The animal face which I felt mine transformed into was the famous [Deus] Leontocephalus of the Mithraic mysteries.' The rest of the quote from *Analytical Psychology* continues 'the figure which is represented with a snake coiled around the man, the snake's head resting on the man's head, and the face of the man that of a lion. This statue has only been found in the mystery grottoes (the underground churches, the last remnants of catacombs)' (p. 98). Elijah leans on a marble lion (p. 248b) and again, the presence of a 'powerful lion' stands outside Elijah's dwelling (p. 249b). Noll's lengthy article on this singular reference needs reconsideration now that there appears such a striking difference between *The Red Book*

and *Analytical Psychology* accounts. Jung had much time to rework this content as shown in the appendix material (*RB*, p. 365), where he reconsiders the Elijah and Salome episode in detail. Noll's insistence that Jung was convinced that he had been 'deified' is now somewhat unfounded given Jung's statement in *Liber Primus* regarding the spirit of the depths and his contribution to healing Jung's immortality (*RB*, p. 230a). Further, given the very brief reference here, Noll's supposition that: 'Jung continued to interpret those experiences as an initiation into a specific grade of the Mithraic mysteries – that of "leo" [which] he never publicly admitted', might now appear as an extreme amplification of the material *sans The Red Book* context. Where Noll is convinced Jung 'believed the process of "becoming one-with-god" was the climax of the initiation process in the Mythraic mysteries', we can now correct considering that Jung's initiation began with the emergence of his visionary faculty and climaxed with the successful transference of libido for Salome's healing. Richard Noll, 'Jung the Leontocephalus', in *Jung in Contexts: A Reader*, ed. Paul Bishop (London: Routledge, 2000), p. 70.

31 Greene, *The Astrological World*, p. 52; *AP*, pp. 94–95.
32 *RB*, p. 252b. Note the biblical similarity of drying Christ's feet with hair in John 12:3 and Luke 7:38.
33 Note in the seminars of 1925, Jung tells how he sweated profusely, thus making the healing of Salome's blindness a similar effect to the healing rain after the Siegfried dream and how it reconciled the tension of the murder; the water announced a cure. Yet, here Jung describes blood, not sweat. This becomes important later in *Liber Secundus* when the role of blood acts as a libido symbol (similar to his first active imagination) as well as a connection for the dead to the living.
34 *RB*, p. 252b.
35 Compared to other figures of the unconscious, like the Red One and the girl in the castle, Salome does not dissolve or disappear, but returns when Jung is hanging from the divine tree. She is seemingly sighted but otherwise unchanged, thus Jung's healing in the unconscious appears to have been a permanent change for her (*RB*, pp. 325b–326a).
36 *RB*, p. 252b.
37 Ibid. Shamadasani indicates in footnote 211 that Salome was like 'a *soror* or *filia mystica* of a hierophant'. Jung would later refer to Toni Wolff as such, a *soror mystica* being a companion of an alchemist. The Chinese symbols (a type of phonetic riddle) that Jung carved into the memorial stone for Toni Wolff can be seen in *The Art of C. G. Jung*, eds. U. Hoerni, T. Fischer and B. Kauffman, B. (W. W. Norton: New York, 2018), p. 163.
38 Elijah and Salome return together at the end of *Liber Secundus* (p. 323a) and in a dream at the end of *Scrutinies* (p. 357b). Salome returns on her own and unhelpful while Jung hangs upside down for three days (p. 325b).
39 *RB*, p. 252b.
40 Ibid.
41 One further notable example is when Jung shrinks the hero Izdubar, his ability to do this comes as a surprise, but once again he proves his confidence in being able to respond and alter conditions within his vision (*RB*, p. 283a).
42 *RB*, p. 246b n. 2.
43 Perhaps it can be suggested that Elijah's presence assists in holding their respective positions so that the necessary shift of libido and, in turn, healing can occur. This shift was not able to happen with Elijah's effort alone.
44 *RB*, p. 246b.
45 *AP*, pp. 143–144; and in Jung, *Notes of the Seminar on Analytical Psychology Given in 1925*, pp. 153–154.

PART III
Liber Secundus

12

THE RED ONE, THE TRAMP AND DEATH

Introduction

26 December 1913

The dynamic that occurred in the 'Mysterium Encounter' proved to be a partial introduction to what Jung would later encounter more fully in *Liber Secundus*: 'the mystery showed me in images what I should afterward live'.[1] Jung alludes to the trials he has yet to endure in order to reap the benefits of the confrontation. There is a prescient sense to what he describes that he has received a notion of what is to come. Fittingly, *Liber Secundus* begins with, 'The door of the Mysterium has closed',[2] as he leaves to set out so that he might apply to his future encounters what he has experienced with Elijah and Salome; dialogue and action in the unconscious.

As *Liber Secundus* begins on 26 December, Jung describes, 'my will is paralysed and . . . the spirit of the depths possesses me'.[3] Perhaps, as a result *Liber Secundus* contains the most extensive and detailed descriptions of Jung's encounters with the dead in the entire work.

What differs here is that Jung describes landscapes, which become more detailed, the encounters with both figures of the unconscious and the dead become more vivid, and the progressive nature of the journey, more apparent.[4] There is a distinct sense that in contrast to the experiences in *Liber Primus*, where the centre of action is with(in) Jung himself, here Jung embarks on a progressive journey. The sequence of scenes details his travels from one locale to another and often includes specifics about terrain, weather and passages of time. Often, in contrast to the setting of Jung's dreams, these landscapes occur in sympathy with what unfolds in terms of action.

The descriptions arise spontaneously and Jung later transcribes them in a more polished form with, at times, numerous commentaries. Although there

100 *Liber Secundus*

is a bewildering array of characters who often appear and disappear at will, we must assume that Jung has considered the original material and worked it while being faithful to the visions as they appeared. All this while crafting an accessible narrative for the reader.

There is a clear sense to the progression of *Liber Secundus* that Jung was delving into the furthest reaches of the psyche, experiencing both his personal and collective unconscious. At times it is obvious he is encountering a figure of his personal unconscious and at other times it is more obvious that the figures make up what could be termed the 'collective dead' or rather the dead found in the collective unconscious. The dead, who return from Jerusalem in the *Sermones*, are such a collective group as are the throngs Jung meets in the chapter titled 'Death'.[5]

What begins at the outset of *Liber Secundus* with a wary and somewhat weary Jung travelling further into his depths, becomes at the end a Jung confident about the dead, his visionary skill and the dead's purpose in appearing.

The Red One

26–28 December 1913

In the first episode of *Liber Secundus*, Jung's interactions with the devil lends clues to his understanding of how figures of the unconscious function differently to those who are the dead.[6] By examining certain details about the first episode in *Liber Secundus*, *by contrast* a fuller picture of Jung's relationship with the dead becomes clear. Figures of the unconscious prove to demonstrate an emotional relatedness and eventually dissolve or disappear, as is seen with the Red One. Similarly the emotive presentation of Salome also falls into this figure category. By contrast the dead, as discarnate souls, have a more objective, distanced and singular quality about them, existing separate and apart from Jung. Although the dead emerge, act and interact with Jung similarly as do figures of the unconscious, they have one overriding distinction; when their discourse is complete, there is no need, nor possibility, that they as discarnates integrate into Jung's personality in the same manner as figures of the unconscious do. As separate soul entities it is not possible for them to participate in the transcendent function's end result, in the same manner, as do figures of the unconscious.

Setting

Jung stands as sentry guard high up in a castle. As he looks out into the distance he sees an approaching red figure, the devil, with whom he has an extended conversation.[7]

Exchange

The Red One, or the devil, greets Jung with a revealing detail; that because Jung was waiting this seemed to call him.[8] This suggests that Jung standing guard over

The Red One, the tramp and Death **101**

the countryside in itself has conjured the devil to him from the unconscious. This fact suggests the Red One to be a figure of Jung's personal unconscious. The devil explains his presence by sharing that during his travels he has been looking for those, like Jung, who have an interest in the 'unseen'.[9] So, the devil also knows that he has been conjured by Jung and by anyone with curiosity about the unconscious. The attraction between Jung and a figure of the unconscious is similar to that of a magnet, in that there is a pull to interact, with the benefit to Jung being to engage in transformation of the libido presented so that it might by the transcendent function be integrated into his personality and thus made available for future endeavours.

Jung confesses that he is not sure why he is standing guard, (perhaps guarding over the structure of the unconscious itself, i.e. the tower castle) but he indicates that extended time with unconscious content allows him in the first instance to experience it, then to understand it more fully. Then he will be able to explain his experiences in psychological terms. This perspective sees Jung the sentry resonating with Jung's spirit of the times, attempting to explain the region of the spirit of the depths in order to justify the direction of his work as Jung the psychiatrist.

He demonstrates his ability to sense the qualities that the devil exhibits, identifying him as 'strange' and 'pagan'.[10] While Jung ponders that the Red One appears to be hiding something, the devil changes colour, becoming 'redder'.[11] When Jung inquires what he is hiding it becomes clear that the one 'shrouded in red' is the devil. The moment Jung has his suspicions, the figure changes colour. A shift occurs again at the very end of the episode when they both change; the devil into a flesh colour and Jung when his green clothes turn to leaves.

The colour conversion and physical change on Jung's part marks not only the conclusion to the conversation, but the reconciliation of its purpose and an example of the transcendent function. Jung's conversation allows him to manage his own perspectives in the conversation without being swayed by the devil's position or opinion. Thus within an active imagination Jung has practised discernment. As sentry, he engages with his opposite and with a part of himself that needed objectifying in order to 'see' clearly. As the conflict of the exchange cools, the colours of each do as well. This suggests a modulating of perspectives, the colour significant of the intensity of each of their positions and their adherence to their respective opinions.

At the very end of the episode the devil, in a trickster gesture, suggests to Jung that he is, in fact, joy and while Jung attempts to grasp this meaning, the devil fades. Fading or disappearing occurs several times in Jung's exchanges and points to his more emotive and personal connection to figures of the unconscious than to the dead. These disappearances point to the successful completion stage of the transcendent function. Jung stresses that the devil was his and the joy the devil confessed to was also his joy. With such an allocation the devil proves to be a projection of Jung's personal unconscious. The devil fading away signifies the energetic resolution of the encounter.

In Jung's commentary of this episode, and assumed to be retrospectively considered, he stresses that he took seriously all the encounters inhabiting his inner world, because he experienced them as real.[12] This was as Elijah instructed; that Jung would be experiencing much more and to write it all down.

102 *Liber Secundus*

This is Jung's approach throughout *Liber Secundus*. In a resolute manner, he confronts and exchanges with every figure he meets. His discoveries in the Mysterium include the possibility that figures of the unconscious present an opportunity for energic resolution as occurred with the curing of Salome's blindness. He would adopt this method of engagement with 'every unknown wanderer' throughout his encounters.

'One of the Lowly'

29 December 1913
This is one of the most complex interactions that Jung has in terms of determining if he is engaging with a figure of the unconscious and therefore a projection, or if the encounter is revealing of the autonomous dead. The episode raises the possibility that the unconscious is a venue of death, which takes the form of energic transformation, while at the same time suggesting the possibility of complex levels of unconscious terrain where figures of the unconscious and the dead exist concurrently.

Setting

On the third night of *Liber Secundus*, Jung wanders in a place covered in snow with an overcast sky.[13] Jung notices a one-eyed, dirty tramp who joins him and they walk and talk while they search for a place to stay overnight. For the first time in the narrative there is a scene suggestive of sequence as well as progression, that is, Jung describes walking from one place to another with a sense of destination in mind while engaging in conversation. Finally, they arrive at an inn for a meal and to sleep, at which time the tramp dies.

The episode shows some of the challenges in trying to identify qualities inherent with both projections and the dead as they appear in the unconscious. The tramp raises questions such as is the unconscious designed to simulate experiences and trains of thought previously untended, in a manner similar to dreams? Perhaps it is too eager to extract criteria from active imaginations given that each occasion is different? Jung as a practitioner is more experienced each time he enters an active imagination and thus more prepared to manage the material he meets there. Further, the episode looks to ask about the perception of dying in the unconscious and what that is exactly.

Exchange

Jung talks with the tramp about his life. He becomes self-conscious when he learns that the tramp spent time in prison, and worries that someone might see him speaking to a 'convict'.[14] This is further confirmed when they arrive at the inn for the night and Jung notes that people there see him as refined and upper class and thus granted him a special place to eat with a table cloth. This suggests the possibility

The Red One, the tramp and Death **103**

that the patrons recognise Jung to be not only a gentleman, but perhaps also an incarnate, which could be the reason for his considered treatment.

The tramp relays the story of the brawl in which he lost his eye and was sent to prison. Literally and figuratively, the tramp sees only a part of himself and his situation. Jung wonders, if Hell contains prisons for those who never experienced such when alive.[15] This reflection suggests a few possibilities: (a) Jung perceives being in Hell; (b) Hell offers the possibility to experience that which was not experienced in life; (c) Jung is currently identifying the tramp as not alive; (d) although the question applies to the tramp, it rightly could be asked of Jung given the situation in which he now finds himself. Has Jung wandered into a prison of his own making, a veritable personal Hell in part because of his struggle to understand what is unfolding? The idea of prison as confinement and the loss of social and personal freedom could be experienced not only *in* Hell, but *as* Hell and so Jung and the tramp find themselves in a collective Hell, both term and terrain.

The tramp's death

As Jung and the tramp retire to their rooms to sleep, the tramp reveals that he has an illness that affects his breathing. The lungs have an association with breath, freedom and life all of which are damaged for the tramp. A short time later, Jung hears coughing, runs to the tramp's room where moonlight is pouring in and he sees the tramp, 'blood is flowing from his mouth . . . He moans half choking . . . I hurry to support him . . . a gentle shudder passes over [him]', then all falls deathly quiet.[16]

THE MOON AND THE DEAD

The appearance of the moon offers some significance in relation to the dead.[17] Jung makes a connection between the dark moon and the place where souls go after death. He is suggesting this is where the tramp's soul went. That he comments here suggests he considered how this episode related to the process of death.[18]

The reference to a 'dead moon' and the soul moving toward death is likened to the nature of the moon's phases of waxing and waning, symbolically representing complementary degrees of consciousness. Although the tramp has expired, Jung's commentary suggests that he retired to the moon where the 'preserver of souls' oversees those with the intention of returning. In *Psychology of the Unconscious*, Jung explains how Native American lore connects the moon to the grandmother: 'In ancient beliefs, the moon is also the gathering place of departed souls, the guardian of seeds; therefore, once more a place of the origin of life of predominantly feminine significance.'[19] There is a regenerative quality to the significance of the moon being a keeper of souls, a transition space before a possible rebirth.[20] Just like the eternal resonance of the moon's presence, death too is eternal.

104 *Liber Secundus*

Jung is left with literal blood on his hands and wonders if there are occasions in Hell to experience death for those who never reconciled their thoughts about it during their lifetime.[21] This question again applies to both the tramp and to Jung. There are two things going on here. For Jung, the question speaks to his need to understand the dead, but in their own spaces of the unconscious, not death seen from an incarnate perspective. And for the tramp, it appears he too like the Austrian customs official has not died correctly, he has not fully understood the ontology of being deceased.

The scene begs some further considerations: Can death occur when already in the underworld or Hell? Is it possible that the tramp had not considered the idea of death up to this point? And if one has never reconciled the issue of death during life, is the emotional and psychological enterprise then encountered after death when foreseeably it is impossible to avoid? Maybe the tramp's issue is that he doesn't know that he is dead? In other words, is it necessary to be conscious of the fact that one is no longer incarnate in order to pass fully into the death state and not have to relive a death in the unconscious? The tramp appears to be one of the soon-to-be dead in the process of passing when they first meet. So, is it possible that Jung's incarnate presence, in fact, facilitates that goal for him?

This might be why Jung has been subject to such an involved and graphic encounter, one from which he emerges with literal blood on his hands. His unconscious has presented him with the opportunity not only to participate and assist in a passing into death, but also to understand this dynamic within the unconscious itself. In this instance Jung helps the tramp realise that he is dead. The question addresses the nature of the unconscious in relation to how the dead appear in psychic space.

The tramp: a figure of the unconscious or dead?

It is possible that the tramp's status, like the Austrian customs official, is unable 'to die properly'[22] and is transitioning to becoming a member of the dead. Yet, what Jung points to in his commentary immediately following the episode suggests otherwise. He notes that the tramp 'wants admittance into my soul . . . I am . . . not destitute enough'.[23]

This comment points to the possibility that the tramp is acting like a figure of Jung's personal unconscious. By wanting admittance into Jung, it is possible that the tramp holds symbolic qualities that Jung has yet to integrate. His embarrassment by the tramp's appearance would suggest as such. The tramp would then be subject to the transcendent function and whose destituteness could eventually be integrated into Jung's personality. Considering Jung also felt that he could learn something from the tramp, gives further credence to the idea that at that moment the tramp might be a figure of Jung's unconscious rather than one of the dead.[24]

Yet, if the tramp *is* one of the dead, he might be playing a role, which simultaneously functions like a figure of Jung's unconscious. This, of course, is

The Red One, the tramp and Death **105**

what makes discerning each type of figure a veritable challenge. Therefore, as a discarnate or one who is on his way to becoming so, the tramp is acting literally as if he is experiencing his own death in order to understand it and symbolically (destitute, dead) as a part of Jung's personal psyche. Jung's query about his destitution resonates not only with the previous questions he poses, but also points to his recognition of what was lacking in himself, making the tramp a suitable projection. The discussion of Hell and the tramp's actual expiration forces Jung to consider what death means within an unconscious context.

This is a complex episode for determining if figures of the unconscious are either figures easily subjected to the transcendent function or the dead *in se*, or perhaps acting as both at the same time. The unconscious here shows itself to be all things to all participants and reveals the multifaceted and multidimensional nature of unconscious encounters. If one is dead and unknowing, perhaps an encounter with an incarnate who also questions the nature of things might raise consciousness in those same places to assist in shifting the necessary libido for both parties.

In the commentary, Jung concludes with a confirmation that the death of the tramp is a cessation of life even in the unconscious and it prompts in him recognition of death's effect in the conscious world. His suggestion of living 'toward death' in life points to a type of mastery over life, which includes the full acknowledgement of death in its many forms.

The episode serves as an energetic continuation of the Siegfried dream. Jung's role in the murder is reconciled by the cleansing rain, a release of tension and the transfer of libido, which prompts him to an acceptance of the sacrifice of his dominant function in favour of a less developed function.[25] The death of the tramp also shifts libido to Jung, but as blood, so that he is forced to question some very basic principles about the nature of endings, asking if life ever really ends or death for that matter? The libido made available to Jung assists him to explore the idea of collective death in the episode 'Death'. The Siegfried dream provided Jung with a death encounter on a personal level, whereas the death of the tramp spoke to Jung in terms of the nature of death in the collective unconscious as a universal experience 'that engulfs the world'.

Jung's level of conscious awareness during the interaction facilitates the tramp's death and in turn Jung receives his libido. It is possible that all manner of consciousness within the unconscious is transferred in some way upon death to the still living. Perhaps, this is what becomes Jung's understanding of the salvation of the dead;[26] that the living benefit most from the consciousness of the dead, and it is the living's duty to be recipient and benefactor of its future use.

Final considerations

Jung's final word on the episode marks the moment when he advocates for the sacred nature of his inner life and the relinquishment of his outer concerns, specifically with regards to his professional commitments.[27] An inner death is what Jung

106 *Liber Secundus*

experienced with the tramp. This kind of death, the loss of an inner perspective, seems too difficult for Jung to bear and reminds him of meaninglessness. And yet outer dying or the conventional notion of death as passing away out of physical form seems more bearable to him.

Although the tramp does not appear in any future scenes of *The Red Book*, there can be no conclusion as to if he disappeared in a similar manner as previous figures of the unconscious or if he simply moved on with an autonomy of consciousness that the dead as souls presumably maintain. Jung uses the libido from the tramp's death for the next stage of his inner journey.

Death

2 January 1914

Setting

After being in a desertscape, Jung wanders out of the desert and towards the north with cooler climes.[28] This terrain differs markedly from the deserts Jung has recently travelled. He finds himself where life meets sea and sky.[29] The description expresses an endlessness, Jung arrives in what could be described as the furthest reaches of the collective unconscious: the 'source', 'womb', 'boundless' and 'immeasurable', the location of Death itself. Jung's experience of getting there is essentially by flight (gliding). This type of movement is distinctly different to the walking he has been doing in previous episodes, indicating the narrative is in a very different terrain and demanding a distinct approach for its exploration.

Jung sees a man standing 'at the last corner of the world' alone and troubled, Jung calls him the 'dark one' and his 'heart has never beaten'.[30] This is the most graphic description in *The Red Book* of the source of the dead and in particular the archetypal image of the keeper of the space as overseer of not only the region but also of those who are passing his way. Jung is open to the experience of feeling the vastness and depth, which death encompasses yet Death does not understand Jung's appearance and asks what he's doing here.

In a similar attribution as Ezechiel makes when he sees Jung and notes he has a body, Death recognises Jung as incarnate. He is surprised that Jung has found himself in the literal land of the dying, the dead or soon to be transformed, because although many do come they are never 'guests' and 'flow past here sadly in dense crowds'.[31] From Death's perspective even the living never return to the world above. This raises questions in terms of how Jung's dead differ from what he discovers being dissolved here.

Exuding an objective, non-emotive and distant quality suggests this stranger is archetypal and perhaps literally Death. He describes to Jung what he oversees; an expanse where all of life and death converge, where all come together 'undifferentiable'.[32]

THE ANCIENTS AND THE UNDERWORLD

There are examples in ancient mythology of those who travel to the underworld as part of a quest or even by necessity and return to the living. They are for the most part heroes. The ancient hero was often noted to be both mortal and immortal, i.e. having one parent a god, this could predispose them with both the desire and ability to complete such a task. In the *Collected Works*, there is only one quote from Virgil's Aeneid and from Book VI specifically, when Aeneas journeys to the underworld:

facilis descensus Averno; noctes atque dies patet atri ianua Ditis; sed revocare gradum superasque evadere ad auras; hoc opus, hic labor est.[33]

[Easy is it to descend to Avernus: the doors of Dis lie open at night and day, but to recall one's steps and escape to the upper world, this is the task, this is the labour.]

A poetic exegesis of the translation sees 'evadere' sitting between an adjective (superas) and its noun (auras) emphasising the difficulty in leaving the underworld. Virgil's repetition of 'hoc', 'hic', this is the task, this the work, places further stress on the difficulty of not only leaving but returning. To make the return journey from the world of the dead and dreams and to make sense of those experiences, to integrate those meanings, that is the real work. Those who were successful in their return include Hercules, Theseus, Aeneas, but also Psyche, Orpheus, Sisyphus and Dante. Odysseus could be included here.[34]

He asks Jung to describe what he sees, presumably because someone incarnate would see something unique to what Death presides over daily. Jung sees a recycling of all living matter; humans, animals and insects as they flow together in a wave of air and sea dispersed and 'dissolving . . . in murky clouds of mist'.[35] Jung wonders if this indeed is the end of all things? Then, Jung describes: 'a sea of blood foams at my feet . . . Blood and fire mix themselves together in a ball – a new sun escapes from the bloody sea'.[36] The newborn sun rising from below making the sea red with blood is, of course, resonant of the same found in Jung's first active imagination. Whereas that presented symbols of death and rebirth, here Jung witnesses how the land of the dead has at its core the facility to rebirth the sun if not life as well.[37] When he contemplated the newborn sun as well as the extreme depths of the scene, he concluded that his 'phoenix ascended'. This suggesting the possibility that the unconscious holds no state of death at all, but only transmutations and rebirth; a recycling of all sorts of matter from one form to another with a possible existence in another part of the unconscious.[38] In his first active

108 *Liber Secundus*

imagination, the newborn sun serves as completion to the vision. Here having faced and observed death and dissolution on a mass scale, the image of the sun suggests a sign of regeneration.

This has given Jung a chance to experience the idea of immortality as defined by a cyclical nature of all energy. The dissolution and breakdown of life produces libido that will be recycled and possibly used again in some other form. The idea is embodied in the reference to the rising phoenix, which itself represents new life from the ashes of the old, fire being the purifying element that makes such libido not just available but useable.[39]

Jung would later speculate that an afterlife could exist as a continuation of a psychic life and could possibly be where 'the hereafter . . . is located'.[40]

Reincarnation

Reincarnation is not a recurrent theme in regards to the dead in *The Red Book*, but rather a peripheral question that would inevitably arise in any study about the dead. It is difficult to discuss the dead and their role in Jung's conception of a psychological model without discussing at the very least its possibility. There are three places in *The Red Book* that suggest that quite possibly Jung experienced a recognition of the idea of reincarnation as a part of his discoveries of the unconscious: 'The Sacrificial Murder', a passage in the 'Nox Secunda' commentaries as well as the episode in *Scrutinies* of Philemon stepping off the wheel of life. Each suggests that reincarnation was perceived by Jung as a dynamic discernible in the unconscious.

Jungian analyst Roger Woolger asks 'Did Jung believe in Reincarnation?' His response: 'Jung does not seem to have accepted actual past life memories until the last decade of his life [and] even then his statements were extremely cautious.'[41] He suggests that Jung might have absorbed what he calls 'memory fragments' of past lives with personality No. 2 being an example.

He shares a conversation between Jung and a colleague, Erlo van Waveren, who discussed a series of dreams with Jung, that he thought indicative of past life memories: 'Whenever [Jung] spoke to me about an incarnation, it was referred to as an ancestor; "ancestral components", "psychic ancestors", "ancestral souls" are all expressions which Professor Jung used.'[42] It would appear that Jung likened such traces in the psychic life of individuals as remnants, or 'psychic heredity' from previous generations as opposed to an objective previous life. Jung's comments in *Memories, Dreams, Reflections* around the question reveal deep consideration and penetrative thought about the possibility, but he remained unsure: 'Whether the karma . . . I live is the outcome of my past lives, or . . . the achievement of my ancestors, whose heritage comes together in me . . . Have I lived before . . . as a specific personality? . . . Buddha left the question open.'[43] Jung is questioning to what degree can the aspirations and goals of a singular personality be attributed to the community of the dead's influence upon him/her?[44] It has been suggested that in Jung's early writings 'there is no personal inherited karma as such, there is only the collective inherited karma of one's ancestors, the archetypes, which one creatively individuates in one's own personality development'.[45] This would suggest

The Red One, the tramp and Death **109**

that we integrate those traces in the process of individuation or in an attempt to become aware of unconscious influences.

Jung's experiences throughout *The Red Book* do not necessarily address the above question, whether he is living another life after a series of previous lives and has inherited personal unfinished business, or if he lives the specific unfinished business of previous generations. And it is unclear how this question reconciles with Jung's experiences of the dead in *The Red Book*. What we do see in Jung's own response is engagement and service to his dead as they intersect with his own life.[46]

Shamdasani interprets Jung's approach to the rebirth question as 'pragmatic' because Jung thought 'one should judge the truth of such conceptions by seeing whether they had a healing or stimulating effect'.[47] Jung's observations of the unconscious clearly included the possibility of reincarnation and his cautious position could have been due to the public reception of such a position as well as the hesitancy that family and colleagues expressed in regards to such ideas. Woolger asks, 'Was Jung's growing belief in reincarnation . . . embarrassing in some way?' An interview with Jung's daughter revealed passages about reincarnation that were 'toned down' as a result of pressure from his family and editors and fear of public sentiment on the matter.[48]

Woolger's final question is: 'Could it be that larger personalities like Jung whom we honor with the term "genius" are able to reabsorb and pass on the psychically inherited remnants of certain creative spirits from previous ages?'[49] It would seem that if Jung was able to do this, we might all in our own way be playing a part in transmitting ideas from the past for their future birth, evolution and integration.

Notes

1 *RB*, p. 254b. This is the last line of *Liber Primus*.
2 Ibid., p. 259a. These gates will open once again at the end of *Liber Secundus* when the mysteries are complete and Elijah and Salome return (*RB*, p. 323b).
3 Stephenson discusses possession as the foundation of Jung's psychology and one that Jung considered contributed to a healthy psychology. Stephenson, *Possession*, p. 259. Lucy Huskinson calls spirit possession a 'catalyst for growth'. Huskinson, 'Analytical Psychology', pp. 71–95, at 92.
4 In contrast to the setting of Jung's dreams these landscapes always occur in sympathy with the action that unfolds. In dreams there is often overlay with regard to action and image for example in the Austrian customs official dream, the dream is set in one time period, but then there occurs an anachronistic appearance of a knight, this is not in sync with the time period of Jung as dreamer.
5 *RB*, pp. 346b and 273b respectively.
6 Ibid. pp. 259–265.
7 Ibid., p. 259a.
8 Ibid.
9 Ibid., pp. 259a–b.
10 This is most likely Jung unable to detect the Germanic characteristics of Goethe's Mephistopheles in his Red One (*RB*, p. 260a, n. 12–14). But Jung is Swiss and for him to have his devil accuse him of being too German certainly again draws the comparison between his devil and Faust's. But, of course, the point the devil makes is that Jung, the sentry, is too conservative in his religious attitude.
11 *RB*, p. 259b.
12 Ibid., p. 260b.

110 *Liber Secundus*

13 Ibid., p. 265a. The description foreshadows the episode as is often the case. For example the scene when Jung travels to Death is described with an equally cold and distant terrain. In the chapter 'Desert', Jung discovers the absence of his soul and says he didn't realise that his soul was 'a desert' (*RB*, p. 235b).

14 *RB*, p. 265b.

15 Ibid. In this episode this is the second time Jung questions conditions in Hell, the first being when he wonders if there are cinemas there for those who didn't enjoy them while they were alive.

16 *RB*, p. 266a.

17 *RB*, p. 267b. Shamdasani in n. 40 refers to Jung's association of the moon being 'a gathering place of departed souls' (*CW*, vol., 5, p. 318). Note fig. 31, the Chalcedon gem depicting souls on the moon. Also useful is to note Hekate's association, not only with the mystery story, and as the one who knew Persephone's kidnapper, but also in her role as guide for the initiates into the mysteries. Kerenyi, *Eleusis*, pp. 36, 79. In *Hekate, Liminal Rites*, D'Este and Rankine note the word 'Brimo was used as a password in the Orphic Mysteries, being recorded on funerary tablets as one of the words the dead soul had to repeat to prove it was an initiate and entitled to enter the paradisiacal Elysian Fields'. Sorita D'Este and David Rankine, *Hekate Liminal Rites: A Study of the Rituals, Magic and Symbols of the Torch-Bearing Triple Goddess of the Crossroads* (London: BM Avalonia, 2009), pp. 171–172. Kerenyi also links Brimo to Hecate: 'Brimo … a designation for the queen of the realm of the dead, for Demeter, Kore, and Hekate in their quality of goddesses of the underworld'. Kerenyi, *Eleusis*, p. 92.

18 The association of the moon dying is an ancient concept, and dealt with extensively in Esther Harding's work *Woman's Mysteries*. She explains about the moon god Sinn and that 'when the moon is bright the god is in his upper-world phase. When the moon is dark the god has gone to the underworld. But he will surely return.' Esther Harding, *Woman's Mysteries Ancient and Modern* (New York: Harper Colophon Books, 1971), p. 90. Jung's reference to the moon being dead possibly refers to the dark moon and associates it with the dead, i.e. the moon is for the dead, even though there is moonlight flooding into the room. Harding describes: 'In psychological terms he who has attained to the realm of the full, or complete moon has gained knowledge of the unconscious, as past, source, origin; he has power in this present world; and has insight into the realm of the future. He has become in a certain sense timeless, he transcends the limitations of time. He has gained immortality. The immortality promised by the moon is not an unending life … It is not a continuation in a state of perfection, but is an ever renewed life like the moon's own, in which diminishing and dying are as essential as becoming' (p. 212). Ancient Hindus consider that the soul's choice at death is either the path of light or the path of darkness. One leads to everlasting light, the other to the world of death and rebirth. Betty Radice, ed., *Bhagavad Gita*, trans. Juan Mascaro (London: Penguin Books, 1962), pp. 41, 8.23–8.26.

19 *Psychology of the Unconscious: A Study of the Transformations and Symbolisms of the Libido*, ed. William McGuire, Supplementary Vol. B (Princeton, NJ: Princeton University Press, 1916), p. 302, §496 (hereafter cited as *POU*). In *Symbols of Transformation* (*SOT*, *CW*, vol. 5, p. 318, §487), Jung includes the picture of the Chaldean gem, first century, in which souls appear to be standing on a crescent moon.

20 See Jung's poetic description of the moon in *RB*, pp. 267a–b.

21 *RB*, p. 266. Jung asked a similar question in the 'Mysterium': 'Am I truly in the underworld?' (*RB*, p. 246). The conditions of conversing with figures of the unconscious incite him to question his surrounds.

22 *MDR*, p. 187.

23 *RB*, p. 266a.

24 Ibid., p. 265b.

25 *AP*, p. 48.

26 Discussed in 'Nox Secunda', p. 297b.

27 Jung resigned from the *Jarbuch* editorship on 27 October 1913, as president of the International Psychological Association on 20 April 1914 and from the faculty of the Medical School on 30 April 1914. Murray Stein notes that this was an attempt to free

himself from 'the spirit of the times'. Murray Stein, 'Carl Jung's Red Book Part 1' [webinar] (22 January 2010), http://ashevillejungcenter.org (accessed 15 November 2010).

28 *RB*, p. 273b. The description here is very similar to what was described in 'One of the Lowly' (*RB*, p. 265a).

29 Ibid.

30 *RB*, p. 274a.

31 Ibid.

32 Ibid.

33 Virgil, *The Aeneid of Virgil*, Books 1–6, ed. R. D. Williams (New York: St. Martin's Press, 1972), Bk VI. pp. 126–129.

34 March, *Cassell's Dictionary*, pp. 343 and 706.

35 *RB*, p. 274a.

36 Ibid.

37 *SOT, CW*, vol. 5, pp. 218, §319.

38 It is unclear here if we are to conclude any reference to reincarnated forms as a result of this episode. See discussion later in this chapter on Jung and reincarnation.

39 'The ancient civilizations of the Near East were familiar with a sun-worship dominated by the idea of the dying and resurgent god – Osiris ... Tammuz, Attis-Adonis, Christ, Mithras, and the phoenix' (*SOT, CW*, vol. 5, pp. 109, §165), similarly stated in *Psychology of the Unconscious* (pp. 102, §188). Although this encounter also feels initiatory, it does not point to any particular mystery initiation other than the dynamic quality of life after death.

40 *MDR*, p. 352.

41 Woolger, *Other Lives*, p. 346. Both Kugler and Olson allude to this shift during Jung's later years, but there is now clear indication in *The Red Book* that this belief was confirmed earlier and that his psychological model begins to look like a means to explain such phenomena. Also appears in Charet, *Spiritualism*, p. 221 n. 147.

42 Woolger, *Other Lives*, p. 346. This is also the language Jung uses when detailing his ancestral spirits dream (*MDR*, p. 338).

43 *MDR*, pp. 349–350.

44 Eugene Taylor explains: 'Indeed the occult for Jung was not a peripheral problem beyond science, but rather at the very heart of his psychology, for the psychic dimension of personality represented not the merely diabolical element within each one of us, but also the unconscious creative ferment ... the achievement of the unique spiritual destiny of each individual.' Eugene Taylor, 'C.G. Jung and the Boston Psychopathologists, 1902–1912', in *Carl Jung and Soul Psychology*, ed. Mark Stern (London: Routledge, 1991), p. 140, cited in Charet, *Spiritualism*, p. 221 n. 147.

45 Coward, *Jung and Eastern Thought*, pp. 100–101.

46 Regarding Jung's comment regarding the question the Buddha left unanswered, was not about reincarnation, but rather about the existence of a self: 'the Buddha felt that the question was misguided to begin with. Why? No matter how you define the line between "self" and "other", the notion of self involves an element of self-identification and clinging, and thus suffering.' Jung explains the same in *Memories, Dreams, Reflections* (p. 349). So, such a position as anatta or no-self doctrine would suggest the inability to reincarnate. Perhaps Jung felt himself in fine company with regards to his own hesitancy to commit to a position. Thanissaro Bhikkhu, "No-Self or Not-Self?" [online] *Access to Insight* (8 March 2011), www.accesstoinsight.org/lib/authors/thanissaro/notself2.html (accessed 22 July 2011).

47 Shamdasani, 'The Boundless Expanse', p. 25.

48 Woolger, *Other Lives*, p. 347.

49 Ibid.

13

DIVINE FOLLY

14, 17, 18 and 19 January 1914

'Divine Folly' and subsequent episodes 'Nox Prima' to 'Nox Quarta' serve as the halfway point of Jung's material in *The Red Book*. This section looks toward the origination of the *Septem Sermones* and serves as its own play within a play, revealing action at various levels of the unconscious.[1]

Setting

The active imagination begins as Jung enters a library located on the right side of a hallway, pulled to make a choice between going right, which he attributes to his thinking function, or going to the left, which is his feeling function.[2] The atmosphere of the library he finds disturbing and intellectually stuffy.[3] Considering Jung's personal life, it is not surprising that he describes the right side of the hallway as such.

He is unsure why he is there but meets a librarian and requests a book by Thomas à Kempis, *The Imitation of Christ*.[4] The significance of the title is important considering his encounter in the Mysterium when he assumed the form of the Crucifixion. He explains to the librarian that the book 'is written from the soul' because for him at least the way of science can disappoint. Jung and the librarian continue an exchange in which Jung advocates a reconsideration of Christianity, i.e. keeping those parts that might work. He then takes the book and leaves the library.

'Nox Secunda'

17 January 1914

Setting

When Jung returns to his active imagination in 'Nox Secunda', he enters a kitchen where he engages in conversation with a cook. The geography of the scene is significant to understand the importance of the arrival of the dead.

The kitchen sits opposite the library where his active imagination took place three days earlier. Having explored the library with its 'conceit' and 'vanity', he moves across the hall where the cook stands at the stove. The alchemical symbolism cannot be overlooked; the cook oversees recipes and mixtures, and assuring the right ingredients contributes to an intended result, something digestible. All of this points to the possibility that on Jung's left side, in the kitchen, a transformation will occur.

He asks if he can enter.[5] What he is waiting for, perhaps not consciously (or, in this case, unconsciously), are the dead who will rush through the kitchen on their way to Jerusalem. He speaks to the cook about the book, *The Imitation of Christ*, which holds interest for them both.[6] To further explain Jung's unconscious vantage when experiencing this scene, in the commentaries he explains that the spirit of the times has chewed over Christianity, analysed to the point of depletion, leaving no mystery. But in the spirit of the depths he can rediscover Christ.[7] The depths invites a resurrection of the Christ story and a reassessment from and in the unconscious. Jung reflects on the way Christ lived prompting him to think that he would like to emulate him.[8] Where the contemplation of the new God appears to evoke Elijah, here the contemplation of the imitation of Christ appears to evoke the collective dead.

The dead arrive

(Note: Jung falls asleep in the kitchen during an already concurrent active imagination with the cook, thus he meets the dead at a deeper level of the unconscious. This becomes clear in 'Nox Quarta'.[9])

This is a seminal moment considering what it prompts. As soon as Jung has this thought, he hears the throng of dead moving through the kitchen on their way to Jerusalem. Like Christ, Jung has raised the dead. Just as Jung thinks about Christ, he hears a strange whirring sound and then shadows 'rush past . . . [a] babble of voices utter . . . "Let us pray in the temple"'.[10] Jung yells to ask where they are going and they respond 'to Jerusalem to pray at the most Holy Sepulchre'.[11]

For the dead to be on their way to pray at Christ's tomb raises some intriguing questions. The Holy Sepulchre, the tomb of Jesus, commemorates his physical death, but also alludes to the idea of resurrection.[12] Now, both the living and dead pray where the human Jesus was resurrected. Yet, what does it mean for the dead to pray at a tomb commemorating a physical death? Are they praying to the Christ who preached to them in Hell before his resurrection or are they looking to Christ's life? Or in him rising anew? Which Christ would be of most value to the collective dead?

Jung responds enthusiastically and wants to join them. One named Ezechiel immediately responds, 'You cannot join us, you have a body. But we are dead.'[13] This is an extraordinary declaration, and although coming from one of the dead themselves, it is this exchange that decisively defines the dead for Jung. Jung's dead are discarnate entities, souls without bodies, perhaps even

114 *Liber Secundus*

the shadows Jung identifies. This exchange could very well not only define for Jung what he had been experiencing in his death dreams the previous years, but also looks to have informed how Jung would see and experience the dead as a separate psychic experience to other figures of the unconscious. Jung is unable to accompany the dead to Jerusalem precisely because he is incarnate, yet this does not stop him from trying.

EZECHIEL

The meaning of the exchange rests with his association of the Biblical prophet known for raising the dead, specifically by bringing life back to human bones.[14] He is now the second prophet that Jung encounters; Elijah also is associated with a Biblical prophet able to raise the dead.[15] The biblical Ezechiel, whose name means 'the power of God', represents the ability to access the future, functioning in a similar role to Jung's spirit of the depths. That he, or one similarly named, appears in Jung's vision of the dead setting off to Jerusalem seems apt. As an Anabaptist advocating a direct relationship with God, here he is unknowing. The episode recalls the question as to why another prophet, Elijah, could not cure Salome of her blindness but instead turned to the incarnate Jung to do so.[16] Ezechiel's inner heat suggests a hunger for knowledge; the ability to master the ways of the unconscious. Jung seems better able to do this for the dead than the dead are.

Discussion

The dead appeal to Jung when they explain that they are going to Jerusalem, but they do not know exactly what is compelling them to go other than although they were believers they are not at peace.[17]

'Jerusalem' has several meanings; 'city of peace' or more literally 'teaching peace'. Yet, the more accurate translation might be 'pointing the way towards completion'.[18] This last possibility considers that the dead return because they have not found their peace and as a result they are not yet complete in their deceased state. Clearly, although the dead were believers, this has not helped them now that they are discarnate, they are still left with the same questions and unfinished business as in life.[19]

Jung wonders why they have no peace and Ezechiel explains: 'It always seems to me as if we had not come to a proper end with life.'[20] This expression resonates with Jung's previous phrase used to describe the customs official who had not learned how to 'die properly' and with the tramp who didn't seem to fully die.[21]

Many suggestions arise as to why the dead haven't experienced a proper end: attachment to incarnate life, attachment to relationships, unresolved emotions, even the unsuccessful transition into levels of the unconscious appropriate or compatible to their incarnate life. Whichever speculation, the exchange reveals that these dead remain unappeased, searching and heading to Jerusalem because they forgot to live something important. Jung is curious as to what that is exactly and Ezechiel does not know, in fact so much so that he asks Jung if he has any idea.[22]

This is an extraordinary question that the discarnate Ezechiel poses to the incarnate Jung. He appeals to Jung's skill of discernment in being alive and incarnate while in the unconscious and two levels deep in an active imagination. Principally, the dead cannot *remember* what they possibly missed while alive.[23] Although they understand and discern their discarnate state as different to Jung's incarnate one, they have not retained details about their own individual lives. They are functioning without the capacity to recall how their condition, when alive, was to affect them as discarnates.

Inner heat

During the discussion Ezechiel reaches out to grab Jung glowing with an 'inner heat'. And Jung responds with 'Let go daimon'.

Ezechiel reaches out with a need and envy to have what Jung so obviously exudes. He sees that Jung is in fact incarnate and possesses a knowing that the dead do not have. The 'inner heat' could be unsated hunger and desire. But equally, it could be that which is reflected back by Jung as how an incarnate appears to the dead; the physical manifestation of the psychological remains of the unlived life. That is, the dead bring with them the life they have not lived. This could be why they are unable to fully transition into a deceased state or to die properly.[24] What Ezechiel wants from Jung is a kind of knowledge that only the incarnate Jung can bestow. When Ezechiel wonders if Jung would happen to know what is missing, he wants not just Jung's knowledge, but the perspective that the incarnate Jung can lend the dead to explain to them their deficiency. Not living his animal refers to the very physical that he has taken over into death as a result of not integrating while alive. This heat can be animal instincts including hunger, sexual drive, mental drive and aspirations. And perhaps these drives have not been integrated on all levels: mentally physically, spiritually and sexually.

Marie-Louise von Franz discusses the very different conditions lived by the dead, specifically a dream she had about her deceased father from which she awoke 'so hot as if with a fever'.[25] Von Franz's father informed her: 'It is not good for either the dead nor the living to be together too long.'[26] As discussed, Jung confirmed for von Franz that she had been with her real father during the dream, not a projection. Von Franz concludes her response was in part due to 'a strong physical reaction against this chill of death, like a call back into the body and into life'.[27] She becomes aware of the physical limitations of these types of encounters and the excessive heat prompts her to remember her incarnate state. Ezechiel's 'inner heat'

116 *Liber Secundus*

confirms the fundamental differences between the living and dead and drives home the point that Jung cannot accompany Ezechiel and the dead to Jerusalem.

Is this 'inner heat' an indication of the transcendent function? The shift allows Jung to differentiate himself from Ezechiel and for him to do the same. But there is an objective quality to Ezechiel's presence and their interaction would appear to be what I have termed interpsychic rapport rather than an active imagination. This dynamic, I have suggested, respects the autonomy of the dead and excuses them from the last stage of the transcendent function, which typically would have Ezechiel as a projection dissolve into Jung's personality. Instead interpsychic rapport has the dead move on to their 'life of the dead' after their exchange.[28]

Jung returns and is led to the madhouse

Ezechiel's lunge towards Jung startles Jung back into the kitchen.[29] The cook is concerned and inquires if anything is wrong with Jung. Due to her reaction, it is obvious that the cook has not experienced nor even seen what Jung has in the same space. It becomes clear that the level of the unconscious where Jung converses with the librarian and meets the cook is different to the realm where he conversed with Ezechiel and witnessed the throng of dead.

The scene that immediately follows is one of the most outlandish and humorous in the entire text and must be considered the reason for the title of the initial episode, 'Divine Folly.'[30] A comedic scene follows in which the librarian rushes into the kitchen 'laughing maliciously', suspicious of Jung's activities and prompted to call the police.[31] In a series of scenes observed by a crowd of onlookers, Jung is hoisted into a white van and admitted to an asylum because he hears voices. That this has occurred just after his encounter with the dead is significant, as the scene appears to act out fears Jung has harboured about the entire enterprise of *The Red Book*.[32]

As Jung is being led away, he remembers he is still clutching the book by à Kempis and employs a type of bibliomancy. Jung wonders what à Kempis would think of his predicament and then lets his eyes fall on the line about temptation.[33] Is this temptation really about the lures of the unconscious in general and the dead more specifically? Presumably, Jung is led away to a mental facility because he was speaking to the dead. Could Jung's confrontation with authority be unfolding due to his guilt over his desire to accompany the dead to Jerusalem? Was the temptation to join the dead so great that, in turn, the scene compensates to the extent that he is led to the 'madhouse' in such a public fashion?

Temptation, as Jung understands it, is not the battle to tame human desires for a more righteous life (perhaps Ezechiel's problem), but rather here temptation is the effect, presence and unacknowledged influence of the dead on the living.[34]

The scene continues as policemen stand to his right and left and he concludes that his pursuits thus far are unacceptable to public life.[35] His acknowledgement of the dead and the actual cost of such a crime, manifests in the form of an arrest. The fact that he is being taken by law enforcers on the left and right reveals that both his approaches – left and right, intuitive and intellectual, feeling and thinking, cook and

Divine Folly **117**

librarian – are being contained.[36] The challenge will recalibrate the correct way of being in the world for him, that is reconciliation between left and right, between the unconscious and conscious, between the dead and the living. In Jung's dealings with the tramp he was slightly embarrassed that someone sees him speaking to a convict, while at the same time revelling in a feeling of reaching the lowest depths in his association with the tramp.[37] Here he is acting out the very real possibility of that rock bottom.

The madhouse

The following few exchanges are worth examining in order to grasp the quandary in which Jung finds himself. One of the doctors (also a professor) declares Jung has a type of 'madness' and Jung agrees.[38] Then the professor asks if he has been hearing voices and not only does Jung enthusiastically confess, but claims that he sought them out. In his defence Jung adds that hearing voices is 'absolutely not abnormal' and that he feels just fine, it is the doctor who dismisses Jung's assessment of his own condition.

The obvious dynamic is the patronising assumption of the professor as doctor (Jung is both) that the patient knows nothing of what he suffers. Jung is battling himself as professor and patient against the establishment of healing attitudes. What emerges is his frustration in the face of a predisposed diagnosis without so much as any personal consideration of his situation as such.

Jung advocates an 'absolutely not abnormal' opinion regarding auditory (and visual) hallucinations. This seems to be comically less confident than 'absolutely normal', either way, Jung is trying to make the point that for him the situation lacks pathology. In fact, what appears to prove this is his resolute confirmation that the voices aren't following him, but rather he pursued them. He is not being haunted by voices, but has sought them out and with this an underlying assumption that the process was both normal and necessary. Not only has Jung pursued the communication with the librarian and the cook, but the dead as well and not just any dead, but those questioning why they are unfulfilled by their lives and their deaths.

The visions and voices manifest as a result of the intuitive method as Jung discusses the book with the cook in the kitchen on the left of the hallway. The kitchen acts like a type of alchemical vessel of transformation, the room of the house designated specifically for transformation of all kinds of nourishment. And Jung's presence preceding the appearance of the dead seems to have facilitated the encounter at the outset.

His confirmation to the professor is undeniably certain. Yet, he hears what he fears most: that a professor (a psychiatrist?) concludes a 'pretty bad' prognosis for recovery due to the nature of what has brought him to the mental ward. Is this not one of Jung's struggles in his professional life, that some of his material was going to convince the public that he was harbouring a personal and very private madness? How would he attempt to convince them otherwise if not to develop a

118 *Liber Secundus*

psychological model, whose central tenets assist in explaining visions with all sorts of figures of the unconscious? This is in part why this scene is a seminal turning point in the narrative. Jung has initiated, encountered and processed his biggest fear while maintaining a clear narrative perspective.

The concluding scene to 'Nox Secunda' sees Jung checked into the hospital.[39] At this point, his clothes are surveyed, that is, his persona is being evaluated. Again the reference to where he is placed in the hospital (to the left and right) reveals his position in relation to the two perspectives he's struggling with. He sees to his left someone staring into space and the one on the right appears to possess a brain whose girth and weight are shrinking. Jung's intuitive side is represented by a person with a fixed gaze, fixed on other interiors, other levels of the unconscious, as Jung did in the kitchen while the cook watched. To his right, his previous way in the world, the life of his spirit of the times, is shrinking. The brain/intellect on which he relied so heavily before grows smaller in relation to the intuitive method he has discovered during his encounters in the unconscious. He is able to sit between the two in silence and balance in observance the effects of the two approaches.

Jung wonders at the end of the episode, if society were eventually to accept this way of thinking, that is, what if we were to invite the dead into our lives or bring the collective into our living'? What if society consciously integrated the collective history of humanity?

Part of Jung's confrontation with the unconscious is the very act of compensation itself, an attempt at rebalancing the unconscious with the conscious attitude.[40] That he was able to emerge with understanding, even several months after such intense encounters is impressive. He grasped that part of what was happening was a redress of his unconscious attitude to align with his conscious way in the world. The appearances of the dead, although extreme, were instrumental in assisting him to see the need for such a rebalance. By considering the dead and considering their exchange seriously, he was engaged in the concept of 'as above so below' introduced in the loggia dream.[41]

'Nox Secunda': commentary on the dead

17 January 1914

This lengthy commentary added to the second night of this episode is the most extensive analysis of Jung's thoughts about the dead in the entire work. Here he reflects in an almost intimate manner his understanding of the dead, their needs, and his relationship to them. What was considered the most authentic exchange with the dead, the Septem Sermones, *now must be considered next to Jung's thoughts here about the collective dead. It must be remembered that commentaries throughout the work were added later and sometimes reworked for several years. It is probable that Jung's thoughts discussed below emerged after his experiences ended and perhaps even long after the composition of the* Sermones.

Chaos

Jung describes how each person has a sense of centre to themselves where there is clarity.[42] He continues to describe a type of layer that covers the chaos.[43] This is as easy to locate as a boundary within oneself and if one searches deeper you can reach the chaos which is 'filled with figures'.[44] Jung has identified the graphic distinction between his personal and collective unconscious, most likely as a result of his encounter with both Ezechiel and the dead.

Jung's visioning now reveals a depth to figures, a dimensional quality that might be evident as a result of his encounters with Elijah and Salome, figures from both his personal and collective unconscious. Such a sustained active imagination would have honed Jung's skill to the qualities of all figures of the collective both dead and projections.

He continues to describe exactly who he discovers. These dead are: 'not just your dead, that is all the images of the shapes you took in the past, which your ongoing life has left behind, but also the thronging dead of human history, the ghostly procession of the past'.[45] This passage could very well be referring to incarnations in past lifetimes. Or the passage might be referring to the personal self having evolved over a single lifetime. Jung appears to suggest that one's own past incarnations along with any residual elements of previous lives can be discerned in the unconscious. The dead here are the veritable treasure that presumably makes up the collective unconscious. And the 'ghostly procession' must include the same dead that Jung has just encountered in the kitchen on their way to Jerusalem.

The passage points to the possibility that the unconscious serves as a holding place for the collective pasts of all peoples, all incarnations, including what could be described as a repository of each deceased person's personal unconscious. Jung perceives the collective archive of history's deceased souls as a residual collection of unconscious content from previous generations. This seems to suggest that at death one carries over one's personal unconscious in spite of the possibility of reincarnation. He continues to describe how the dead live alongside the living as they gaze 'greedily' through one's eyes, or see the world literally through you. That they 'moan and hope' points to their purpose in appearing in the first place. It is not the individual deceased relative here desiring what Jung has to offer as an incarnate, but rather it is the collective dead who look to finish their lives in death and look to do so through the work of the living Jung.[46] The practically universal denial of a post-mortem existence Jung calls 'cluelessness' and reveals his frustration with this traditional viewpoint. He emphasises that just because one does not see the dead does not mean they're not there: 'You seem to believe that you can absolve yourself from the care of the dead . . . Do you think that the dead do not exist because you have devised the impossibility of immortality?'[47] If you doubt their active influence, he challenges, the dead are as easy to find as looking and listening.

With the dead in and part of the chaos, Jung finds what waits on the other side are choices, decisions, mistakes, regrets and paths not taken, but considered.

120 *Liber Secundus*

The boundary between man and the chaos not only divides the conscious from the unconscious, but also serves as a threshold for the repository of choices and life directions not taken. It seems apt that the collective dead share an unconscious terrain not only with memories of all past human lives, but with all that was not lived, that is the choices and paths not taken.

These passages reveal how Jung came to understand the dead as first presented in *Memories, Dreams, Reflections*. They are their unredeemed acts passed down through human history and their sighs are the sound of their unrequited desires left so by incomplete lives. Shamdasani suggests that Jung's 'theology of the dead ... does not take the form of literally saving the souls of the dead, but [involves] taking on the legacy of the dead ... answering their unanswered questions'.[48] This is Jung's redemptive effort on their behalf. And if this redemption is not undertaken, then possible haunting conditions might ensue. While you are busy dismissing the dead of their immortal possibilities, they are busy waging an often silent battle to impose their will and preferences.[49] Such a dynamic results from being ignored, and as a result the dead have the ability to drive the passions and desires of the living. Neglected, the community of dead hope to become an acknowledged part of life. This might suggest that their life emerges from their effect on the living.

This type of dead are the very ones who have in life suffered. They exercise power over the living if they had not reconciled the same power during their lives (perhaps as Ezechiel's inner heat reveals). They were broken by life's circumstances and were unable to reconcile, therefore they remain unappeased with an inability to move towards resolution, dissolution or any type of atonement.

Toward the end of this commentary, Jung asks the reader directly: 'Have you entered the beauty of their thoughts?'[50] He is asking not only if you are paying attention, but is suggesting how to access the dead in the unconscious; through the very needs they are expressing. In essence his question is, 'What efforts have you made to assist them in understanding not only their lives but their deaths as well?' The lack of attention and the psychological repercussions as a result of such inattention, this is the true haunting.

Instruction for the dead

At this stage in the narrative, Jung expresses a deep connection to his responsibility for the dead. In his warning of how to engage, he reveals both acceptance as well as reverence in service. He makes distinctions not only between the living and dead but also between the dead and other figures of the unconscious.[51] Working with the dead takes solitary dedication and a deep loneliness that will unknowingly overwhelm the living.[52] Jung's efforts here are his secret business and exist as a covenant between him as an incarnate and his dead for their salvation.

Speaking aloud about the mysteries dispels their sacred nature and relationship to the work, because such work with the dead is likened to the 'tree of divinity'.[53] Severing the relationship with the dead is like separating Jung from himself and his ancestral lineage. He equated the work with the dead to that with the soul, but

Divine Folly **121**

now the entire project sits directly with the divine. The reverence that Jung feels for his work in answering the dead is dedicated and he hears their needs and does so 'with love'.[54]

If the connection to the dead is not recognised and realised in some manifested way, all that is left is their haunting. But, if a sense of connection is restored by the living, then their salvation can occur. The living with their conscious attitude toward the dead allow for temptation to be recognised as the dead's requests for recognition. Jung stresses that such conscious acknowledgement of their efforts is 'hidden and strange' but the result will be 'the wellspring of your best work'.[55] With this there is satisfaction of being conscious of one's directions with the dead's blessings.

All of this can occur by finding one's dead, which requires an introspection in much the same way as finding one's soul.[56] A by-product of soul searching (Jung's at least) is encounters with the community of the dead who in their various manifestations appear once one's orientation to soul is established. In fact a sense of resolution dawns at the end of the commentary when Jung welcomes his soul's return.[57] This occurs as if he has earned her appearance through his acceptance and understanding of his dead.

'Nox Tertia'

The third night of this cycle of active imaginations, Jung converses with his soul about madness and she encourages him not only to embrace it but to live with it. At this point the professor walks in to find Jung incoherent, revealing once again that he has moved between levels of the unconscious in a similar fashion as he did in the cook's kitchen.

He shifts from the collective unconscious or 'chaos' to his personal unconscious as he describes the disorientation of being committed to the madhouse.[58] The physical description suggests his emotional and mental state are like being in the ocean, swaying on the waves and unsteady.[59] This is a physical and psychological locator for Jung and his inability to gain a foothold is expressed by the sensations of being on a ship. He moves from experiencing the ocean as a physical sensation, to observing a ship, to being on the ship, all the while still in his bed in the hospital.[60] Thus, within his active imagination, once again, he is having a further vision, that is he is experiencing levels of depth and distance within the unconscious, in a similar manner as he did in the cook's kitchen.[61]

Since Jung raises the suggestions about chaos it is possible that he is experiencing the passengers on the ship as the collective dead who see his participation as ghostly. The whole encounter leaves Jung feeling unsettled and disoriented. He appears to have reached his most desperate moment of incomprehension. A sense of true madness has gripped him as he describes being literally at sea and at the mercy of the unconscious as ocean, which plays with his literal and emotional balance. In addition to being overwhelmed by the symbols and images of the psyche he is equally unprepared from his scientific/intellectual perspective to manage and understand their meaning.

122 *Liber Secundus*

Jung then refocuses from his conversations on the ship back to the hospital bed where he engages with a fellow patient who asserts that they are indeed in Hell.[62] Jung suffers from seasickness as he grabs his bedrails to steady himself.

'Nox Quarta': back to the kitchen

19 January 1914

Jung is confused and does not know if he is asleep or awake, dead or alive when he hears laughter and emerges from a 'blind darkness' to find the cook waking him.[63] The cook informs Jung that he has been sleeping for an hour. This is the second time the cook has awakened Jung, the first being after the appearance of the dead on their way to Jerusalem.[64] Jung has used the cook's kitchen as a launching point into the collective unconscious from which he has emerged with definitive ideas about the dead and the living's relationship to them.

What Jung has experienced in these active imaginations is the reality that throughout his encounters, he knows he must counteract his confrontations with some safe place either with his soul or in his physical life. When he awakens from the dream he is still in the level of the personal unconscious, which began with the cook in the kitchen. He has arisen closer to consciousness than the deeper levels in which appeared the chaos of the community of the dead.

Although the course of four active imaginations lasted over six nights, Jung managed to return to the same place in the cook's kitchen after the series. The time in the mental ward was a 'dreadful play' and he felt as if he were watching himself go through the motions of being committed to the madhouse in a type of paranoia dream.

Jung bids the cook goodbye and thanks her for 'the accommodation', almost as if she assisted in his explorations. He leaves the kitchen to return the book to the other side of the corridor and wonders if the librarian understands what goes on in his kitchen. He asks the librarian if he's had an incubation sleep there, to which the librarian responds that such an idea had never occurred to him.[65] Jung suggests an incubation sleep to a figure of the unconscious, which raises the question if such a practice is even an option for a figure, or is it simply accessible to an incarnate Jung travelling deeply into the collective unconscious. Jung confidently leaves the kitchen knowing he has survived his encounters in all levels of the unconscious as well as with the community of the dead.[66]

'Nox Quarta' commentary: the incest taboo

The madhouse episodes lead to in-depth speculation as to what exactly Jung has been doing with the dead. The commentary addresses questions but it is not clear to whom; to himself, the spirit of the depths or perhaps his soul? He invites the dead to a similar ancient ritual of drinking blood in order to speak and be heard. Recognition, devotion and a rightful place in the psyche seems to be what Jung is

Divine Folly **123**

exploring when he wonders if really what the dead want is simply love. He even asks what it would be like 'being in love with the dead'.[67] Such an idea might lend a clue to how Jung feels about his work with them. Love, not blood, might be the currency the dead most value and might be the connection they seek in the living incarnate Jung.

Jung seems to be really distracted by a type of compulsion or 'craving' to speak with the dead and this introduces a sexual quality to the connection. He then begins to recount the biblical story of Elijah who raises the child from the dead but with decidedly sexual overtones. The result of Elijah's actions is to raise the child from the dead but Jung wonders in fact if the act is an 'ambiguous impure pleasure'.[68]

Could Jung have a desire for a 'lusty commingling' for the dead?[69] Is raising the dead really like this? Describing it as such ushers in the discussion of the incest taboo. Considering raising the dead as incest implies a process of begetting, because the encounters arise from immersion in the same unconscious as the dead reside. The retelling of the biblical Elijah raising the dead child and here with sexual undertones gives the story an intriguing reframing. Has Jung tapped into a sexual feeling or is he attempting to liken his work with the dead to an incestuous obsession, one he can't quite shake?

To raise a child from the dead certainly seems to call on powers not of this world, to go from death and its domain back to life itself, might be deemed as a 'holy evil' pursuit, an evil not unlike sexual intentions towards a child. But just as such sexual advances can be initiated by the need to be empowered and to feel power, Jung identifies the ability, in fact, his ability to raise the dead with similar satisfaction.

Raising the dead also begs questions such as, 'If one can do it, should you?'[70] Jung explains the dynamic:

> [T]he fundamental basis of the 'incestuous' desire does not aim at cohabitation, but at the special thought of becoming a child again, of turning back to the parent's protection . . . it is not incestuous cohabitation which is desired, but the rebirth.[71]

Raising the dead is a type of rebirth although one wonders if it introduces a degree of self-service in the same manner as incestuous desires, that is, is Jung raising the dead for his own satisfaction? Incest involves an inversion of libido into the unconscious, and with it a draw Jung is unable to withstand. Perhaps he is suggesting that contacting the dead with intention and the resultant relationship is akin to the trials and struggles of the incest taboo? If so, this would prove to be a fundamental quality that distinguishes the dead from other split-off parts of the psyche; that Jung, in fact, calls on or raises his dead, but that figures of the unconscious quite possibly appear themselves as a result of their inherent disengagement from the psyche. Considering the spirit of the depths' command to awaken the dead, this

124 *Liber Secundus*

could be Jung's answer. This unfolds as a long-term relationship outside the scope of integration into his personality, i.e. outside the dynamic of the transcendent function. The discussion thus far has focused on the pivotal relationship of each to Jung, not in the initiation of each type of figure at the outset. It is not clear when figures emerge, if Jung draws them near or if they appear independently. It seems that there is no clear distinction in the initial presentation of how the dead and figures of the unconscious come to interact, rather the dynamic of the exchange and their conclusion seems more apt to point to their nature.

The biblical scene of Elijah and the dead child here suggests a possible lust 'with corpses'. It is exact in detail to 2 Kings 4:32, but added is the sexual nuance. The scene shows the idea of raising the dead to life holds parallel to begetting, not necessarily copulation. I suggest that Jung perceives 'commingling' with the dead to be a specific type of focus and dedication of mental energy, what Hollenback would call 'recollection'. This energic investment during interpsychic rapport requires an immersive commitment to see the exchange to its conclusion that is to raise the dead to complete the exchange and to release the connection back to them. This takes a quality of energy he identifies as lustful.

Notes

1 One of the most perplexing parts of the *Septem Sermones* is its opening line, 'The dead returned from Jerusalem not having found what they sought.' Stephan Hoeller, *The Gnostic Jung and the "Seven Sermons to the Dead"* (Wheaton, IL: Quest Books, 1982), p. 44. Scholars have attempted to glean meaning from this initial sentence, yet *The Red Book* confirms exactly when the dead left for Jerusalem (17 January 1914) and why (to pray at the holy sepulchre). They set off for the holy city a full two years before they returned, and incited Jung to write/channel the *Sermones*. During that intervening time Jung continued to struggle with the content that originally emerged between November of 1913 and April of 1914. He was to reconsider and write commentary about the original material for another two years, at which time in April of 1916, with the haunting of his house, the dead reappeared to discuss the content of what he would write as the *Septem Sermones ad Mortuos*, included in *The Red Book* as *Scrutinies* (*RB*, p. 346b).
2 *RB*, p. 295b.
3 Ibid., p. 292a.
4 The title of Thomas' book is significant because Jung uses it to discuss his understanding of the idea of imitation. He is taken both by the idea of imitating Christ, but sees also the complication inherent in imitation, He advocates clearly that the method of living by religious law no longer holds meaning for him and that the true teaching is to be found within, which *The Red Book* proceeds to demonstrate.
5 *RB*, p. 294a.
6 This is known to be a form of divination called bibliomancy, a method by which answers to questions were obtained by opening the Bible to a random passage and interpreting it as an answer.
7 *RB*, p. 295b.
8 *RB*, p. 245b,
9 *RB*, p. 302.
10 Ibid., p. 294a.
11 Ibid., p. 294b. This detail is not mentioned or included in the previously published versions of *Septem Sermones*.

12 Arthur McMahon, 'Holy Sepulchre', in *The Catholic Encyclopedia*, Vol. 7 (New York: Robert Appleton, 1910), www.newadvent.org/cathen/07425a.htm (accessed 28 April 2011).

13 Ibid.

14 Ezechiel 37:1–14.

15 2 Kings, 2:3.

16 *RB*, p. 252b.

17 Ibid., p. 294b.

18 'The place name Jerusalem (pronounced yerushalaim in Hebrew) is a combination of two words. The first is "yeru" meaning "flow". This word has several applications such as the flowing of water in a river, the throwing of something as being flowed out of the hand or as the flowing of a finger in the sense of pointing out the way one should go. This last use is the use in the name yerushalaim. The shalayim is from the word shalam meaning complete and whole (the word Shalom is also derived from shalam, while it is usually translated as peace it more means to be complete or whole). When these two words are put together they mean something like "pointing the way to completeness".' Jeff A. Benner, *Biblical Hebrew E-Magazine* 8 (October 2004), www.ancient-hebrew.org/emagazine/008.doc (accessed 15 February 2008).

19 This looks to be what prompted Jung's statement regarding the need to guide both the dead and figures of the unconscious (*MDR*, p. 338).

20 Consider this alongside the idea appearing in Jung's previous material of not dying 'properly' or fully.

21 *RB*, pp. 266a–b. This becomes a pivotal point when Philemon discusses why the dead are requesting to be taught by him in the *Sermones*.

22 *RB*, p. 294b.

23 *MDR*, p. 338.

24 Jung's own explanation in the commentary regarding this inner heat includes the idea that animals live in communion with one another in a socially balanced way, where the natural order is kept intact with the environment and with one another (*RB*, p. 296a).

25 Von Franz, 'Archetypes Surrounding Death', p. 18.

26 Ibid.

27 Ibid.

28 Stephens, 'Active Imagination and the Dead'.

29 *RB*, p. 294b.

30 This episode actually occurs in 'Nox Secunda', but these four nights' entries come under the action of 'Divine Folly'.

31 *RB*, p. 294b.

32 Ibid., p. 298a.

33 Ibid., p. 294b.

34 *RB*, p. 297b.

35 Ibid., p. 295.

36 'On the right is my thinking, on the left is my feeling' (*RB*, p. 295b).

37 *RB*, p. 265.

38 Ibid., pp. 266a–b.

39 Ibid.

40 Here Jung reflects on his lifetime thus far overburdened in a sense with his thinking function, an approach that only got him so far (*RB*, p. 295 n. 178).

41 *AP*, p. 40.

42 *RB*, p. 295b.

43 Ibid., p. 296a. This description is resonant of the 'effectual' quality Jung describes about figures of the unconscious and the dead (*RB*, p. 260b).

44 *RB*, pp. 295b–296a.

45 Ibid., p. 296a.

46 *MDR*, p. 339.

126 *Liber Secundus*

47 *RB*, pp. 297b–298a.
48 Shamdasani, 'Carl Gustav Jung and *The Red Book* (part 1)'.
49 *RB*, p. 296a. The hauntings here appear to suggest how the dead take hold and remain so in an almost obsessive way.
50 *RB*, p. 296b.
51 He then quotes Isaiah 24:66. This is significant because *Liber Primus* began with a quote from Isaiah about prophecy, and here at the commentary's end is a reference that only the body dies, not the wishes, dreams or even man's evil disappears at death and so man carries these with him into the next world.
52 *RB*, p. 296b. Jung alludes here to the conflict experienced by Christians when the dead return to the living, for example: Leviticus 19:31, Leviticus 20:27 and Isaiah 8:19. The dead are the living's business, it is up to the living to precipitate healing so that they may be able 'to die properly' or find peace in death.
53 *RB*, p. 296b. Jung's association of the mysteries to the dead once again links initiation with speaking to the dead and affecting the necessary change that the living are able to instigate. The passage also speaks to Ezechiel's question if Jung happened to know what the dead were missing in death (*RB*, p. 294b). His hope appears to be that the incarnate Jung is able to perceive something that the discarnate Ezechiel cannot. Jung offers his services to the dead for such questions and his efforts in *Septem Sermones* appear to be further effort to assist the dead in their 'salvation'.
54 *RB*, p. 297a.
55 Ibid., p. 297b. Jung suggests that this type of work, soul work and knowing one's dead, assists with understanding life.
56 Conversations with the soul often occur nearby those encounters with the dead. For example the discovery of Jung's spirit of the depths initiated his encounter with his soul. After Jung visits the site of Death, his soul appears in the episode shortly thereafter titled 'Sacrificial Murder'. And below after this section on chaos, his soul appeared (*RB*, p. 298a). The soul also dives into the collective unconscious for Jung after Elijah raises the dead boy (p. 305a).
57 *RB*, p. 298a.
58 This is a continuation of the work from January 18.
59 *RB*, p. 298b.
60 This series of sequential perspectives appeared previously when Jung gazed into the crystal to see the Crucifixion and then suddenly assumed the crucified position in the 'Mysterium Encounter'.
61 Here the passengers on the ship identify Jung's incarnate state is like a ghost, which indicates that from the unconscious he appears altered in relation to others participating on the ship at the same time. The detail of appearing as a ghost is significant and resonant of the Austrian customs official dream when a ghost also emerged within the unconscious setting (see Chapter 6 this volume).
62 *RB*, p. 298b.
63 Ibid., p. 302a.
64 Ibid., p. 294b.
65 Incubation or the ancient form of dream healing, required the ill person to sleep overnight in a Temple of Aesculapius and to discuss with a priest the next day any dreams and symbols that emerged. The symbols were thought to hold the seed of healing. Jung's mention here points to him sensing that everything that unfolded between him falling asleep in the hospital and waking up was healing in that he emerged with an understanding of the role of the dead in his life. For a thorough discussion of incubation see Carl A. Meier, *Healing Dream and Ritual* (Einsiedeln, Switzerland: Daimon Verlag, 2003).
66 When Jung emerges from the library he pulls back a green curtain to find a cast of characters in the anteroom, a theatre, and the characters all resemble Jung. The definitive point to the scene is towards the play's conclusion, when Jung emerges from the scene to 'become one with' himself. That his self has descended into the kitchen, further into the

unconscious, then back into the building where he began seems a symbolic interpretation of his active imaginations. His conscious now emerges back to life and need not remain in the madhouse (*RB*, p. 303a).

67 *RB*, pp. 294a–b.
68 Ibid., p. 304a.
69 Ibid.
70 Mary Douglas notes in her book, *Leviticus as Literature*: 'The Pentateuch did not just ignore its ancestors. It violently hated to be in communication with them ... The surrounding peoples in the Mediterranean and Aegean regions all had cults of the dead, Egypt, Assyria and Babylonia ... and Canaan. But in the Pentateuch there is no sign of it. If it had been deliberately removed before the books were edited, why?' Mary Douglas, *Leviticus as Literature* (Oxford, Oxford University Press, 1999), p. 99. The point is that in the biblical tradition there is strong opposition to contacting the dead.
71 *POU*, §342. Useful here is Liz Brodersen's discussion in *Taboo, Personal and Collective Representations, Origin and Positioning within Cultural Complexes* (London: Routledge, 2019), p. 85.

14

PHILEMON AND THE POISONER

The future in the past

22 January 1914

The scene is resonant of the same in the episode 'Death'. Jung manages to touch something deeply as he did with Death. He asks his soul to dive into the depths and bring to him whatever she finds. This can be taken literally but also signifies Jung's advanced ability to vision. By sending his soul, he is directing his intention, he is in control of his actions as well as his soul's actions within the unconscious. By commanding his soul, he is commanding his vision. Previous scenes such as with Seigfried and the Mysterium with Salome see a frightened and confused Jung unknowing, while slowly learning his power in the unconscious. Here he orders his soul and she works to his bidding. And what does Jung do? Accepts the depths and her gifts. This literal dynamic is likened to Jung's ability to now vision in the deepest unconscious himself, although he is using his soul, he now has unimpeded visual access. This is a first.

She returns with a list of items representative of a true archive of human history; mythologies, languages and former cultures.[1] The plunder draws attention to the depths she finds beyond Jung's personal unconscious. Although she does not mention the literal dead, his soul returns with the archival content residing in and as the collective unconscious. After seeing such extensive historical remnants in the abyss, Jung concludes that if you don't complete your life the dead will in fact pursue you to live it, to live your destiny: 'Everything must be fulfilled'.[2]

The knowing Jung gains here is how the dead influence the thoughts and possible directions the living can take. Is Jung describing an element of haunting if the dead beseige? It is only haunting if the awareness of the dead in relation to one's own life is not considered, otherwise decisions, compulsions and drives might just be the dead attempting to find expression via the living.

Philemon the magician

When Jung meets Philemon, he wonders as a magician if 'he conjure[s] up immortality'.[3] Here Jung sees magic as incomprehensible and this would certainly include the majority of what Jung has experienced thus far in the unconscious. Philemon points to magic that resides within everyone, precisely what Jung uncovered in the loggia dream, the presence of soul. Philemon stresses that by accessing the chaos not only is magic an inevitable by-product, but the dead must be included in this category.[4] Magic also suggests the ability to manifest anything from the chaos including both the dead and figures of the unconscious. His concluding reveal is not only that he is a lover of soul as his name indicates, but also a guide and trusted companion of the dead.[5] Jung can see spirits and shades surrounding Philemon in a bluish light and he concludes that humanity for Philemon is in fact the dead themselves. They are everywhere for Philemon waiting to hear his wise words.[6] And one blue shade in particular with a wound to his forehead caught Jung's eye, with whom Philemon spoke intently; it was Christ.

These shades appear blue in the unconscious and are similar to Jung's vision in the 'merry garden' of coloured light appearing haloed behind men, just after the Siegfried dream. Jung associates Philemon with his role as instructor to Christ as he enters death.[7] Jung wonders of his own significance if he can consort with Philemon, the teacher of Christ, and doubts his worthiness of such company. What is Jung saying about his own readiness if he were to take instruction from Christ's own teacher? After all, Christ went to Hell to minister to the dead. What exactly has Jung been doing with his dead thus far?

The poisoner

Jung engages in a lengthy exchange with the serpent from the Mysterium, at the end of which he concludes he has integrated the wisdom of the serpent from the beyond. This is likened to incorporating not just libido, but if we understand serpents to be heroic ancestors from the past then the serpent's appearance signals that Jung has learned from his encounter with Elijah and Salome, he has learned from the dead. But, he still wonders what lies ahead.[8] He asks his serpent to go into the depths and when he does he thinks he has found Hell. There he sees a man hanging.[9] Again, similar to when he sent his soul to dive into the depths, Jung is able to direct figures and events in the unconscious, a sign of a type of mastery of his abilities in these spaces.

What follows is a conversation Jung has with the hanged man who poisoned his parents and wife. He relays he committed the crime for God and although he loved his family, he wanted to facilitate their passage from a troubled life to an everlasting peace. For the murder, the man was condemned to hang to death. The most intriguing part of the exchange are details that the man describes about his condition of life in death.[10] The exchange is seminal in demonstrating Jung's curiosity and need to understand the nature of the dead and their surroundings.

130 *Liber Secundus*

He is interested in what Hell is like for the dead. As an incarnate visitor, he cannot discern the same reality that the poisoner experiences. Once again Jung recognises the dead as a discarnate soul entity, but the difference in this passage is the state or nature of their existence in what appears to be Hell.

Although the murderer has a level of awareness and even memory of his incarnate past and a sense of his present, there exists a quality of stasis. He perceives that his relationship ties have carried over, but not as strongly as in life and he appears unaffected that those connections have not continued. His status eludes him and even contemplating his existence doesn't seem to prompt in him a desire for self-reflection; he's simply unsure of who he is. Jung's curiosity urges him to share more, but it is the idea of not having a sense of self that Jung is interested in hearing more about. The poisoner shares his brief interactions with his wife and there is a distinct lack of emotive resonance in how the poisoner describes his relationships at this point. His hope that his family might be quickened to a paradise of sorts seems not to have unfolded. Rather, it appears he has experienced nothing as a result of his decisions.

When alive the poisoner had the desire to know what it was like to speak to the dead, but now this holds no interest. The lack of emotion and cognition is so extreme that when Jung suggests that perhaps the murderer is in Hell, he expresses his utter lack of concern and wonders aloud if he can leave, he is unaware even of his ability to move.[11] There is neither desire nor permission, but simply thought that leads to action. The serpent elaborates on the conditions where the poisoner has found himself; there is only 'motion . . . surg[ing] back and forth in a shadowy way. There is nothing personal whatsoever'.[12]

Jung discusses with the serpent the idea of balancing the opposites and the serpent suggests that 'the dead will soon become extinct'.[13] This particular idea is intriguing, almost as if to say when all psychological tensions on earth become reconciled there will be no reason for a storehouse of inherited wisdom to be made available because the unconscious will be ever present in consciousness.[14] When this happens, the dead will be justly honoured in the lives of the living. Up to this point the dead have served a purpose in pointing out the dynamics of the unconscious and how it can serve as a self-regulating system, yet the reconciliation of the unconscious with the conscious could very well make the purpose of the dead redundant.

Commentary

Looking back on his experiences with the dead Jung shows growth in his assessment of how the unconscious serves. By diving in headlong into his experiences, his skills grew to makes sense of what he saw. These active imaginations have strengthened Jung's abilities and shored his emotional reserves such that he was beginning to sense a resilience in the face of personal challenges. That is, his commitment to his unconscious was in fact renewing his spirit of the times. At this stage Jung concludes that his efforts to understand the unconscious began to empty it, as he says 'the immortal in me is saved' and he was 'no longer threatened by the dead'.[15]

The dead were seen and heard by the incarnate Jung, they did not integrate into his personality, rather they were satisfied and returned to their own lives in death. Jung in a sense is describing how bringing unconscious content into his day aligned his unconscious to his consciousness and not only satisfied his dead but also himself – he became right with his dead.

By facing all that the dead wanted from him, to be seen and acknowledged and in turn redeemed, he served their needs and thus that part of his unconscious is answered. His work with the dead is done, even though the dead did not disappear. By the wisdom of his soul and his dead, he received the teachings that the spirit of the depths was urging him to pursue in *Liber Primus*. Although the dead do not totally disappear, they continue to wait in line, seeing what the living, and what Jung, will do next.

Notes

1 *RB*, p. 305b.
2 Ibid., p. 308b.
3 Ibid., p. 312a. In a comedic sense Jung decides that the elder man working in his garden with his elderly wife Baucis is most likely a retired magician and now appears 'pensioned'.
4 *RB*, p. 314b. This is the same chaos in Jung's 'Nox Secunda' commentary in which he discusses how easy it is to find and hear the dead (*RB*, p. 296a).
5 Jung's comparison of Philemon to snakes might more concretely link Philemon to the dead and more specifically to a lineage of ancestry.
6 *RB*, p. 316b. RB, p.316b. This description is similar to that of the shades in Book VI of the Aeneid when Aeneas approaches the banks of the Styx (1.282–294). Note the description of chaos as a part of the underworld (1. 265).
7 In *Scrutinies*, the last scene of the work shows Philemon in his garden again speaking to Christ (*RB*, p. 359a).
8 *RB*, p. 322a.
9 Ibid.
10 Ibid., p. 322b.
11 Later, Jung discusses the poisoner's atmosphere as 'gray and impersonal' because he killed his parents and wife and did so for his own wishes. This could be the reason as to why the murderer experiences the Beyond as he does. Note that Jung does not experience the same conditions, but rather comments on what he sees.
12 *RB*, p. 322b. The detail is similar to the quality described when Jung meets Death and sees the throngs of dead meeting their dissolution (*RB*, p. 274a).
13 Ibid.
14 Jungian Jeffrey Raff recounts: 'Marie-Louise von Franz made a statement that the individuated person lives in the world of active imagination: that the ego does not identify with the outer world, nor the inner world, but with the imaginative world – which includes both of the others. The conscious ego that is united with the manifest self experiences life from a central position based in the imaginative worlds and neither identifies with outer life events nor inner archetypal states.' It would seem that attention to the dead and their influence on the living would not only balance the unconscious and conscious but a by-product of such balance would be a self centred with and in both perspectives. Raff, *Alchemical Imagination*, p. 62.
15 *RB*, p. 323a and the same sentiment, p. 230a.

PART IV
Scrutinies

15

SCRUTINIES

Introduction

19 April 1914

Scrutinies, the third and final part of *The Red Book*, begins the very day, 19 April 1914, that *Liber Secundus* ends.[1] It comprises new material added intermittently up to and including what has been known previously as Jung's monograph titled *Septem Sermones ad Mortuos*, or *Seven Sermons to the Dead* (whose start date is 29 January 1916). There is a considerable amount of material leading up to the *Sermones* that now necessitates a revision and expanded interpretation of the work.[2]

It will be a dedicated task for future scholars to reframe the *Sermones* in light of its original presentation embedded amidst new material here, including Jung's commentaries. A sensible approach might be to recast the work outside of a Gnostic context as Basilides, who was previously credited as relaying most of the material to Jung, we now know was added later to the text, during Jung's composition of the calligraphic volume.[3] Philemon, along with Jung, serves as the principal narrator. Reconsidering the *Sermones* in light of this version confirms Jung's comment in *Memories, Dreams, Reflections* that he was answering the dead and their questions and that he was moved to express information from Philemon.[4] Jung is clear of the work's authorship, even fifty years later, and in spite of its unorthodox method of transcription.

Scrutinies stands as an extension to the narrative begun in *Liber Secundus* with the actual *Sermones* composing the last part of the section as a whole. With the *Sermones* now positioned physically and chronologically towards the end of *Scrutinies* after significant preceding material, the question as to the work's overall significance must be asked.

It is an 'exotic and unconventional'[5] work both in style and content, and unlike any other Jung would write. It serves as a culmination as it marks the end of

136 *Scrutinies*

Jung's confrontation with his unconscious, but also contains hints of the seminal psychological material that Jung would explore throughout his professional life.[6] The content of both Jung's commentaries and the scenes preceding the sermons themselves suggest that Jung was attempting to discern the dead in his personal unconscious next to the collective dead and still again alongside other figures of the unconscious sharing the same psychic space. Where in *Liber Secundus* the narrative made clear Jung's opinions about the dead and their relationship to the living, in *Scrutinies* this dynamic is further elaborated. Jung discovers that the living's responsibility to the dead is not only to consider them the 'unanswered' but by doing so in the first instance is to validate them as the independent and discarnate entities that Jung experienced them to be.[7]

Previous scholars have fully discussed the content of the *Sermones* and made ample connections to Jung's psychological architecture as a result.[8] So my aim here is to consider *Scrutinies* within the context of Jung's engagement with the dead, his whole-hearted commitment along with the course this relationship was to take. Revealed here also is a glimpse into Jung's state of mind as the end of his confrontation with and updated orientation to the unconscious.

The episodes also introduce a different voice to Jung's narrative voice, here called 'I', as well as an extended conversation that I suggest is with the deceased Hélène Preiswerk.

WHY HELLY PREISWERK?

There are a few reasons why I propose that the shade who guides Jung to lead a Mass for the dead is Helly Preiswerk, his cousin and the subject of his doctoral thesis. Their exchange is an important one and reveals a few details that make her an obvious choice as the shade who Jung addresses as 'my beloved'. Although Jung was enamoured by many women and was involved with several, including his wife, the content of the exchange and his obvious affection, makes 'Helly' a most likely choice.[9] Helly died on 13 November 1911, almost four years before this dated entry.[10] Although Jung referred to Sabina Spielrein as 'my beloved', her death on 11 August 1942 in Russia at the hands of the Germans makes her still living at the time of Jung's visions here. Maria Moltzer's last dated correspondence was 1934 and Toni Wolff at this time had been a steady and stalwart guide for Jung during his confrontation. By 1916 Helly had died, and seeing that she played such a prominent role in Jung's dissertation by showing him the mediumistic dynamic, her role in assisting Jung at this stage seems the most likely choice for the identity of the shade.

'Helly' and Jung perform a ritual Mass for the community of the dead, which prepares them to receive the teachings Philemon and Jung deliver together. Where previously the *Sermones* appeared as a text loosely punctuating the end to his confrontation, now it can be interpreted as his vocation in service to the dead.[11] His work and dedication to the dead elaborated in the 'Nox Secunda' commentary can be seen in action in the preparatory Mass and the composition of the *Sermones* themselves. Not only did Jung continue his work as a psychiatrist, but equally his devoted effort to the discarnate community.

The writing of the *Sermones* served as the beginning of the end to Jung's confrontation. Jung describes in *Memories, Dreams, Reflections* how just before the haunting of his house he began to notice a change in himself.[12] According to Aniela Jaffé, the *Sermones* served to amalgamate 'the most essential ideas in his fantasies, and is therefore both a review of the phase of introversion now drawing to an end and a preview of work to come'.[13]

Jung's soul, or at least her voice, returns claiming that she was in a different world.[14] He accuses her of only desiring human blood and she agrees that nothing surpasses it. This confession attributes his soul's happiness to her ability to partake in the life of the living. By drinking human blood, she consumes the libido that connects her to the living, incarnate Jung.[15] This is the same method that the dead use to maintain contact and yet, she is not one of them.[16] Her qualifier of specifically 'red' blood suggests the heat or passion of human life that not only fuels her ability to ascend and exist in the realms where she resides, but also allows her to return to Jung. His soul proceeds to show him the bloody battlefields of fallen souls. And it is Jung's 'I' who groans under the duress and responsibility of needing to carry them himself.[17]

This scene reveals the possible residual psychic pressure of World War I coming to an end. The immense loss of life and sheer numbers look to have weighed on Jung's 'I' and his encounter reveals a need to pull the dead up to the light. Jung resists and quotes Luke 9:60 to his 'I': 'let the dead bury their dead'.

Jung displays a confidence about the dead that has evolved due to his intense encounters in *Liber Secundus*. He addresses an 'I' who is assuming the role of psychopomp and who feels responsible for guiding the dead to the light, and feels equally the weight of that responsibility in the literal 'hauling them' himself. When Jung addresses the souls' fates, it is unclear if he means that everyone meets their fate at the moment of death, or that the dead have a fate in death, their new life as discarnates, their life in death, which is fated. This is not clear.

Although Shamdasani considers the 'I' to be Jung's shadow, the tone of Jung's gloomy 'I' could equally be considered the spirit of the time, who most likely holds no notion as to how to serve the dead nor any desire to do so. As Jung is now familiar with the perspective of the spirit of the depths, he is able to encounter the inherent cycle of life in death. When he quotes Luke 9:60, his project with the dead is not to confirm their physical demise with burials, but rather to confirm a continuation of life in death. Jung as incarnate narrator appears more assured if not philosophical about his work as he moves into *Scrutinies*.

His soul intercedes and demands 'compassion', for his 'I', which she claims binds life and death. Implied is that compassion or the desire to understand the plight of the dead and their yearning for an alliance with the living, links the

138 *Scrutinies*

living and their ability to comprehend them. Equally, compassion is what has really assisted Jung with his visioning of the dead, considering that compassion is needed to understand not only the process of active imagination, but also the personal material that has emerged as a result. It is self-compassion for his efforts that has permitted him to understand the dead.

Again, the blood, which the soul requests, is the physical libido representing this compassion. Jung, his soul and the 'I' are all addressing the condition in which the dead inevitably find themselves and each perspective here is slightly different. Yet, they each have an articulated opinion as to their role with the dead.

The deceased 'Helly'

On 2 December 1915, Jung recounts that in his active imagination three deceased shades approached.[18] One of them made a whirring sound like 'the wings of the sun beetle . . . I recognized her. When . . . still alive, she recovered the mysteries of the Egyptians for me, the red sun disk'.[19]

Jung associates this shade with someone, when alive, who taught him the Egyptian mysteries, i.e. the idea of survival in the afterlife, and considering Helly's mediumship abilities, this makes a likely connection. The description of the red sun disk and the whirring of the sun beetle also recall the images in Jung's first active imagination that signified rebirth.[20] Jung addresses the Egyptian symbols in his 1925 seminar referring to his first active imagination where he credits his 'beloved' with showing him the mystery of after-death survival.[21] If we consider the shade to be Helly, then with her return as a shade shows her re-enacting the Egyptian mysteries.

As the conversation continues she cries for Jung to find a symbol one they can follow.[22] As a result a rod is placed in Jung's hand and he interprets it as a phallus, Helly calls it HAP. A surprise is Helly's satisfaction at the phallus being a symbol of procreation and, in this instance, of rebirth.[23] Later in the exchange, she equates HAP with a sunken church in which the living and the dead form a community.[24] With HAP being an operative symbol for the deceased's needs, the exchange continues.

Helly associates thinking with Jung's physical body. She discerns that 'thought' affects Jung's appearance and her perception of him in the unconscious. It is not simply that the body holds a type of knowledge, rather, the incarnate Jung, while in the land of the dead, holds a perspective, which yields knowledge accessible to the discarnate Helly. Helly encourages Jung to drink blood and other fluids from a carcass (resonant of the 'Sacrificial Murder' episode). Previously, the dead were seeking the blood of the living Jung. Here, the dead Helly suggests that the living Jung partake in the same. The gesture appears to drain life from death and looks to be a metaphor for Jung's journey thus far in *The Red Book*.[25]

Jung is repulsed by the suggestion, even if it means that the living and dead remain close. Her purpose is to give Jung the knowledge he needs.[26] That the dead need 'the life juices of men' recalls the Nekyia episode of the Odyssey and the blood required to form the connection necessary to speak with the dead in the first instance. Although

Helly suggests there is learning to be had by Jung in the land of the dead, he is horrified. The intimate connection they shared reflects back to a time when she taught Jung unknowingly about the 'mystery' through her unimpeded access to the unconscious through her mediumship. This is the mystery, Helly's legacy, which is her ability to speak to the dead, just as Jung is doing now.

THE DEAD'S LEGACY

In *Memories, Dreams, Reflections*, Jung recounts a vision of his neighbour, whose funeral Jung had attended the previous day. As he lay awake thinking about him he describes seeing him at the end of his bed beckoning him to come to his own house. Jung followed him to his study where his friend stood on a stool and showed him a book. The next day he went to the house to see if the book was in fact there: there was the stool and the books with red binding, the books of Emile Zola, one of which was titled *The Legacy of the Dead*.[27] Jungians Marlan and Miller found, in fact, no book by Zola with that title. They called this episode a 'fiction' but one that must have had a lasting effect on Jung.[28] The point of Jung's story, in a sense, proved itself. The idea of legacy, as with his neighbour, is associated here with both the deceased themselves and their ability to communicate to the living. This account shows a visitation dream with veridical details confirmed by Jung the next day; a dream whose psychic terrain was accessible and confirmed by the apparition of his deceased neighbour. That there was no book by Zola by that description or title need not be the detail of significance here, neither would this need to be proved in order to make the dream either meaningful or true for Jung. Rather, the significance might be served by the stool, which Jung found in the very position as it appeared in the dream.

There appears a sense with Helly's emotional pleas for Jung's participation that she is appealing to him as an incarnate, that she is asking Jung to atone for the scientific position of his dissertation, which presented communication with the dead as intrapsychic.[29] Perhaps Jung is now reconsidering that position. And who better than his research subject to return as a discarnate, and by virtue of their discussion, prove his findings incorrect?

Helly's life as a discarnate

Helly proceeds to describe the nature of her life as one of the deceased. When Jung calls to her to teach him about spirits her response is similar to his soul, to grant her blood so she has access.[30] Once again she confirms that blood contains the libido necessary to initiate and maintain the connection between the living and dead. Jung suggests that she take it from his heart. She begins to describe the sensations of being one of the dead as being like birds flying over the ocean and feeling the

140 *Scrutinies*

pull to earthly sensations and animal nature that spirits yearn for. For Helly the pull is Jung's incarnate self that she wishes to 'cling to earth'.

Helly expresses such dedication to the living Jung that she literally wishes to be reincarnated as one of his dogs. Helly feels Jung holds such deep value not simply as an incarnate, due to their emotional relationship while she was alive, but also because of their dedicated interest in her mediumship abilities. From this exchange perhaps it can be assumed that Jung's feelings went deeper than previously thought.[31] That dogs serve as dedicated companions to the living is revealing and shows the deep urge for Helly to incarnate even in animal form if only to serve him and his interests as an incarnate. This reveals her condition, which is representative of other deceased who are 'still near and incomplete' (similar to how Toni Wolff felt closer to earth than Emma). Helly yearns for what she left incomplete confirming again the perception that the deceased feel that their lives and deaths have left unanswered questions that must be addressed to and by the living.[32]

Helly does something ritualistic when she whispers the word 'Brimo', indicating she is an integral part of Jung's initiation into the depths. Not since Jung's encounter with his deceased father has he interacted with someone so closely related. The gesture is similar to the priestess officiating at Eleusis who announces the birth of a son from the goddess of the dead.[33] The utterance of 'Brimo' signals a birth in death and marks the initiates' ability to see and hear the goddess. Jung sees and hears his 'deceased beloved' yet responds frustrated and overwhelmed that perhaps his initiation was not completed with Elijah and Salome but continues still. He feels the pressure of such intense exposure and exchange with the dead and perceives a further expectation from Helly, which he feels obligated to fulfil. Jung expresses his problem with the encounter, which is basically 'Should I live with shadows instead of with the living?'[34] And he bemoans her desire still to seek from him, the living, had she not used her time wisely when alive? The pressure and obligation Jung feels builds and he begins to perceive the real costs of the demands of the unconscious in all of its forms.

The focus on the eternal is essential to understanding this dynamic with Helly. Jung speaks to a seminal quality important for the 'success' of the dead as discarnates, to identify the immortal value while still alive. He blames those incarnates who made no notice of the dead and lived their lives wholly unaware of the immortal part of themselves. In a similar manner as with the tramp, as well as with the dead on their way to Jerusalem who forgot to live something, they did not contemplate life to include a consideration of death. By ignoring this, the dead pass over unprepared and some, like the tramp, even unaware of their status of being dead. Jung's frustration lies with them now demanding of him further work because they haven't done theirs.

Helly identifies the real Jung, his soul, and what the living see as his shadow. Her point is that the living only experience a part of Jung, and take advantage of him, not seeing how important he is to the community of the dead.[35] Yet, he does not want to die in order to grasp the discarnate perspective. Therefore, Helly is

Scrutinies **141**

able to perceive the 'mark' that the living wear once they have consorted with the dead.[36] Even in the unconscious realm, Jung exhibits his sincere dedication. Helly's caveat is, 'Do not commingle with any of the dead'.[37]

These are extraordinary instructions with considered knowledge of the community in which she inhabits. While alive, Helly was in service to the deceased and now is assuming the same role in the beyond as their spokesperson. Yet, what is the difference between the community she refers to above and the commingling that she addresses here? Is a unified community of the living conscious of the dead healing for both parties while commingling might potentially be detrimental to both?[38] Where community points to a shared enterprise of perspectives both living and discarnate, might commingling imply a lack of benefits from such a perspective? Commingling might suggest seeking one another out for no particular purpose, but it also might suggest an extended connection with unintended consequences. Thus, von Franz's comment is apt that asserts the dead are so different to the living that it is a challenge to coexist for any length of time.

Mass for the dead

Just as Mass is conducted in the name of Christ as representative of eternal life, in some oddly parallel way, this Mass is conducted in Jung's name for the community of deceased. This Mass for the dead by the dead prepares them to receive the teachings of the *Sermones*. Helly invokes the blood necessary for the connection to be made and maintained.[39] The Mass is similar with ritual imagery and symbolism pointing to a holy order of rites for the dead.

Helly speaks to the dead *as if* she is Jung and therefore conducts the Mass on his behalf. She is assuming the same role as she did when alive, as medium passing on information between the dead and the living. Here she establishes the connection through the incarnate Jung, and the information passes from the living Jung through the deceased Helly to the dead. This is the same dynamic that occurs with Philemon and Jung when they deliver the sermons.[40]

One way to consider the dynamic is that Jung is channelling the deceased Helly, who in turn is speaking to the collective dead. The difficulty is that when Helly addresses the dead, she is speaking as if she is Jung and it is not clear if she in fact is channelling Jung. Religion Scholar W. Hanegraaf states:

> The term channelling refers to the conviction of psychic mediums that they are able, under certain circumstances, to act as a channel for information from sources other than their normal selves. Most typically, these sources are identified as discarnate 'entities' living on higher levels of being, but the complete range of channelled sources mentioned in the literature contains almost everything to which some kind of intelligence might be attributed [and] . . . communication with spirits of the recently departed – as in classical spiritualism – is not characteristic of New Age channelling.[41]

142 *Scrutinies*

Thus this type of communication, that will appear again when Philemon delivers the sermons, in a similar role to that of Helly, appears unique to Jung in that typical channelling involves information derived *from* discarnates delivered *to* incarnates. In this instance, both the Mass and the *Sermones* are for the benefit of the dead. Just as the Catholic liturgy signals the body and blood of Christ, here the dead need the body and blood of the incarnate Jung for the completion of the ritual for the eventual understanding of the *Sermones*. The purpose is to raise the dead so that they will gain 'speech and life' through Jung.

It is unclear if it is Jung or Helly who instigates the Mass, but it appears to be an effort toward building a collective communion between them both. The purpose of the Mass is to resurrect the dead and to reach a common goal by which living and dead might coexist with full awareness of one another.[42] Is this the same as Jung living with the unconscious, by using the dead as metaphor? I would say no, this type of coexistence is different, this is more than acknowledging unconscious influences, this is about recognising who the dead are, their interest in Jung's life at this particular time and how the dead look to Jung to carry on the psychospiritual lineage of their concerns.

This scene parallels the Catholic Mass narrative in which the body and blood of Christ serve as the symbols for rebirth and immortality. The Mass is an opportunity to remember the life and sacrifice of Christ as he himself conducted the ritual at the Last Supper.[43] Through the format of the Mass, the deceased Helly and incarnate Jung assist the collective dead in remembering their condition as incarnates so that they might better orient and embrace their lives as discarnates.[44] The invocation begins with Helly invoking the dead in Jung's name.

She knows what the living need to say to the dead and what the dead need to hear from them. Who better to serve as a medium than one who acted in the same role while alive? The blood here is a reminder of the corporeal reality that the deceased once knew. Helly describes a beneficence that results if the living and dead become mutually aware of one another's intentions. If the living understand the possible influence the dead have on their desires, this could yield an ease in making manifest their desires. This important affirmation shows the degree of dedication Jung and Helly felt for the dead. Jung acknowledges the possible derivation of his desires to be the result of the dead's influence on him and considers the sacrificial fire to be his driving passion.

The Mass makes clear that the intentions of the dead are different in nature to that of figures of Jung's personal unconscious. Their desires are made manifest by the acts of the living as well as the livings' acknowledgement. Figures of the unconscious, although equally autonomous, have as their derivation the personal unconscious into which they will eventually integrate.

Helly's explanation of the prayer stresses that the dead are unsettled because men have forgotten them. Even deceased, the dead maintain that their human nature inherently explains their need for redemption from the living. Salvation comes in the form of their recognition. Their still present human nature facilitates their orientation to the living even in their discarnate state. Humanity suggests

Scrutinies **143**

that knowledge is a cyclical affair, requiring it to cycle through the dead and living in order to advance further understanding on the part of both. This is resonant of Jung's ideas, discussed previously,[45] that although the dead have access to an unlimited amount of knowledge by way of the unconscious, knowledge needs an incarnate perspective to be applicable.

Helly finds it laughable, as does Jung, that by forgetting the dead the living can continue their lives. The result of such an approach is a more agitated community of the dead. They still need recognition and as Jung raged in *Liber Secundus*, just because reason has erased the dead does not mean they have disappeared. In fact, due to this seeming neglect, the dead are in 'a frenzy', which accounts for their collective appearance for the *Sermones*.

Philemon and Jung's soul

In Jung's commentary added after the Mass, Philemon, who appeared in 'The Magician' in *Liber Secundus*, now returns.[46] Jung describes, 'he came alongside me invisibly, and I felt the presence of the good and the beautiful'.[47] Jung has become sensitive enough to perceive what is not visible even in the realm of the unconscious, a skill that he has acquired as a result of his journey through the regions.[48] To perceive the invisible within the unconscious might prove to be the culmination of Jung's visionary discernment, and indicates a depth of skill and insight within the unconscious.

Philemon asks as to why exactly have the dead not moved on? And he determines because they still are 'craving . . . power'. It would seem that this desire for power is not simply wanting more, but rather not having found an exact expression of the power they had when alive.[49]

Philemon observes the dead yearning for what the living Jung might take for granted, that is the life force that the incarnate condition maintains. The essence of this desire for power is more specifically about empowerment, and the feeling that the dead seem to exhibit of not feeling seen and heard and therefore legitimised in their new state. Their *unlived* power in life translates as disempowered in death, and could be partially responsible for not having 'crossed over to the other side', not having come to their proper end. That Philemon is able to perceive this quality in the dead in the same psychic space proves his status as teacher and friend of the dead, and also shows his depth of purpose with them.

Notes

1 *RB*, p. 226a. Shamdasani justifies this as the reason to include it in *The Red Book*.
2 The most important detail being that the dead who return to haunt Jung before the writing of the *Sermones* actually left for Jerusalem two years previously in the episode 'Nox Secunda'.
3 *RB*, p. 206. Shamdasani confirms that Basilides' authorship was added after Jung's completion of the *Sermones* in the *Black Books* and only then when it was transcribed into calligraphic form. This inclusion would appear as an intentional distancing from the work

144 *Scrutinies*

on Jung's part. Stephan Hoeller calls this move 'a trickster-like scholarly fiction' as Jung gave out several copies with the subtitle 'written by Basilides'. It would have appeared that Jung's part in the production was simply a translation into the German of Basilides' work. For a full discussion of the Gnostic connections to the *Sermones* see Shamdasani's footnote with full bibliography (*RB*, p. 346 n. 81) and Stephan Hoeller's thirteen taped lectures covering the entirety of *The Red Book*, confirming his steadfast Gnostic perspective. Stephan Hoeller, *Exploring C.G. Jung's Red Book*, BC Recordings, part 10, http://bcrecordings.net/store/index.php?main_page=index&cPath=6 (accessed 18 February 2010).

4 *MDR*, pp. 339 and p. 215 respectively. Deirdre Bair includes an extended version of this passage, but not cited: '[Philemon] formulated this thing that was not me and expressed everything that I had not thought . . . Until the *Septem Sermones*, it was only said by him. Then it was demanded of me that I say it myself . . . The *Septem Sermones*, that was when Philemon simply lost his absolute autonomy and I had to say it myself.' Bair quotes Jung's opinion about the *Sermones* (probably from the Protocols) that the *Sermones* emerged from 'raw material that flows forth, but that just does not contain the entire person. One must not overestimate the unconscious' and then, 'I always said: there is this talk, but it isn't I who is talking. I only hear it, and I perceive it as regrettably poor. I was simply swept up by this stream and felt as if I were in it. But throughout that process I always preserved my critical view. I gnashed my teeth, so to speak, because I didn't agree with it at all.' Bair, *Jung*, pp. 291–292, 295.

5 James Heisig, 'The VII Sermons: Play and Theory', *Spring* (1972): 207.

6 Heisig's article is a fine examination of the psychological concepts to be found in the *Sermones* and those that Jung was to elaborate. Although written almost forty-six years ago, I suggest this to be the clearest and most concise analysis of the *Sermones* to be found in English.

7 *MDR*, p. 217.

8 Robert Segal and Stephan Hoeller. Shamdasani's thorough footnote covering the Gnostic treatment of the work serves, in fact, as a comprehensive bibliography of the treatment of the *Sermones*. Now that Basilides is not in the forefront of the sermons' composition history, the Gnostic theme does not need to remain the only method by which to read the *Sermones* and I suggest an alternative reading below that adjusts the work to an updated understanding of the dead who were to receive the teachings.

9 Sabina Spielrein, Maria Moltzer and Toni Wolff are just three of the women with whom Jung was thought to be emotionally involved. In a letter to Freud, Jung said about Maria Moltzer and Martha Boddinghaus: 'Between the two ladies there is naturally a loving jealousy over me.' John Kerr, *A Most Dangerous Method* (New York: Alfred A. Knopf, 1993), p. 299. Hillman credits a possible love relationship with Hélène to 'transference, participation mystique, or love' suggesting that it was 'only to be expected'. Hillman, 'Some Early Background', p. 132. Bair says about Helly that she 'probably had a school girl crush on Carl'. Bair, *Jung*, p. 48. See also Bair's description of Jung's womanising and its effect claiming: 'the marriage . . . had veered precipitously toward divorce . . . as the gossip about Carl's possible infidelity coupled with [Emmas'] life in the Burghölzli fishbowl had finally become too much' (pp. 108–113). Catrine Clay discusses the climate of Jung's lectures at the medical school during this time: '[I]t was not only Jung's students who were spellbound; the lectures were open to the public and soon he had a large following of wealthy Zurich women who had too much leisure on their hands. Here they found an outlet for their underused intellects and often for their underused emotions too, what with talk of erotic complexes repression, and this new world of the unconscious . . . Carl's lectures were soon the best act in town and the medical students complained that they often could not find a seat in the lecture theatre, so popular were they with the so-called *Pelzmäntel* – fur-coat – brigade.' Catrine Clay, *Labyrinths: Emma Jung Her Marriage to Carl and the Early Years of Psychoanalysis* (London: William Collins, 2017), p. 98.

10 Bair, *Jung*, p. 80.

11 Aniela Jaffé, 'Phases in Jung's Life', *Spring* (1972): 177.

Scrutinies **145**

12 *MDR*, p. 215.

13 Jaffé, 'Phases in Jung's Life', p. 178.

14 Shamdasani explains Jung's soul followed the new born God (Izdubar). What is confusing is that there is no indication in *Liber Secundus* that this is the case, apart from Shamdasani's detail (*RB*, p. 226a). Here, she explains where she has been. Added to the confusion, after the birth of the new God, she appears in the episodes: 'The Way of the Cross' and 'The Gift of Magic'. She dives into the depths to bring forth knowledge of humanity's history and gives Jung the magic rod (p. 335a).

15 In fact Jung suggests that the soul is the representative of the self in the realm of the spirit of the depths, a discussion he has after the birth of the new God. Jung is working towards a definition of the self, but experiencing the various realms of the unconscious and drawing conclusions as a result. Here the soul is on the move and experiences events apart from Jung's conscious awareness of them, including disappearing with the new born God.

16 *RB*, p. 335a. Note previous references to blood as libido appear in the following episodes: the deceased tramp in 'One of the Lowly', 'Sacrificial Murder' in addition to the deceased shade in this chapter. Jung also invites his soul/Helly to drink directly from his heart (*RB*, p. 340).

17 *RB*, p. 340b.

18 Ibid., p. 339.

19 Ibid., pp. 339a–b. The whirring sound is the same that the dead make in the cook's kitchen (*RB*, p. 294a). This particular description recalls similarities in Jung's work on the Miss Miller fantasies (*Psychology of the Unconscious* and *Symbols of Transformation*), in particular the 'Song of the Moth' in which Jung explains: 'Under the symbols of the "moth and sun" we have dug down into the historic depths of the soul, and in doing this we have uncovered an old buried idol, the youthful, beautiful, fire-encircled and halo-crowned sun-hero' (*POU*, p. 102, § 187, in *SOT*, *CW*, vol. 5, p. 109, § 164). It is important to remember that Jung never met Frank Miller (in addition to there being no record of when she died) so this discounts the possibility that she is the deceased shade.

20 *RB*, p. 237b. In Jung's first active imagination, the scarab appears, here it is called the sun beetle (p. 237b). The newborn sun also appears during Jung's exploration of 'Death' (pp. 273b–274a).

21 *MDR*, p. 204; *AP*, p. 48.

22 *RB*, 339b.

23 Shamdasani helps elucidate the association of the word HAP and its possible importance. Jung had a copy of a book titled *The Egyptian Heaven and Hell* by W. Budge in which Jung marked a particular passage that discussed how the four children of Horus had significant roles in protecting the deceased while in the underworld. Jung had underlined this detail. This suggests that the deceased had underworld protection, as if guarding the soul after death was important enough that it warranted the services of Egyptian deities. Perhaps this suggests that Jung himself is being watched over in the underworld and perhaps by the deceased Helly. Perhaps Jung is associating HAP with protection in the underworld. Helly could be the one seeking protection or offering it to the incarnate Jung. Or perhaps, she seeks the symbol HAP as necessary protection for them both.

24 *RB*, p. 342a. The mention of the phallus recalls Jung's first memory of a childhood dream, in which he discovers an underground chamber with a throne on which sits a phallus (*MDR*, pp. 26–27).

25 In *Liber Secundus*, Jung discusses the effects of dedicating such intense time to the dead (*RB*, p. 323a).

26 *RB*, p. 339b.

27 *MDR*, p. 344.

28 Stanton Marlan and David Miller, 'What Is the Legacy of the Dead? Jung's Memories and the Case of Zola's Missing Book' *Spring* 77 (2007): 277–282.

29 Under Jung's discussion on *heightened unconscious performance* he concludes: 'The image enters consciousness without the mediation of the senses, intrapsychically' (*CW*, vol. 1, §139).

146 *Scrutinies*

He asserts that his study of Helly found her abilities to be 'something quite out of the ordinary', and in an additional concluding paragraph added later to the thesis, he explains what he set out to do in the study was to 'counter general opinion, which dismisses so called occult phenomena with a contemptuous smile, by demonstrating the manifold connection between these phenomena and the subjects covered by medicine and psychology' (§149 and n. 135). Jung's dissertation was an attempt to pursue serious scientific research on what he speculated in the *Zofingia* lectures regarding after-death survival.

30 *RB*, p. 340a.
31 We do not know the last time Jung and his cousin saw one another. We know he met up with her in Paris and took her and her sister out several times. At this stage Jung had plans to return to Zurich and shortly after to marry Emma. We also know that Helly returned to Switzerland, opened her own tailor shop and worked until her death at the age of 30. See Bair, *Jung*, pp. 52, 69, 80. Significant too is Helly's dress made for Emma, which was his favourite and in which Emma appeared in one of Jung's most profound visions of her (*MDR*, p. 327).
32 This sentiment is expressed by the hordes of the dead heading to Jerusalem who forgot to live a part of their lives (*RB*, p. 294b).
33 Kerenyi, *Eleusis*, pp. 92–93.
34 *RB*, p. 340b.
35 Ibid. The thought, 'Since I belong to you' addresses Helly as a member of the community of the dead and does not indicate the same meaning, as it did with Salome, that she might be a projection of Jung's personal unconscious.
36 *RB*, p. 299 n. 198.
37 Ibid., p. 342a.
38 Von Franz, 'Archetypes', p. 18.
39 *RB*, p. 342a. Again, during the Mass: 'Take eat, this is my body, that lives for you. Take eat, drink this is my blood, whose desire flows for you. Come celebrate a Last Supper with me for your redemption and mine.'
40 *RB*, p. 346b.
41 Wouter Hanegraff, *New Age Religion and Western Culture: Esotericism in the Mirror of Secular Thought* (New York: State University of New York Press, 1998), pp. 23 and 24 respectively.
42 Note again, this would not be possible if the dead were projections of Jung's personal unconscious, these dead are interested in working with Jung, not being integrated into his personality. Although the successful dynamic of active imagination and the transcendent function appears here, the end result does not.
43 Adrian Fortescue, 'Liturgy of the Mass', *The Catholic Encyclopedia*, Vol. 9 (New York: Robert Appleton, 1910), www.newadvent.org/cathen/09790b.htm (accessed 16 July 2011).
44 It must be remembered that this Mass parallels the Catholic liturgy not the Catholic Mass for the dead, which assists souls in their quest for everlasting peace. These dead are not at peace and only through the teachings of the *Sermones* that point out to them their discarnate nature will they find that peace and move on to their life of the dead.
45 See Chapter 6 this volume, subsection 'What the dead know'.
46 *RB*, p. 342b.
47 Ibid.
48 Jung was also able to perceive 'tangled invisible beings' in *Liber Primus* (*RB*, p. 240b).
49 *RB*, p. 342b. This description recalls Jung's conversation with Ezechiel before his departure to Jerusalem (*RB*, p. 294b). Philemon's discussion of the dead is similarly continued in the commentary after the first sermon.

16
THE *SEPTEM SERMONES*

Introduction

As the *Sermones* is greatly enhanced in *The Red Book* version, it is necessary to reconsider them in terms of what we now know about the dead. The dead are seeking knowledge because neither their trip to Jerusalem nor the unconscious where they now find themselves can reveal what they need to know in terms of how to live as discarnate souls. As souls without bodies, they do not understand themselves in their new surroundings and they turn to both Jung for his incarnate perspective and Philemon for his discarnate one. Philemon, now somewhat of an amalgamation of Jung's No. 2 personality, the spirit of the depths, and Elijah, understands the nature of the unconscious as one of its members and is primed to share with the dead what he knows. They have been prepared for such learning by the Mass in which Jung offered them his body and blood through Helly. The ritual brought a sacrosanct quality to work and prepared the dead to *hear* Philemon.

Jung feels called to answer the questions that are most prevalent to the dead in their state as discarnates. Therefore the *Sermones* become an opportunity for Jung to experience how the dead experience themselves in their reality. They reveal themselves and the unconscious as lacking enough oppositional tension for either significant self-reflection or for change to occur; they are souls in a sea of the unconscious with little to no reference point for self-definition and it is through their insistence that Philemon explains to them their condition. Although it would appear that Jung's incarnate state assists in qualifying the teachings for the dead in some way, it is Philemon who after each of the *Sermones* bends down to touch the ground as if to literally ground the knowledge on their behalf.

The *Sermones* therefore serve as an instrument to calibrate the unconscious perspective for the dead.[1] Jung's role is not simply as scribe and witness but is active and at times critical of both Philemon's content and methods. His incarnate

148 *Scrutinies*

vantage permits the dead to gauge themselves and, by contrast, assists them in pursuing their lives as discarnates. [2]

A brief summary of the *Sermones* shows the dead initiating the request to be taught:[3]

Sermon 1: 'You have what we desire.'[4]

Sermon 2: 'We want to know about God. Where is God? Is God dead?'[5]

Sermon 3: 'Tell us more about the highest God.'[6]

Sermon 4: 'Speak to us about Gods and devils.'[7]

Sermon 5: 'Teach us . . . about the church and Holy Communion.'[8]

Sermon 6: Philemon addresses spirituality and sexuality.[9]

Sermon 7: 'We forgot to mention one thing, that we would like you to teach us about men.'[10]

The course of the *Sermones* begins with the dead inquiring about God and ends with their inquiry about man, suggesting that the dead are suffering from an overwhelming lack of orientation. Since they start with God, this indicates that they are looking to orient themselves first amidst the vast unconscious landscape where they now find themselves. As they end their search with a question about man, they are looking not just to remember their lives, but to understand incarnate life from their current vantage as discarnates. In a sense they are looking to understand their lives so that they might understand their deaths. This is not dissimilar to Jung's question about the tramp who might be experiencing death because he had not considered it during his life.[11]

THE BIRTH OF CONSCIOUSNESS

Erich Neumann in his work *The Origins and History of Consciousness* discusses the development of consciousness or as he explains:

> Mythological accounts of the beginning must invariably begin with the outside world, for world and psyche are still one. There is as yet no reflecting, self-conscious ego that could refer anything to itself, that is, reflect. Not only is the psyche open to the world, it is still identical with and undifferentiated from the world.

In this respect, it would appear that discarnates, not fully passed over into death, have found themselves with these same challenges. Further: 'Only in the light of consciousness can man know. And this act of cognition, of conscious discrimination, sunders the world into opposites, for experience of the world is only possible through opposites.'[12]

After the first sermon, Philemon explains that the dead whom he teaches are those who perished in the war and now 'still hover over their graves'.[13] They simply didn't know themselves beyond their understanding of belief in their faith. Philemon instructs them to understand their lives in order to find a peaceful death.[14] Thus, Philemon's project is to explain a type of psychocosmology to discarnates who are not fully transitioned, so that they may understand how their faith failed them in both life and death. The seminal point is that they recognise what they knew about being discarnate while alive. It appears that knowledge about post-mortem conditions could possibly assist one with one's discarnate state so that unlike the Austrian customs official and the tramp, they might die properly.

RUDOLF STEINER ON GUIDING THE DEAD

Rudolf Steiner shares some similarities with Jung on the post-mortem state:

> One who has a connection with a departed soul can remind that soul of what it knew of the spiritual world while on the earth. This is possible by reading to the dead . . . thus instructing that soul, so to speak . . . This enables us to bridge the abyss that separates us from the dead.

He goes on to say, 'What we are touching upon here is the fact that the spiritual thoughts nurtured by souls here on earth can not only be perceived but be understood by the souls beyond', suggesting, as evidenced from Jung's interactions with the dead including their instruction, that it is the knowledge during life about after death survival, which appears to be the currency that assists the dead in increasing their consciousness as discarnates.[15] In a parallel manner: 'It is often emphasised that the purpose of reading the Bardo Thotrol to a dead person is to remind him of what he has practised during his life. This "Book of the Dead" can show us how to live.'[16]

In the last sermon, Philemon provides the dead with a vision of man by attributing him to a gateway through which one moves from the outer world of Gods to the inner one of man. This description captures the idea of going from boundlessness to inhabiting a physical body. Towards the end of the *Sermones*, Philemon attempts to remind the dead of the process of entering the 'gateway' of a human body. Where the dead find themselves now is the vastness, because they have left behind their lives as men, and inhabit an 'inner infinity'.

150 *Scrutinies*

The goal of the *Sermones*

What makes the *Sermones* such a singularly odd text, is not simply its Gnostic language, but the perspective from which it is written; it is Philemon who explains the conditions of life and death to the dead from their point of view, as souls without bodies. This is, in part, why the teachings themselves need to come from Philemon, because it is he who not only shares their unconscious terrain, but understands it well enough to articulate it in a manner that they can grasp.

The goal of the *Sermones* according to Charet is as follows:

> [Jung] taught them about the nature of reality, the supreme god, gods and devils, the church, spirituality and sexuality, and lastly about human beings. But, in a sense, the entire message was about human beings, their world, their dreams, and their destinies.[17]

Although the teachings can be read as being about man, I would say the message really is about the dead themselves; *their* supreme god, *their* gods and devils, *their* church and in particular *their* new community as discarnates. As they grow to perceive all of this and how it differs from that which they experienced in their incarnate lives, they not only are able to cross over fully into a state of death, but will also grasp how to live with themselves now.

The overall goal of the *Sermones* is really the process of individuation and while the first sermon explicitly outlines this idea, the other sermons support how individuation is operationalised.[18] The most important point is that individuation 'does not involve striving after static and abstract ideals forged consciously, in isolation from the unconscious but means remaining true to one's libidinal base'.[19] The libidinal base is not just understanding who one is exactly, but knowing it.

Thus, each sermon is an attempt to explore individuation in terms of each realm of experience; the experience of God as a singular and vast entity, then as it applies to the experiences of plural gods, the community and finally to men. This process reveals how man lives in and with his world of experience.

But the real question is how does this entire idea of individuation apply to discarnates? Heisig further suggests: that 'the text goes a step further in defining the individuation process whereby one originates as an individual by distinguishing the power of one's ego consciousness from the powers that transcend it, i.e., gods and demons'.[20] This requires looking again at the transcendent function and how it applies to the dead.[21] If the purpose of the transcendent function is to increase consciousness by integrating unconscious material, then what does this process look like for the dead, who might just be the ones contributing that unconscious content? In other words, if the result of active imagination, or more specifically interpsychic rapport, is an increase in consciousness, then what is the immediate effect on the dead during the same exchange? Do conversations Jung has with the dead raise the consciousness of the dead? He suggests as much.[22] So what would raising the consciousness of the dead look like? The answer seems to point to

The *Septem Sermones* **151**

using memory in order to incite examination of one's life and grow an awareness of death while alive.[23] That is, arriving in a discarnate state seems to be assisted by having had an awareness, or an idea or even an expectation as to what the discarnate state would be like. In Steiner's perspective it is having a notion of spiritual ideas fostered during one's lifetime; 'spiritual thoughts nurtured by souls here on earth can not only be perceived but be understood by the souls beyond'.[24]

In *Memories, Dreams, Reflections,* Jung discusses a dream from one of his students in which she arrives in the hereafter to find that she must give a lecture about her life, and the dead were eager to hear of her acts and decisions. Jung notes the possibility that the dead yearn to understand what takes place in incarnate life.[25]

As the incarnate perspective integrates the unconscious to become more aware, then this new awareness must in turn affect the level or capacity of the dead themselves. What assists them is very specific. It is not any incarnate perspective that can assist the dead with their own individuation, but an incarnate state fully aware of the dead and their influence.[26] This is evident in Jung's dream of his father when he returns to ask Jung about marriage. The important point to mention here is that Jung treats his father like a discarnate who returns looking for information that will assist him in his continued life as a discarnate. This encounter and, in particular, the manner in which Jung discusses it, is obviously not a case of Jung encountering a projection of his psyche in the form of his father, because he is equally intent on providing his father with what he will need to meet his mother when she arrives in the hereafter. Could this encounter be interpreted as being about Jung and his own marriage? Perhaps, but Jung himself links the dream to prescience about his mother's death.[27]

This is why both Jung and Philemon together are present for the teachings of the *Sermones*. It is their mutual awareness and their common goal, which makes the *Sermones* effective. If Philemon were to have been the sole voice for the dead, there would not be enough oppositional tension for the teachings to be applicable. As Jung is witness, scribe and participant, his presence allows the incarnate perspective to acknowledge or mirror the teachings, and in turn, allows for enough contrast in perception to facilitate learning on the part of the dead. This triangulation is similar to what occurred with Jung, Elijah and Salome during her cure. Elijah, as representative of the dead and the realm of the depths, has been with Salome forever and has been unable to cure her or even never considered to do so. It is Jung's incarnate presence that facilitates the shift of libido that restores Salome's sight. With the *Sermones,* Jung's incarnate presence permits the delivery of the teachings, because in part, he is fully aware of the dead.

Posing the question about how the transcendent function works for the dead points to why the *Sermones* occur in the first place. The *Sermones* offer Jung an opportunity to explain to discarnates their surroundings, and offer the dead an opportunity to learn how to become more conscious. The process affords each a closer examination of the other's condition. Only when the last question is answered, after the dead hear about man, are they satisfied and their condition or 'heaviness fell . . . and they ascended'.[28] In confirmation of the teachings, they

152 *Scrutinies*

received the understanding that they've sought, and now sated they are able to move on and pass fully over into their deceased state. As Jung becomes more comfortable with the community of the dead and their questions, his understanding of them increases, as does their ability to perceive an incarnate self with new connections with the dead. As Steiner emphasised, souls

> filled entirely with thoughts, concepts, ideas and sensations taken solely from the material world – cannot be perceived at all from the other world . . . But a soul filled with spiritual ideas . . . a soul glowing and illuminated by spiritual ideas – is perceptible from the other world.[29]

Sermons 5 and 6

Philemon discusses church and Holy Communion by introducing the ideas of sexuality and spirituality as opposites. Although possibly an unorthodox pairing, both spirituality and sexuality are regenerative practices or perspectives in which 'the world of Gods is made manifest'.[30]

The sexuality of man is more earthly and his spirituality more heavenly while woman's spirituality is more earthly and her sexuality more spiritual. Philemon warns if one does not differentiate these two concepts in one's essence then one will not be able to discern oneself from the Pleroma or the vastness, which would appear to be the same quality of the unconscious that the dead currently are experiencing.[31] The difference here of course is that the transition that the dead make to the final state of being deceased still might enable them an opportunity to glimpse the incarnate state they've just left and thus finally accept the limitless quality they now experience.

These two concepts are not so much opposites to be reconciled but perspectives that might be grasped by souls without bodies. If Philemon presents the idea of spirituality, these souls might not understand the idea in terms of the 'utterly boundless' nature of the unconscious. But by introducing the idea of sexuality, the dead might understand by recalling sexuality of the physical body as an expression of spirituality. Essentially these two concepts exemplify the difficulty for discarnates to perceive their surroundings and to conceive of a manner in which they might gain more consciousness. With this example, Philemon assists the dead with the possibility of relating back to a spiritual orientation from their physical lives. If they are able to recall in their essence, sexuality as a spiritual expression within the body, this might work toward augmenting their level of consciousness.

Philemon continues the discussion of the two ideas in the sixth sermon when he designates the serpent and the dove as representing qualities of sexuality and spirituality respectively: The serpent as a representative of the region of the dead, as a deceased ancestor embodies important qualities. It provided the energy necessary to complete the curing of Salome, and also located the hanged man for Jung and served as Elijah and Salome's companion. The serpent appears as not only a symbol of transformation because as a reptile it sheds its skin for rebirth, but:

The wisdom of the serpent, which is suggested by its watchful lifeless eye, lies essentially in mankind's having projected into this lowly creature his own secret wish to obtain from the earth a knowledge he cannot find in waking daylight consciousness alone. This is the knowledge of death and rebirth forever withheld except at those times when some transcendent principle, emerging from the depths, makes it available to consciousness.[32]

The dead here contemplate the ideas of sexuality and spirituality while in transition themselves, and can possibly relate to the snake as representative of the same space. They too must see in themselves the same qualities that the serpent represents, i.e. the knowledge just beyond the reach of incarnate man, that of death and rebirth. The bird as the essential spirituality in man was seen in the loggia dream. There the bird, having turned into a girl then back again, demonstrated the inherent spiritual value of the human being. Most importantly, the dove represents the spiritual knowing of those who are deceased, who have reached an arrival in their deceased state and have achieved a break with their physical bodies. Thus the dead might readily perceive these two symbols. Here the dead claim they have known for a long time the information Philemon relays.

While incarnate the dead had the thick and fleshy presence that the body provides but were 'thin' on spiritual perspective. Again similar to the tramp, they did not attend to spiritual questions even with regard to their faith. Although they claim they know what Philemon teaches, do they understand how to apply it in a landscape of non-differentiated unconsciousness? If they know what Philemon teaches, how is it that they've found themselves in this predicament, not having crossed over fully? The wealth of knowledge of the dead is useless if it cannot apply in their present circumstances.[33]

Between the sixth and seventh sermons Philemon speaks of stepping off 'the wheel of creation' and Jung describes it as 'an indescribable mystery'.[34] This is the third scene suggestive of the notion of reincarnation. It is an extraordinary moment in the narrative and one that does not appear in the previous versions of the *Sermones*. As a result of trying to grasp what Philemon means by stepping off the wheel of fate, Jung experiences a transformative glimpse of Philemon himself and the purpose of their project in the *Sermones*. Jung assumes Philemon's countenance and experiences Philemon within his own physical body. He senses Philemon's voice as his own and hears and sees what Philemon hears and sees.[35] By Philemon stepping off the wheel, Jung experiences a growth peak, a quickening, which seems to release Philemon from rebirth and perhaps even from his status as teacher of the dead.

This process could be considered the ultimate moment of individuation or reaching a pinnacle of the objective form. Philemon has become realised as a result of his role as teacher of the dead. Yet, it is Jung who physically experiences this moment of Philemon's objective form. In one respect, Jung's No. 2 has aged and matured along with Jung's willingness to include him in the course of his living, and at this pivotal moment, Philemon is able to step out of the

154 *Scrutinies*

cycle of life and creation. Jung as an incarnate is 'truly bound to the wheel', yet the proximity of such a perfected experience is not so far away that Jung cannot feel the wheel stand still for him, too. This scene explains more fully the detail that was not included in previous versions, that is after each of the sermons was complete Philemon bent down and touched the ground, resonate of the Buddha's gesture, the *bhumisparsha mudra* or 'calling the earth to witness'.[36] This detail, along with the scene described above, links Jung's experience of the dead with a moment of witness to a possible cessation of rebirth, and possible goal for the community of discarnates.[37]

In a similar manner as with Jung's travels in *Liber Secundus*, when he arrived at Death and witnessed the profound process of dissolution of living beings, here he has encountered a moment of lucid knowing by way of Philemon. One suggestion is that Philemon is able to step off the wheel due to Jung's incarnate involvement with the *Sermones*, in the same way Jung was involved with Salome's cure. When Jung requests that Philemon teach him what has transpired, Philemon describes saving a sense of his experience from 'the revolving wheel of endless happenings'.[38]

Philemon describes how to keep his essence apart from the cycle of birth, and all that goes along with a personal identity tied to a physical body. Where Philemon was touching the ground after each sermon, similar to the Buddha, here he appears to experience the cessation of rebirth as a moment of enlightenment. But, it is left open the conclusion of how this moment affects the incarnate Jung. Does the ability of Philemon, as Jung's No. 2 personality, to cease rebirth affect Jung and his immediate future in any way? Future interpretation might do justice to this question.

The Tibetan Book of the Dead

From the presentation of the *Sermones*, it is possible to see the architecture of Jung's thinking in his commentary to *The Tibetan Book of the Dead*, written in 1935.[39] His exposition of dying as a psychological process for a Western audience reveals a certain understanding that he gained from teaching the dead at this time.[40] In the essay he stresses that 'metaphysical assertions . . . are *statements of the psyche* and are therefore psychological'.[41] Once again this is Jung's way of stressing his empiricist position with the focus of the psychic experience rather than needing to confirm its veracity. What Nagy calls Jung's 'doctrine of knowledge through experience' is at work here while he explains the psychological stages of the discarnate process.[42]

Not only does he use language appropriate to a Western understanding of an Eastern book of the dead, but he links the dynamic of individuation to consciousness and soul. He begins by stating how westerners minimise the importance of soul by comfortably replacing the idea with the concept of mind and 'consciousness, as the invisible intangible manifestation of the soul'.[43] He explains how the purpose of such teachings, as in the Bardo Thödol, were always the object of secret initiations culminating . . . in a figurative death which symbolized the total character of this reversal.[44] And, in point of fact, the instruction given in the Bardo Thödol serves to recall to the dead man the experiences of his initiation . . . for the instruction is . . . nothing less than an initiation of the dead into the Bardo life, just as the initiation of the living was a preparation for the Beyond.[45]

In simple terms this explains the idea of dying before one dies. The initiation allows for a path to become clear so that at the moment of death there is familiarity for the course of what is to follow.[46] Similarly when he speaks about the book as describing 'a way of initiation in reverse, which . . . prepares the soul for a descent into physical being' this must have reminded Jung of his seminal encounter with Ezechiel.[47] That the distinguishing factor between the dead and living is a physical body and also the means by which the orientation of soul is determined. Providing commentary for *The Tibetan Book of the Dead*, gave Jung an opportunity to see his teachings to the dead reencountered in an Eastern context.

Such Eastern influence is seen in Philemon touching the ground, 'calling the earth to witness'[48] and stepping off the wheel of creation.

This seminal moment finds Jung feeling the cessation of creation and experiencing himself becoming Philemon. Or perhaps Jung's perception is not a case of shapeshifting into Philemon, but rather is more of a glimpse of what Philemon's role as No. 2 has been, a glimpse of Philemon glimpsing the life of Jung. The scene confirms the first words the spirit of the depths uttered to Jung about man being an endless expression of eternity. In a sense the scene confirms Jung's thought: 'when we once grasp the meaning of the conscious and the unconscious together, we become aware of the ancestral lives that have gone into the making of our own lives'.[49] This episode shows when he recognises how Philemon has contributed not only his No. 2 perspective but how his transitoriness lives inside and alongside Philemon's ancestral presence.

Thus the spirit of the depths and Philemon appear to frame the entirety of *The Red Book* experience in regard to man's relationship to the dead. With the beginning the discovery of the spirit of the depths and ending with Philemon in conversation with Christ, these two not only link their respective perspectives to the dead, but also to the region, each serving Jung in terms of depths, vision and underworld perspective.

The last sermon

This extraordinary occurrence is followed by the last sermon on man. Considering the dead find what they were pursuing in the end, they leave. Philemon's discussion after the final sermon is equally suggestive of the overall purpose of the work and what the dead needed to learn in order to fully cross over. Philemon's voice here is very much like the spirit of the depths at the very beginning of *Liber Primus*, whose first words serve to remind Jung that man is the

156 *Scrutinies*

expression of life's continuous manifestation of 'becoming and passing away'.[50] He is describing the experience of incarnate man. Thus the dead come to learn how man is a gateway in which 'the entire future streams into the endlessness of the past'.[51] The last statement, of course, refutes Philemon's implication that the dead have dissolved into ash. Rather, he implies that they have experienced what he has, they have stepped off the whirling circle of births. The dead may now remain in the unconscious, in their being, in their life of the dead, having understood their essence both as incarnates and discarnates and now able to surrender their 'transitoriness'.

It could be said that the *Sermones* served their purpose for Jung, Philemon and the dead. Although it appears that Jung grasps an understanding of the cyclic nature of life and death, there exists some ambiguity here if this cycle of births is in fact a cycle of rebirths. In addition to the single passage in 'Nox Secunda' commentary and the references discussed regarding Emma Jung and Toni Wolff, Jung remained noncommittal about reincarnation.[52] Jung wants to resolve such a question within an active imagination, and appears keen to be taught how exactly to get off the wheel of existence himself, as Philemon has done.

Yet, there is still the question whether these dead, now 'sole beings', are able to reincarnate or not. Is this episode in which the dead appear to step off the wheel of rebirth in the same manner as Philemon as a result of the sermons, meant to indicate that in fact reincarnation is a possibility? Does this not assume that since they had been subjected to it they had reincarnated before? This is not clear, although Jung seems interested to be taught what Philemon knows in terms of breaking the cycle, not necessarily being gifted with the impossibility of reincarnating himself. It does seem remarkable that such encounters as have been discussed in *The Red Book* regarding Jung and his dead, would not produce more substantial possibilities in the direction of reincarnation as an experience, but perhaps this is the scene that suggests the possibility and then again, perhaps this topic was one Jung was happy to have left unresolved.[53] Either way, Philemon's experience comes down to this: to recognise one's incarnate life as an 'eternal moment' is a powerful acknowledgement, spiritual knowledge of a kind that assists the dead most in their incarnate and discarnate lives.

Notes

1 Bair's assessment of the *Sermones* describes its purpose as a, 'highly stylised, carefully delineated guidebook, a kind of self-help text book (albeit in archaic language) for successful individuation and peaceful acceptance of the collective unconscious'. Bair, *Jung*, p. 296. Shamdasani calls them: 'a comprehensive psychotheological cosmology'. Shamdasani, 'The Boundless Expanse', p. 19. Hoeller says: 'The dead have rejected and been rejected by Christianity.' Hoeller, *Exploring C.G. Jung's Red Book*, n.p.

2 Greg Mogenson's perspective is useful: 'Though death is frequently imagined as a state free from the conflicts of life, it would be an error to assume that death actually resolves these conflicts. The "diffuse omniscience" of the hereafter tends to blur the distinction between the opposites, making it impossible for the dead to struggle with them as the living do.' It is at this point that I disagree with Mogenson: 'At death

The *Septem Sermones* **157**

the process of individuation is arrested. To the extent that the dead were unable to individuate in life, they become dissolved into the collective unconscious. It is in this sense that they are "unredeemed"'. Mogenson, *Greeting the Angels*, p. 112. The question if the dead individuate must be seen as the exercise of the Sermons themselves, as it appears their reception to learning from Jung and Philemon ends with them having understood their discarnate state, certainly this unto itself is individuation.

3 The presentation here is consistent in content with previous versions, and varies in terms of terminology, which could be due to translation preference. Apart from Philemon being the principal narrator of the teachings, we see Jung's role at times questioning Philemon's choices and methods. This is new in *The Red Book* version, which shows Jung as a much more active participant in the teachings and commentary than previous published versions.

4 *RB*, p. 346b. A fuller discussion of this line appears below as there is more to the beginning of the *Sermones* here than previously known. The *Sermones* begin on p. 346b (#1), then consecutively: pp. 348b (#2), 350a (#3), 351a (#4), 352a (#5), 353a (#6), 354a (#7).

5 *RB*, p. 348b.

6 Ibid., p. 349b.

7 Ibid., p. 351a.

8 Ibid., p. 352a.

9 Ibid., p. 353a.

10 *RB*, p. 354a. Barry Jeromson's summary of the *Sermones* is useful in 'Systema Munditoius and Seven Sermons: Symbolic Collaborators in Jung's Confrontation with the Unconscious' *Jung History* 1, no. 2 (2005–2006) [online] Philemon Foundation, www.philemonfoundation.org/publications/newsletter/volume_1_issue_2/systema_munditotiusand_seven_sermons_symbolic_collaborators_in_jungs_confro (accessed 22 May 2008). For a further discussion see Greene's treatment of the above in *The Astrological World*, p. 143.

11 *RB*, p. 266a.

12 Erich Neumann, *The Origins and History of Consciousness*, trans. R. F. C. Hull, Bollingen Series, XLII (Princeton, NJ: Princeton University Press, 1954), pp. 6 and 104 respectively.

13 *RB*, 348a.

14 Ibid., p. 348b.

15 Steiner, *Staying Connected*, pp. 46–47 and 30 respectively. This particular lecture of Steiner's was delivered in February 1913.

16 Francesca Fremantle and Chogyam Trungpa, *The Tibetan Book of the Dead* (Boston, MA: Shambhala, 2000), xx; *RB*, p. 354a. A further examination of some of Steiner's ideas seen in his lectures, 'The Nature of Man' describes specifically, 'Man's Sevenfold Nature'. The layers of man's nature appear as such: the physical body, the etheric body ('responsible for nutrition, growth and reproduction'), the astral body ('the seat of all that we know as desire passion, and so on'), the 'I am' ('the name the soul uses only of itself, the God begins to speak within that individual soul'), the *Spirit Self* ('Whatever part of the astral body has been thus transformed by the "I"'), *Life Spirit* ('what he has transformed in the etheric body by his own efforts') and finally *Spirit Man* ('the highest achievement open to man on Earth' a type of integration and awareness of all of the above). Richard Seddon, ed., *Rudolph Steiner* (Berkeley, CA: North Atlantic Books, 1988), pp. 23–26. The reason this material is of interest here is that both the Sevenfold Natures and the *Seven Sermones* look to explain to man and to the dead respectively their condition so as to best prepare both for survival in the afterlife. Jung possibly was aware of Steiner's lectures seeing this one was delivered in 1906. The similarities between the two men are notable, such as their interest in Goethe (Steiner having been an editor of Goethe's works) and they both lived and worked in Switzerland with Steiner establishing his spiritual centre, the Goetheanum, originally built in 1913 in Dornach near Basel (ibid., pp. 8–9). A comparison of the two can be found in Gerard Wehr's *Jung and Steiner: The Birth of a New Psychology* (Great Barrington, MA: Anthroposophic Press, 1990), in which Wehr points out, 'Both Steiner and Jung had a particular and profound relationship with the dead' (p. 12).

158 *Scrutinies*

17 Charet, *Spiritualism*, p. 266.

18 Heisig, 'The VII Sermones'.

19 Ibid., p. 211. Shamdasani explains the relationship between the soul and analysis by quoting Jung's explanation: 'The soul seems to detach from the body pretty early and there seems to be almost no realisation of death ... Whatever we do and try analysis is the first steps towards that goal.' Shamdasani, 'The Boundless Expanse', p. 24.

20 Heisig, 'The VII Sermones', p. 214.

21 Barry Jeromson suggests the *Sermones* and Jung's mandala sketch, called Systema, 'resonate with Jung's transcendent function in action.' Jeromson, 'Systema Munditoius', n.p.

22 *MDR*, p. 358.

23 Again, 'Nox Secunda' commentary (*RB*, pp. 297b–298a). And Steiner: 'Many people consider it childish to involve themselves with thoughts of the spiritual world, but this is exactly how they deprive souls after death of needed nourishment.' Steiner, *Staying Connected*, p. 63.

24 Steiner, *Staying Connected*, p. 30.

25 *MDR*, p. 336.

26 Analyst Susan Olson discusses individuation after death and shows a degree of equanimity toward both the objective existence of the dead *in se* and the advantages of a subjective interpretation that the dead in dreams can offer. She undoubtedly favours a consistent subjective interpretation grounded in the dreamer's experience of the personal psyche, but she does give Jung credit when it appears 'in his after-death dreams of his wife and his friend [Jung] assume[s] that the dream-figures of the dead represent "objective" beings inhabiting, the "afterlife" and undergoing individuation in the "spirit" mode of existence.' Olson, *By Grief Transformed*, pp. 188–191.

27 *MDR*, pp. 344–345

28 *RB*, p. 354b.

29 Steiner, *Staying Connected*, p. 29.

30 *RB*, p. 352a. Shamdasani notes (n. 112) Jung's reference of this in *AP*, p. 29.

31 *RB*, p. 352b.

32 Henderson and Oakes, *The Wisdom*, pp. 36–37.

33 *RB*, p. 353b.

34 Ibid., p. 353b. It is significant that between the sixth and seventh sermons Philemon speaks of stepping off 'the wheel of creation. That is just before the dead ask to be taught about men.

35 Ibid. This again is similar to Jung's experience with Elijah and Philemon when he assumed the gesture of the Crucifixion (*RB*, p. 252b).

36 Glossary of Southeast Asian Art, www.art-and-archaeology.com/seasia/glossary.html (accessed 22 July 2011).

37 The repeated scene of Philemon touching the ground resonates with the Buddha's mudra, but what occurs just following Buddha's calling the earth to witness is: 'Bu Devi (the Earth goddess) confirms Buddha's past meritorious lives, by wringing out her hair at the Buddha's feet' (ibid.). This is impressively similar to Salome's gesture immediately before her sight is restored (*RB*, p. 252b).

38 *RB*, p. 252b.

39 Yates notes that Jung wrote the commentary the year his sister died and revised it in 1953 when Toni Wolff died. Yates, *Jung on Death*, p. 5.

40 Yates states: 'In the context of World War I, Jung wrote the "Seven Sermons to the Dead" noting the correspondence between the world of the dead, the land of the ancestors, and the collective unconscious'. She also specifies that Jung interpreted *The Tibetan Book of the Dead* 'as a parallel to withdrawing one's projections'. Yates, *Jung on Death*, pp. 4–5.

41 C. G. Jung, 'Psychological Commentary on *The Tibetan Book of the Dead*' (1935), in *CW* vol. 11, § 831–858.

42 Nagy elaborates, 'through acknowledgement and acceptance of the realities of personal experience we come at last to true self-knowledge and to the transcendent center of

The *Septem Sermones* **159**

the personality, to the self.' Marily Nagy, *Philosophical Issues in the Psychology of C.G. Jung* (New York: SUNY Press, 1991), p. 19.

43 *CW*, vol. 11, §835 and §838.

44 The reversal refers to 'the standpoint . . . needed before we can see the world as 'given' by the very nature of the psyche' (*CW*, vol. 11, §841).

45 *CW*, vol. 11, §841.

46 It must be noted that there are indications in the commentary that appear as if Jung is distancing himself from some of his earlier opinions regarding the dead. Although he sees such initiation as an attempt to 'restore to the soul the divinity it lost at birth' (*CW*, vol. 11, §842), he distinguishes a psychological "Beyond" as 'not a world beyond death' (§841). So while he states clearly the West has 'rationalized the . . . psychological need [for the soul's immortality] out of existence' he lauds the instructions in *The Tibetan Book of the Dead* as 'the highest application of spiritual effort on behalf of the departed' (§855). Although he affirms the existence of psychic facts, it is unclear if he is advocating an Eastern approach or if in his attempt at commentary he is comforted by such distance that psychological explanations afford (§857).

47 *CW*, vol. 11, §854.

48 Glossary of Southeast Asian Art.

49 *AP*, pp. 143–144.

50 *RB*, p. 354b. *Liber Primus*, p. 230a. And again, in *MDR*, p. 265. Here it would appear that Philemon suggests that the dead have dissolved into ash because they understood their lives and deaths. But the dead ascended like 'smoke', no mention of ash, so I suggest they disappeared into their lives as the dead.

51 *RB*, p. 354b.

52 Ibid., p. 296a. Also *MDR*, pp. 349–350. Shamdasani is the only scholar who links Jung's passage about a series of dreams indicating reincarnation (*MDR*, p. 351) with Jung's dreams of Toni Wolff.

53 *MDR*, pp. 349–350.

17

AFTER THE LAST SERMON

Death, Elijah and Salome

Considerable material follows the last sermon, dated 8 February 1916, to the last entry, dated 1 June 1916. The majority of this final material does not concern the dead. The last episode of import following the seventh sermon and the ascension of the dead, involves a visitation by Death who says that he comes far from the East.[1] Considering the implicit references to Eastern ideas with Philemon touching the ground after each sermon and his stepping off the wheel of creation, it does not seem surprising that this figure comes from the East. He states that he brings relief from suffering.[2] When Jung asks him why he is so dark and admits that he is frightened of him, he states that Jung will be 'veiled'. This is perhaps a more developed notion of Jung's 'mark', which appeared with his physician as well as with the woman in the garden party dream.[3]

Death is not preparing Jung for his own death, but to be one who will continue with full awareness of death and the dead in life. As if the marking of those who have consorted with the dead is equally available to Jung in the form of a veil as one who is in service to the dead. The covering is visible not only *at* night, but *to* the night or to the dead and allows for Jung's protection. His warmth will be protected in life and in death, due to his work with both incarnates and discarnates. There is a sense of transformation into maturity or embodied knowledge shown by the transiting from a solar self to a stellar one.

Immediately after this exchange, Philemon asks Jung to ponder the dark one's message at which time he touches Jung's eyes and reveals to him 'the immeasurable mystery'.[4] This, of course echoes the same gesture used by the spirit of the depths, when he first initiated Jung into his visionary faculty.[5] Where Jung was able to see the depths when this was done previously with the spirit of the depths, here Jung is able to grasp the cosmos, 'in the brilliance of countless stars'.[6] Thus, Jung experienced a final initiation in which he balanced his journey through the depths with a glimpse of the heavenly heights, again similarly resonant of his out-of-body experience many years later.

The last of Elijah and Salome

On 3 May 1916, Jung sees Elijah and Salome in a dream and they seem unaware of all that Jung has experienced in his life and in the unconscious since their last meeting almost two years before, on 9 February 1914 (before Jung hung on the divine tree with Salome as company at the end of *Liber Secundus*).[7] Even with Elijah's ability as prophet, and his association with both Jung's No. 2 and the spirit of the depths, he is not aware of how much Jung has changed or what changes have occurred during his life and this surprises him.[8]

This is a fundamental shift in Jung's understanding of the dynamics of his psyche.[9] Before, Jung experienced Elijah and Salome as part of or an aspect of his soul. This particular encounter has led him to reflect and now conclude that by separating them and attributing them to the daimonic category, they can act as relational agents. Jung has now ushered them outside the domain of his soul. This represents an enormous growth curve from the Jung in *Liber Primus* who struggled to perceive competing material in the unconscious, to the Jung who can objectively evaluate his interactions to determine their own nature. This confirms that for the dead to reap the benefits of incarnate growth, they must be informed of it. Thus Elijah, as a representative of the community of the dead, would have needed to interact with Jung or to be informed by an incarnate perspective in order to know anything about man.

Interestingly, Jung still credits them the quality of knowing both past and future, which appears to reflect the quality of the unconscious in general. It is Salome who first recognises the need and indeed the benefit of change.[10] Revealingly, Salome gives away her nature, as a figure of Jung's unconscious, she will change and morph as Jung has throughout his encounters, but, she will need Jung in order to do it. Elijah, who questions the viability of the multiple, has no need or desire for change or growth. He attempts to show Jung that there really is nothing new, the past is similar to what will come.[11] This is, in fact, an expression of Elijah's nature, a consistent reference point in the unconscious landscape, firmly planted in the land of the dead. But it is Salome who whispers her last words to Jung, full of possibility that in a sense she is partial to 'being and multiplicity'.[12] Salome's nature is to change and shift presumably as Jung does. As Jung comes to the realisation that they have remained unaware of him during their mutual time apart, she becomes more cognisant of the same realisation, which in turn is reflected by her statement. Even emerging from the unconscious after two years, Elijah seems to have maintained his demeanour as representative of the dead and Salome still situates herself more personally in relation to Jung.

Conclusion

Scrutinies, as the last section of *The Red Book*, sees Jung having gained a sense of orientation and mastery in relation to the dead. The *Sermones* embedded in this larger section now looks to have been written specifically for the dead and offers guidance

162 *Scrutinies*

in terms of managing a discarnate existence in the unconscious. The emphasis on the reality of the soul's survival after death is an obvious prerequisite for the work and now looks to reveal further how the unconscious accommodates at the very least a notion of survival of the soul in a psychic existence. In one respect it is an appropriate end to *The Red Book* as it reveals a Jung confident enough in what he has gleaned about the dead in his previous encounters to offer advice in the form of teachings. The most seminal point to the *Sermones* is that it suggests the possibility that individuation occurs in a post-mortem state and is further assisted by the degree to which one practised considered awareness of the life of the dead while still living. Thus knowledge of the dynamics of the unconscious while alive appears to assist in locating that same quality when discarnate.

The Mass on behalf of the dead and the *Sermones* prepare the dead, in search of the 'light' that will assist them to pass over completely, as they currently inhabit a half-life, half-dead state. Therefore the *Sermones* must be reframed as a text tailored as a guide for the dead so that they may reach their complete state as discarnates. The teachings, delivered as a combined effort with Jung's incarnate perspective and Philemon's discarnate one assist the dead to grasp their lives as men and their lives as discarnates.

Notes

1 *RB*, p. 354b. It is unclear if this is the same figure who Jung meets in the episode 'Death' in *Liber Secundus*.
2 Ibid.
3 *RB*, p. 355a. There is a line from the last sermon, which appears to manifest in this exchange: 'The star is the God and the goal of man' (*RB*, p. 354a). There is also a sense of transformation into maturity or spiritual knowledge transiting from a solar self to a stellar one.
4 *RB*, p. 355a. This echoes a similar gesture when the spirit of the depths opened Jung's eyes when he initiated Jung into his visionary process (*RB*, p. 237b).
5 *RB*, p. 237b.
6 Ibid., p. 355a. This figure acts in the role of a celestial mother who is asked by Philemon to accept Jung as her child. Here it appears Philemon announces his release from service to Jung, but he wishes to pass on the responsibility to this celestial mother figure. She won't accept him until he cleanses himself of the impurities of commingling with men. This is a reversal of the attitude that the dead are unclean.
7 *RB*, pp. 323b. They both return and Jung claims: 'The cycle is completed and the gates of the mysteries have opened again' (*RB*, p. 325b).
8 *MDR*, pp. 337–338. It is unclear what their state or activity might have been in the meantime, but given the vivid description of their abode and the activity there, perhaps in a similar manner they returned to their equivalent of lives of the dead. Although Salome is not a member of the dead, they both might still be engaged in the same manner as Jung's father and mother in the fish lab dream (*MDR*, p. 239).
9 *RB*, p. 357b.
10 Ibid., p. 358a.
11 Ibid.
12 Ibid.

PART V
Beyond *The Red Book*

18

POST-*RED BOOK* IMPLICATIONS

Jung's professional writings after his confrontation with the unconscious and the writing of the *Sermones* see him attempting to grapple with some of the issues that the literal dead posed to his model of the psyche. In 1919, he delivered a lecture on 'The Psychological Foundations of Belief in Spirits' at the Society of Psychical Research. By way of his discussion of complexes, Jung attempts to situate the literal dead in the unconscious dynamic while identifying them as a psychological experience. It is his accommodation regarding souls and spirits, which suggests that he is bridging the ideas of split-off soul parts of the psyche *and* other peoples' souls:

> It is impossible to speak of belief in spirits without at the same time considering the belief in souls. Belief in souls is a correlate of belief in spirits. Since, according to primitive belief, a spirit is usually the ghost of one dead, it must once have been the soul of a living person. This is particularly the case wherever the belief is held that people have only one soul. But this assumption does not prevail everywhere; it is frequently supposed that people have two or more souls, one of which survives death and is immortal. In this case the spirit of the dead is only one of the several souls of the living. It is thus only a part of the total soul – a psychic fragment, so to speak.[1]

This appears to be an accommodation allowing for discarnates to appear in the unconscious alongside split-off soul fragments, while also leaving open the possibility of unconscious material subject to the transcendent function and that which is not. Yet, the confusion arises when Jung proceeds to discuss 'the existence of unconscious complexes that normally belong to the ego, and of those that normally should not become associated with it. The former are the soul-complexes, the latter the spirit-complexes'.[2] Is the presence of spirit-complexes or 'those that

166 Beyond *The Red Book*

normally should not become associated with it' in actuality referring to discarnates or others' souls? These would certainly fall into a category of souls being *in se* without the desire to be attached or merged into another personality. In his essay in 1939, titled 'Concerning Rebirth', Jung would define an 'ancestral soul' as 'the soul of some definite forebear' and 'for all practical purposes, such cases may be regarded as striking instances of identification with deceased persons'.[3] It certainly seems that Jung is alluding to the dead *in se* and our ability to be in contact with them on some level.

Additionally, when Jung states: 'Spirits are not under all circumstances dangerous and harmful. They can, when translated into ideas, also have beneficial effect' and that they are 'therefore either pathological fantasies or new but as yet unknown ideas' this is an unconventional approach to their definition.[4] This supposition allows for spirits to serve as a psychological catalyst for personal, cultural, or even political change and seems in the absolute a creative explanation for the presence and influence of the dead. Addison captures this idea best:

> Jung felt that the dead and the weight of human history, of Christian history, are being neglected in the (his) present day, and that they are a living presence within the soul requiring reanimation to enable our own living. Through listening and creating a potential space within a larger continuity between two mysteries, namely: those who in past aeons have preceded us and that which we are destined to become, a relativisation takes place that sets our own transient existence and imminent concerns in a universal context. In recollecting the forms that animate us, the deeply personal connecting back through history, including Jung himself, the present becomes animated by the past, and the result is an affirmation of life.[5]

And yet, it is also resonant of Jung's own discoveries outlined in his 'Nox Secunda' commentary where he suggests the effect that the dead have on the living is not only to drive passion but to be 'the wellspring of [one's] best work'.[6] Here is the possibility that the *content* that the dead bring to the exchange might possibly differ from the dynamic of other split-off parts of the psyche that work their way back to the personality.[7] That is, the dead in fact are not symbols at all, but it is their message, whatever that might be, which influences the actions, decisions and future of the living.[8]

Notes

1 *CW*, vol. 8, §577.
2 Ibid., §587, in more explicit terms: 'Spirits … viewed from the psychological angle, are unconscious autonomous complexes which appear as projections because they have no direct association with the ego' (§585).
3 *CW*, vol. 9, §224.
4 Ibid., §596 and §597 respectively.
5 Ann Addison, '*Lament of the Dead: Psychology After Jung's Red Book* by Hillman, James & Shamdasani, Sonu', *Journal of Analytic Psychology* 60 (2015): 281–285.

Post-*Red Book* implications **167**

6 *RB*, p. 297 n. 188.
7 In a now well-known reconsideration Jung would state in this essay his doubt about the existence of spirits. The original quote reads: 'I see no proof whatever of the existence of real spirits and until such proof is forthcoming I must regard the whole territory as an appendix of psychology.' In 1948 he would footnote this sentence and claim: 'After collecting psychological experiences from many people and many countries for fifty years, I no longer feel as certain as I did in 1919 when I wrote this sentence. To put it bluntly I doubt whether an exclusively psychological approach can do justice to the phenomena in question.' He would credit research in parapsychology as well as physics, which he claimed 'opens up the whole question of the transpsychic reality immediately underlying the psyche' (*CW*, vol. 8, §600).
8 Australian musician Nick Cave movingly states: 'Dread grief trails bright phantoms in its wake . . . these spirits are ideas, essentially. They are our stunned imaginations reawakening after the calamity. Like ideas, these spirits speak of possibility. Follow your ideas, because on the other side of the idea is change and growth and redemption.' Paula Mejila, 'The Brutality and Tenderness of Nick Cave's Newsletters', *The New Yorker* (9 November 2018), www.newyorker.com/culture/culture-desk/the-brutality-and-tenderness-of-nick-caves-newsletters (accessed 9 November 2018).

19

CONTEMPORARY CONTEXT

Jung emerged greatly changed by his experiences at the end of *Scrutinies*. His open and committed engagement with the unconscious and the dead might have implications in a contemporary context. These are two areas that might look to Jungian research to help explain and more specifically engage in what could be going on with patients and clients who have had anomalous experiences involving the dead.

The dynamic occurring in the process of induced after-death communication (IADC) begins with the practice of eye-movement desensitisation reprocessing (EMDR), and its general purpose is to address trauma or post-traumatic stress disorder (PTSD) in an expedient way.[1] The method finds that those who have experienced trauma benefit from specific eye-movement patterns that access emotions tied to the trauma. Patients have found that the process works quickly and requires few sessions. Therapist Allan Botkin discovered during the EMDR process that one Vietnam veteran had a spontaneous vision of a deceased friend with immediate positive effects. Directly following the vision, the veteran experienced relief from his symptoms, particularly his grief.

Botkin's discovery stresses not the traditional route to grief therapy, which 'helps survivors . . . by fully accepting the finality of death and severing their bonds with the deceased', but rather: 'Instead of encouraging acceptance of the feelings of disconnection and withdrawal from emotional attachment to the deceased, IADC therapy actually provides psychological resolution through the profound, life-changing experience of reconnection with the deceased.'[2] The method involves having the patient engage in rapid eye-movement patterns while simultaneously concentrating on their sadness and grief. What follows in Botkin's case studies is a spontaneous vision of the deceased and a very brief exchange. The process appears not only to have an immediate effect but a lasting one. Patients more importantly discover a renewed relationship to the deceased:

Contemporary context **169**

I had worked with Sam, a 46-year-old patient at the VA hospital, on other traumatic memories of his Vietnam War experience, but he had avoided bringing up this one because it was too painful. While in Vietnam he had developed a close relationship with Le, a 10-year-old orphaned Vietnamese girl . . . Sam and Le developed a special relationship . . . After several months, Sam decided to adopt Le and bring her home . . . however . . . all orphaned Vietnamese children on the base were to be sent to a Catholic orphanage in a distant village . . . Sam, in tears, helped load Le and the other Vietnamese children onto a . . . truck to take them to the orphanage . . . [when] shots rang out and bullets zipped past . . . Sam realized . . . he saw [Le] laying face down . . . her torso was blown open from a bullet that entered from behind . . . the incident was Sam's undoing.[3]

Botkin tried EMDR with Sam, whose grief had been debilitating for the last twenty-eight years. As the eye-movement exercises began there appeared a noticeable relief of sadness. When Botkin instructed the final eye movement Sam relayed:

When I closed my eyes I saw Le as a beautiful woman with long black hair in a white gown surrounded by a radiant light. She seemed . . . more content than anyone I have ever known . . . She thanked me for taking care of her before she died. I said 'I love you, Le' and she said 'I love you too, Sam' and she put her arms around me and embraced me. Then faded away.[4]

Botkin describes how elated Sam was and knew he had communicated with Le: 'I could actually feel her arms around me.'[5] Botkin assessed this as a grief hallucination but in his professional experience could not account for its wholly positive effect. This type of therapeutic method, guided by a trained EMDR practitioner, was able to facilitate a healing through an encounter with the deceased. Botkin's research relays case-study discussions that are all similar in how they unfold with the end result being a type of 'reconnection'. What he has discovered from repeated experiences is patients are 'renewed by an uplifting experience that gives them the feeling of a different but satisfying and permanent new relationship . . . they continue their bond knowing their loved one is OK and imminent. The experience of reconnection heals.'[6]

There are a few aspects to this dynamic that appear similar to Jung's encounters with his dead. In IADC there seems an ability very quickly to connect to the personal unconscious for a brief period of time, which could be the process of active imagination or interpsychic rapport. The real healing, of course, is the dissipation of burdened sadness that seems to lift immediately after the encounter. It seems that what is integrated back into the mourner's personality is the libido connected to the emotion of grief locked in an historical moment of loss. This previously bound emotion when released, in a sense, returns to the mourner to healing effect.

Could this grief simply be bound to the lost object and therefore the vision is simply a figure of one's personal unconscious? Perhaps. But the 'feeling' and sentiment of

170 Beyond *The Red Book*

knowing where the dead are and perhaps where to find them appears to be at the core of the healing, not simply the unravelling of the moment of loss. Jung's encounter in France with the deceased Emma might have been moving because Jung knew where she went, in addition to the comforting notion that she was still working on herself. In both the IADC work and Jung's instance, the visioning itself is the method that incites not only connection but the deeply meaningful reconnection.

Jung's visioning also helps contextualise the work that analyst Roger Brooke has conducted, also with war veterans, with respect to the dead. Brooke discusses the dreams and repetitive nightmares that soldiers have for years after returning home and he demonstrates how working in the space of active imagination (or interpsychic rapport) is a method that heals. He tells the story of one vet who could not shake his first killing of 'an enemy combatant'. But over the years the nightmare morphed and moved emotionally closer to home. Rather than the dream showing killings in the Middle East, they moved to shadows in his own home, involving his children. Brooke guided the vet to look at the dream closely at which time the vet admits about his first killing that 'he saw himself in that man's suicidal courage'. The vet goes on to speak to the insurgent and says, 'I shall remember you with respect as a fellow warrior. Go to Allah and rest in peace.' This gesture is not only acknowledgement of the deceased and the tie that binds them, but is also an offering, an energetic exchange that heals them both.[7] This is what Jung would call the care and work on behalf of the dead.

The Red Book material might be a valued contribution to contemporary practitioners who are engaging with clients who have anomalous experiences. Like Jung, both Botkin and Brooke did not have an intention to work with the dead, but rather with those who are suffering. In both instances the work was tied up with traumatic grief and unresolved business with the dead. Such open-minded acceptance and space for the dead to make their case, is in short, a healing gesture for the living who sit burdened in the consulting room.

Notes

1 Allan Botkin, *Induced After-Death Communication: A New Therapy for Healing Grief and Trauma* (Charlottesville, VA: Hampton Roads, 2005).
2 Ibid., p. 30.
3 Ibid., pp. 10–11.
4 Ibid., p. 11.
5 Ibid.
6 Ibid., p. 30. This research affirms the Continuing Bonds research that results from what appears to be a process of grief resolution that people engage in naturally.
7 Roger Brooke, 'An Archetypal Approach to Treating Combat Post-Traumatic Stress Disorder', in *Outpatient Treatment of Psychosis; Psychodynamic Approaches to Evidence-Based Practice*, ed. D. L. Downing (London: Routledge, 2017), pp. 190–191.

20

CONCLUDING THOUGHTS

C. G. Jung and the Dead offers the opportunity to examine chronologically the neglected theme of the dead in Jung's personal material during his intense confrontation with the unconscious, while also engaging for the first time in a detailed analysis of how the theme of the dead emerges throughout *The Red Book*. These discussions reveal how Jung developed and used his visionary skill to discover and grow his relationship to the unconscious from literal encounters with the dead, to an understanding of how they live in the unconscious and alongside the living.

In this respect perhaps *The Red Book* might be considered a possible Book of the Dead for the Western psyche. Traditionally, Books of the Dead are texts whose principle function is to provide detailed instructions in preparation for death. Such texts have also offered a way to become an initiate into the mysteries before death, such that upon death, the initiate has an experiential understanding of the transition before it occurs.[1] The instructions often appear obtuse but look to prepare the reader with foreknowledge so as to make the transition from life to death recognisable. These instruction manuals allow the living to experience details about the potentialities of experience that they might encounter. This is one way *The Red Book* material can be read, as demonstrating the varied terrain and content that the newly deceased might possibly meet during the transition from life to death. Jung conducted his journey through the unconscious meeting all sorts of figures, including the dead, and learning how to manage what he encountered. This has not provided a guidebook in the precise manner of *The Tibetan Book of the Dead*, but rather has outlined an example of the terrain of any journey involving the unconscious and to this effort has assisted in preparing those who wish such foreknowledge with a taste of what the unconscious possibly holds. And although Jung's caveat aims to stress that this journey was his own and was about *his* unconscious, the work still gives curious journeyers a taste of what such an encounter might hold for them.

172 Beyond *The Red Book*

As the episodes of the book detail Jung's method of active imagination and interpsychic rapport in action, *The Red Book* shows this method and its process thoroughly. In these terms, the content assists with making visioning the unconscious more conscious. As Jung came to understand that analysis was a preparation for death, due to its orientation to soul, equally, the material assists with the same goal; an orientation to (of) the soul for the purpose of understanding both life and death.

The dead were instrumental in assisting Jung to understand all aspects of what would become his psychological model. By initiating him into his visioning, with their insistent presence, Jung began to answer their question to him: 'What are you going to do about us, how are you going to explain us?' In this sense, tending to this question posed by the dead proved to be Jung's individuation. How he visioned his dead and other figures of the unconscious is how he became more conscious and how he came to translate dynamic personality elements. And as he discovered what the dead were saying, he uncovered his personal ancestral lineage, what it feels like to inherit such a lineage and to emerge into the world to communicate such an idea. He discovered the importance of caring for the dead and what exactly that requires. This is best expressed when he described his life in the Tower in Bollingen:

> There is nothing to disturb the dead, neither electricity, light nor telephone . . . my ancestor's souls are sustained by the atmosphere of the house, since I answer for them the questions that their lives once left behind . . . It is as if a silent, greater family, stretching down the centuries, were peopling the house.[2]

His visioning journey delivered him to this.

With Jung's geography of the unconscious and the explicit details of how he visioned the dead and related to them, he provided not only a method to raise consciousness toward a fuller more expressive life, but at the same time, has shown the path toward the final journey into death. With the express focus of soul in both instances, *The Red Book* might earn its place as a Book of the Dead for the Western psyche with Jung its committed and dedicated steward.

Notes

1 Stanislav Grof, *The Ultimate Journey: Consciousness and the Mystery of Death* (Ben Lomond, CA: MAPS, 2006), pp. 77–78.
2 *MDR*, p. 265.

BIBLIOGRAPHY

Ackroyd, Peter. (1995). *Blake: A Biography*. New York: Ballantine Books.

Addelson, Betty. (2005). *The Lives of Dwarfs: Their Journey From Public Curiosity Towards Social Liberation*. New Brunswick, NJ: Rutgers University Press.

Addison, Ann. (2015). '*Lament of the Dead: Psychology After Jung's Red Book* by Hillman, James & Shamdasani, Sonu'. *Journal of Analytical Psychology* 60, 281–285. doi: 10.1111/1468-5922.12148_1.

Baeur, E., Belz, M., Fach, W., Fangmeier, R., Schuppe-Ihle, C. and Wiedemer, A. (2012). 'Counselling at the IGPP-an Overview'. In Kramer, W. H., Baeur, E. and Hövelmann, G. H., eds., *Perspectives of Clinical Parapsychology: An Introductory Reader*. The Netherlands: Stichting Het Johan Borgman Fonds.

Bair, Deirdre. (2003). *Jung: A Biography*. New York: Back Bay Books.

Belz, Martina. (2012). 'Clinical Psychology for People with Exceptional Experiences in Practice'. In Simmonds-Moore, Christine, ed., *Exceptional Experiences in Health: Essays on Mind, Body and Human Potential*. Jefferson, NC: McFarland.

Benner, Jeff A. (2004). *Biblical Hebrew E-Magazine* 8 (October) [online]. Available at hebrew.org/emagazine/008.doc (accessed 15 February 2008).

Bergquist, Lars. (2013). *Swedenborg's Dream Diary*. West Chester, PA: Swedenborg Foundation.

Bernstein, Jerome. (2005). *Living in the Borderland: The Evolution of Consciousness and the Challenge of Healing Trauma*. Hove, UK: Routledge.

Bianco, Simone, Sambin, Marco and Palmieri, Arianna. (2017). 'Meaning Making After a Near-Death Experience: The Relevance of Intrapsychic and Interpersonal Dynamics'. *Death Studies* 41(9), 562–573. doi: 10.1080/07481187.2017.1310768.

Bishop, Paul. (2010). '*The Red Book* in Relationship to German Classicism' [lecture], Jung's *Red Book* Conference, San Francisco Jung Club, 4–6 June.

Blalock, Sarah and Holden, Janice. (2018). 'Preparing Students to Counsel Clients with Potentially Spiritually Transformative Experiences'. *Counselling and Values* 63, 31–44.

Botkin, Allan. (2005). *Induced After-Death Communication: A New Therapy for Healing Grief and Trauma*. Charlottesville, VA: Hampton Roads.

Brodersen, Liz. (2019). *Taboo, Personal and Collective Representations, Origin and Positioning within Cultural Complexes*. London: Routledge.

174 Bibliography

Brome, Vincent. (1978). *Jung: Man and Myth*. London: House of Stratus.

Brooke, Roger. (1991). *Jung and Phenomenology*. London: Routledge.

Brooke, Roger. (2017). 'An Archetypal Approach to Treating Combat Post-Traumatic Stress Disorder'. In Downing, D. L., ed., *Outpatient Treatment of Psychosis: Psychodynamic Approaches to Evidence-Based Practice*. London: Routledge.

Bhikkhu, Thanissaro. (2011). 'No-Self or Not-Self?'. *Access to Insight*, 8 March [online]. Available at www.accesstoinsight.org/lib/authors/thanissaro/notself2.html (accessed 22 July 2011).

Bulkeley, Kelly. (1995). *Spiritual Dreaming*. New York: Paulist Press.

Bulkeley, Kelly and Bulkeley, Patricia. (2005). *Dreaming Beyond Death: A Guide to Pre-Death Dreams and Visions*. Boston, MA: Beacon Press.

Burkert, Walter. (1987). *Ancient Mystery Cults*. Cambridge, MA: Harvard University Press.

Burkert, Walter. (1987). *Greek Religion*. London: Wiley-Blackwell.

Burleson, Blake. (2005). *Jung in Africa*. London: Continuum.

Cameron, Rose. (2016). 'The Paranormal as an Unhelpful Concept in Psychotherapy and Counselling Research'. *European Journal of Psychotherapy & Counselling* 18(2), 142–155.

Cavalli, Thom. (2002). *Alchemical Psychology: Old Recipes for Living in a New World*. New York: Tarcher/Putnam.

Charet, F. X. (1993). *Spiritualism and the Foundations of C.G. Jung's Psychology*. New York: SUNY Press.

Clay, Catrine. (2017). *Labyrinths: Emma Jung, Her Marriage to Carl and the Early Years of Psychoanalysis*. London: William Collins.

Chodorow, Joan, ed. (1997). *Jung on Active Imagination*. Princeton, NJ: Princeton University Press.

Coward, Harold. (1985). *Jung and Eastern Thought*. New York: SUNY.

Dannenbaum, S. M. and Kinnier, R. T. (2007). 'Imaginal Relationships with the Dead: Applications for Psychotherapy'. *Journal of Humanistic Psychology* 49(1), 100–113.

D'Este, Sorita and Rankine, David. (2009). *Hekate Liminal Rites: A Study of the Rituals, Magic and Symbols of the Torch-Bearing Triple Goddess of the Crossroads*. London: BM Avalonia.

Douglas, Mary. (1999). *Leviticus as Literature*. Oxford: Oxford University Press.

Dourley, John. (2014). *Jung and His Mystics: In the End It All Comes to Nothing*. London: Routledge.

Drob, Sanford. (2012). *Reading 'The Red Book': An Interpretive Guide to C.G. Jung's Liber Novus*. New Orleans, LA: Spring Journal Books.

Frantz, Gilda. (2010). 'Jung's Red Book: The Spirit of the Depths'. *Psychological Perspectives* 53(4), 391–395.

Fremantle, Francesca and Trungpa, Chogyam. (2000). *The Tibetan Book of the Dead*. Boston, MA: Shambhala.

Fortescue, Adrian. (1910). 'Liturgy of the Mass'. *The Catholic Encyclopedia*, Vol. 9. New York: Robert Appleton [online]. Available at www.newadvent.org/cathen/09790b.htm (accessed 16 July 2011).

Giegerich, Wolfgang. (2010). 'Liber Novus, That Is, the New Bible: A First Analysis of C.G. Jung's Red Book'. *Spring* 83, 361–411.

Glossary of Southeast Asian Art (n.d.). [online]. Available at www.art-and-archaeology. com/seasia/glossary.html (accessed 22 July 2011).

Green, Celia and McCreery, Charles. (1994). *Lucid Dreaming: The Paradox of Consciousness During Sleep*. London: Routledge.

Greene, Liz. (2018). *The Astrological World of Jung's Novus Liber*. London: Routledge.

Bibliography

Greyson, Bruce. (2013). 'Getting comfortable with near death experiences. An overview of near-death experiences'. *Missouri Medicine*, 110(6), 475–481.

Greyson, Bruce. (2014). 'Congruence Between Near-Death and Mystical Experience'. *International Journal for the Psychology of Religion* 24(4), 298–310.

Grof, Stanislav. (2006). *The Ultimate Journey: Consciousness and the Mystery of Death*. Ben Lomond, CA: MAPS.

Grubbs, Geri. (2004). *Bereavement Dreaming and the Individuating Soul*. Berwick, ME: Nicolas Hays.

Hanegraaf, Wouter. (1998). *New Age Religion and Western Culture: Esotericism in the Mirror of Secular Thought*. New York: State University of New York Press.

Hannah, Barbara. (1973). *Jung: His Life and Work*. New York: G. P. Putnam's Sons.

Harding, Esther. (1971). *Woman's Mysteries Ancient and Modern*. New York: Harper Colophon Books.

Heisig, James. (1972). 'The VII Sermones: Play and Theory'. *Spring*, 206–218.

Henderson, Joseph. (2005). *Thresholds of Initiation*. Ashville, NC: Chiron.

Henderson, Joseph and Oakes, Maud. (1963). *The Wisdom and the Serpent: The Myths of Death, Rebirth, and Resurrection*. Princeton, NJ: Princeton University Press.

Hillman, James. (1976). 'Some Early Background to Jung's Ideas: Notes on C.G. Jung's Medium by Stefanie Zumstein Preiswerk'. *Spring*, 123–136.

Hillman, James. (1979). *The Dream and the Underworld*. New York: Harper Perennial.

Hoeller, Stephan. (1982). *The Gnostic Jung and the "Seven Sermons to the Dead"*. Wheaton, IL: Quest Books.

Hoeller, Stephan. (2010). *Exploring C.G. Jung's Red Book*. BC Recordings: Part 10 [online]. Available at http://bcrecordings.net/store/index.php?main_page=index&cPath=6 (accessed 18 February 2010).

Hoerni, U., Fischer, T. and Kauffman, B. eds. (2018). *The Art of C.G. Jung*. New York: W.W. Norton.

Hollenback, Jess. (1996). *Mysticism: Experience, Response, Empowerment*. University Park, PA: Penn State University Press.

Hollis, James. (2013). *Dispelling the Ghosts Who Run Our Lives*. Ashville, NC: Chiron.

Homans, Peter. (1995). *Jung in Context*. Chicago, IL: University of Chicago Press.

Homer. (1963). *The Odyssey*, trans. Robert Fitzgerald. New York: Anchor Books.

Huang, Hsinya. (2006). 'Blood/Memory in N. Scott Momaday's *The Names: A Memoir* and Linda Hogan's *The Woman Who Watches Over the World: A Native Memoir*'. *Concentric: Literary and Cultural Studies* 32(1), 191–195.

Hunter, Jack. (2017). 'Ontological Flooding and Continuing Bonds'. In Klass, Denis and Steffen, Edith Maria, eds., *Continuing Bonds in Bereavement: New Directions for Research and Practice*. London: Routledge.

Huskinson, Lucy. (2010). 'Analytical Psychology and Spirit Possession: Towards a Non-Pathological Diagnosis of Spirit Possession'. In Schmidt, Bettina and Huskinson, Lucy, eds., *Spirit Possession and Trance: New Interdisciplinary Perspectives*. London: Continuum.

Ingerman, Sandra. (1991). *Soul Retrieval: Mending the Fragmented Self*. New York: HarperSanFrancisco.

Jaffé, Aniela. (1971). *Jung's Last Years*. Dallas, TX: Spring.

Jaffé, Aniela. (1972). 'Phases in Jung's Life'. *Spring*, 162–190.

Jaffé, Aniela. (1979). *Apparitions: An Archetypal Approach to Death Dreams and Ghosts*. Irving, TX: Spring.

Jaffé, Aniela. (1989). *Was C.G. Jung a Mystic? And Other Essays*. Einsiedeln, Switzerland: Daimon Verlag.

176 Bibliography

Jeromson, Barry. (2005–2006). 'Systema Munditoius and Seven Sermons: Symbolic Collaborators in Jung's Confrontation with the Unconscious'. *Jung History* 1(2) [online]. Available at www.philemonfoundation.org/publications/newsletter/volume_1_issue_2/systema_munditotiusand_seven_sermons_symbolic_collaborators_in_jungs_confro (accessed 22 May 2008).

Jung, C. G. (1896). *The Zofingia Lectures*, trans. Jan Van Heurck, in *The Collected Works*, Suppl. Vol. A. London: Routledge.

Jung, C. G. (1916). *Psychology of the Unconscious: A Study of the Transformations and Symbolisms of the Libido*, ed. William McGuire, in *The Collected Works*, Suppl. Vol. B. Princeton, NJ: Princeton University Press.

Jung, C. G. (1935). 'Psychological Commentary on *The Tibetan Book of the Dead*', trans. R. F. C. Hull. In *The Collected Works*, Vol. 11. Princeton, NJ: Princeton University Press.

Jung, C. G. (1936). 'Individual Dream Symbolism in Relation to Alchemy'. In *Psychology and Alchemy*, trans. R. F. C. Hull, *The Collected Works*, Vol. 12. Princeton, NJ: Princeton University Press.

Jung, C. G. (1943). On the Psychology of the Unconscious'. In *Two Essays on Analytical Psychology*, trans. R. F. C. Hull, *The Collected Works*, Vol. 7. Princeton, NJ: Princeton University Press.

Jung, C. G. (1951/1969). 'On Synchronicity', in *The Structure and Dynamics of the Psyche*, trans. R. F. C. Hull, *The Collected Works*, Vol. 8, 2nd ed. London: Routledge & Kegan Paul.

Jung, C. G. (1955/1969). 'Synchronicity: An Acausal Connecting Principle', in *The Structure and Dynamics of the Psyche, The Collected Works*, Vol. 8, 2nd ed. London: Routledge & Kegan Paul.

Jung, C. G. (1956). 'On the Nature of Dreams'. In *The Structure and Dynamics of the Psyche*, trans. R. F. C. Hull, *The Collected Works*, Vol. 8. Princeton, NJ: Princeton University Press.

Jung, C. G. (1956). 'The Psychological Foundation of Belief in Spirits'. In *The Structure and Dynamics of the Psyche*, trans. R. F. C. Hull, *The Collected Works*, Vol. 8. Princeton, NJ: Princeton University Press.

Jung, C. G. (1956). *Symbols of Transformation*, ed. William McGuire, trans. R. F. C. Hull. In *The Collected Works*, Vol. 5. Princeton, NJ: Princeton University Press.

Jung, C. G. (1957). 'On the Psychology and Pathology of So-Called Occult Phenomena'. In *Psychiatric Studies*, trans. R. F. C. Hull, *The Collected Works*, Vol. 1. Princeton, NJ, NJ: Princeton University Press.

Jung, C. G. (1959). 'A Typical Set of Symbols Illustrating the Process of Transformation'. In *The Archetypes and the Collective Unconscious*, trans. R. F. C. Hull. In *The Collected Works*, Vol. 9. Princeton, NJ: Princeton University Press.

Jung, C. G. (1966). 'Picasso'. In *The Spirit in Man, Art and Literature*. London: Routledge.

Jung, C. G. (1969). 'Psychology of the Transference'. In *Practice of Psychotherapy*, trans. R. F. C. Hull, *The Collected Works*, Vol. 16. Princeton, NJ: Princeton University Press.

Jung, C. G. (1970). 'Psychology and Religion: West and East', trans. R. F. C. Hull. In *The Collected Works*, Vol. 11. Princeton, NJ: Princeton University Press.

Jung, C. G. (1975). *Letters: 1951– 1961*, Vol. 2. Princeton, NJ: Princeton University Press.

Jung, C. G. (1977). *Mysterium Coniunctionis*, ed. William McGuire, trans. R. F. C. Hull, *The Collected Works*, Vol. 14. Princeton, NJ: Princeton University Press.

Jung, C. G. (1989). *Analytical Psychology: Notes of the Seminar Given in 1925*, ed. William McGuire. Bollingen Series XCIX. Princeton, NJ: Princeton University Press.

Jung, C. G. (1992). *Letters: 1906–1950*, Vol. 1. Princeton, NJ: Princeton University Press.

Jung, C. G. (2009). *The Red Book*, ed. Sonu Shamdasani, trans. Mark Kyburz. New York: W. W. Norton.

Jung, C. G. (2012). *Introduction to Jungian Psychology: Notes of the Seminar on Analytical Psychology Given in 1925*, ed. Sonu Shamdasani. Bollingen Series XCIX. Princeton, NJ: Princeton University Press.

Jung, C. G. and Jaffé, Aniela. (1961/1995). *Memories, Dreams, Reflections*, trans. Richard Winston and Clara Winston. London: Fontana.

Jung, Emma and von Franz, Marie-Louise. (1970). *The Grail Legend*. Princeton, NJ: Princeton University Press.

Kast, Verena. (1988). *A Time To Mourn*. Einsiedeln, Switzerland: Daimon Verlag.

Kerr, John. (1993). *A Most Dangerous Method*. New York: Alfred A. Knopf.

Kerenyi, Carl. (1991). *Eleusis: Archetypal Image of Mother and Daughter*. Princeton, NJ: Princeton University Press.

Kingsley, Peter. (1999). *In the Dark Places of Wisdom*. Point Reyes, CA: Golden Sufi Center.

Knight, Michele. (2013). *Ways of Being: The Alchemy of Bereavement and Communiqué*. Unpublished doctoral thesis, University of Sydney. Available at https://ses.library.usyd. edu.au/handle/2123/13764 (accessed 16 May 2008).

Kugler, Paul. (2005). *Raids on The Unthinkable: Freudian and Jungian Psychoanalyses*. New Orleans, LA: Spring Journal Books.

Lachman, Gary. (2012). *Jung the Mystic: The Esoteric Dimensions of Carl Jung's Life and Teachings*. New York: TarcherPerigee.

Launer, John. (2017). *Sex and Survival: The Life and Ideas of Sabina Spielrein*. New York: The Overlook Press.

Luke, Helen. (2003). *Dark Wood to White Rose: Journey and Transformation in Dante's Divine Comedy*. New York: Parabola Books.

Main, Roderick, ed. (1997). *Jung on Synchronicity and the Paranormal*. Princeton, NJ: Princeton University Press.

Main, Roderick, ed. (2004). *The Rupture of Time: Synchronicity and Jung's Critique of Modern Western Culture*. Hove, UK and New York: Brunner-Routledge.

Marlan, Stanton and David Miller. (2007). 'What Is the Legacy of the Dead? Jung's Memories and the Case of Zola's Missing Book'. *Spring* 77, 277–282.

March, Jenny. (1998). *Cassell's Dictionary of Classical Mythology*. London: Cassell.

Mason, Su. (2010). 'Spiritual Healing: What Is It? Does It Work and Does It Have a Place in Modern Healthcare?' *Royal College of Psychiatrists*. Available at www.rcpsych.ac.uk/pdf/ Su%20Mason%20Spiritual%20Healing%20in%20Modern%20Healthcare.x.pdf (accessed 5 October 2018).

Mathes, Charlotte. (2006). *And the Sword Shall Pierce My Heart: Moving from Despair to Meaning After the Death of a Child*. Ashville, NC: Chiron.

McMahon, Arthur. (1910). 'Holy Sepulchre'. In *The Catholic Encyclopaedia*, Vol. 7 [online]. New York: Robert Appleton. Available at www.newadvent.org/cathen/07425a.htm (accessed 28 April 2011).

Meier, Carl A. (2003). *Healing Dream and Ritual*. Einsiedeln, Switzerland: Daimon Verlag.

Mejila, Paula. (2018). 'The Brutality and Tenderness of Nick Cave's Newsletters'. *The New Yorker*, 9 November. Available at www.newyorker.com/culture/culture-desk/the-brutality-and-tenderness-of-nick-caves-newsletters (accessed 9 November 2018).

Merchant, John. (2012). *Shamans and Analysis: New Insights on the Wounded Healer*. London: Routledge.

Meyer, Marvin. (1987). *The Ancient Mysteries A Sourcebook*. San Francisco, CA: Harper & Row.

Miller, David. (2004). *Hells & Holy Ghosts: A Theopoetics of Christian Belief*. New Orleans, LA: Spring Journal Books.

Mogenson, Greg. (1992). *Greeting the Angels: An Imaginal View of the Mourning Process*. New York: Baywood.

Moore, Peter. (2016). *Where Are the Dead? Exploring the Idea of an Embodied Afterlife*. London: Routledge.

178 Bibliography

Nagy, Marilyn. (1991). *Philosophical Issues in the Psychology of C.G. Jung*. New York: SUNY Press.

Neumann, Erich. (1954). *The Origins and History of Consciousness*, trans. R. F. C. Hull. Bollingen Series, XLII. Princeton, NJ: Princeton University Press.

Neumann, Erich. (1955). *The Great Mother*. Princeton, NJ: Princeton University Press.

Noll, Richard. (1994). *The Jung Cult*. New York: Simon & Schuster.

Noll, Richard. (2000). 'Jung the Leontocephalus'. In Bishop, Paul, ed., *Jung in Contexts: A Reader*. London: Routledge.

Oeri, Albert. (1970). 'Some Youthful Memories of C.G. Jung'. *Spring*, 182–189.

Ogden, Daniel. (2001). *Greek and Roman Necromancy*. Princeton, NJ: Princeton University Press.

Olson, Susan. (2010). *By Grief Transformed: Dreams and the Mourning Process*. New Orleans, LA: Spring Journal Books.

Pilard, Nathalie. (2015). *Jung and Intuition: On the Centrality and Variety of Forms of Intuition in Jung and Post-Jungians*. London: Karnac.

Radice, Betty. (1962). *Bhagavad Gita*, trans. Juan Mascaro. London: Penguin Books.

Raff, Jeffrey. (2000). *Jung and the Alchemical Imagination*. York Beach, ME: Nicolas-Hays.

Raff, Jeffrey. (2002). *Healing the Wounded God*. York Beach, ME: Nicolas-Hays.

Roxburgh, Elizabeth C. and Evenden, Rachel E. (2016). '"Most People Think You're a Fruit Loop": Clients' Experiences of Seeking Support for Anomalous Experiences'. *Counselling and Psychotherapy Research* 16, 211–221.

Roxburgh, Elizabeth C. and Evenden, Rachel E. (2016). '"They Daren't Tell People": Therapists' Experiences of Working with Clients Who Report Anomalous Experiences'. *European Journal of Psychotherapy & Counselling* 18(2), 123–141.

Savage-Healy, Nan. (2017). *Toni Wolff & C.G. Jung: A Collaboration*. Los Angeles, CA: Tiberius Press.

Seddon, Richard, ed. (1988). *Rudolph Steiner*. Western Esoteric Masters Series. Berkeley, CA: North Atlantic Books.

Shamdasani, Sonu. (1998). *Cult Fictions: C.G. Jung and the Founding of Analytical Psychology*. London: Routledge.

Shamdasani, Sonu. (2008). 'The Boundless Expanse: Jung's Reflections on Death and Life'. *Quadrant* 38(1), 9–30.

Shamdasani, Sonu. (2010). 'Carl Gustav Jung and *The Red Book* (part 1)', *Library of Congress Webcasts* [online], 19 June. Available at www.loc.gov/today/cyberlc/feature_wdesc. php?rec=4909 (accessed 6 June 2011).

Shamdasani, Sonu. (2012). *C.G. Jung: A Biography in Books*. New York: W.W. Norton.

Shamdasani, Sonu. (2015). '"S.W." and C.G. Jung: Mediumship, Psychiatry and Serial Exemplarity'. *History of Psychiatry* 26(3), 288–302.

Sherry, Jay. (2008). 'Carl Gustav Jung, Avant-Garde Conservative'. Unpublished doctoral thesis, Freie Universität Berlin.

Silverman, David, ed. (2003). *Ancient Egypt*. Oxford: Oxford University Press.

Skea, Brian. (1995). 'Trauma, Transference and Transformation: A Study of Jung's Treatment of His Cousin, Hélène, A Jungian Perspective on the Dissociability of the Self and on the Psychotherapy of the Dissociative Disorders'. *The Jung Page*, 23 February [online]. Available at www.cgjungpage.org/learn/articles/analytical-psychology/802-a-jungian-perspective-on-the-dissociability-of-the-self (accessed 10 May 2009).

Smith, Evans Lansing. (2001). *Descent to the Underworld in Literature, Painting, and Film 1895–1950: The Modernist Nekyia*. London: Edwin Mellen Press.

Stein, Murray. (2005). 'Individuation: Inner Work'. *Journal of Jungian Theory and Practice* 7(2), 1–13.

Stein, Murray. (2010). 'Carl Jung's *Red Book*: Part 1' [webinar], 22 January. Available at http://ashevillejungcenter.org (accessed 15 November 2010).

Stein, Murray. (2010). 'Critical Notice: Jung, C.G., *The Red Book: Liber Novus*'. *Journal of Analytical Psychology* 55, 423–434.

Steiner, Rudolf. (1999). *Staying Connected: How to Continue Your Relationships With Those Who Have Died*, ed. C. Bamford. Great Barrington, MA: Anthroposophic Press.

Stephens, Stephani. (2015). 'Active Imagination and the Dead'. *International Journal of Jungian Studies* 2 December, 1–14.

Stephens, Stephani. (2017). 'The Spectre and Its Movement: The Dynamic of Intra and Transgenerational Influence'. International Association of Jungian Studies Conference, Capetown, South Africa.

Stephenson, Craig. (2009). *Possession Jung's Comparative Anatomy of the Psyche*. Hove, UK: Routledge.

Stevens, Anthony. (1990). *On Jung*. London: Taylor & Francis.

Streit-Horn, Jenny. (2011). 'A Systematic Review of Research on After-Death Communication (ADC)'. Unpublished doctoral dissertation, University of North Texas, Denton. Available at https://digital.library.unt.edu/ark:/67531/metadc84284/m1/1.

Swedenborg, Emanuel. (2010). *Heaven and Hell*. West Chester, PA: Swedenborg Foundation.

Taylor, Eugene. (1991). 'C.G. Jung and the Boston Psychopathologists, 1902–1912'. In Stern, Mark, ed., *Carl Jung and Soul Psychology*. London, Routledge.

Taylor, Eugene. (1991). 'Jung and His Intellectual Context: Swedenborgian Connection'. *Studia Swedenborgiana* 7(2), 47–69.

Taylor, Eugene. (2007). 'Jung on Swedenborg, Redivivus'. *Jung History* 2(2) [online] Philemon Foundation. Available at www.philemonfoundation.org/publications/newsletter/volume_2_issue_2/jung_on_swedenborg (accessed 15 March 2009).

Totton, Nick. (2007). 'Funny You Should Say That: Paranormality, at the Margins and the Centre of Psychotherapy'. *European Journal of Psychotherapy & Counselling* 9(4), 389–401.

Turner, Edith. (1993). 'The Reality of Spirits: A Tabooed or Permitted Field of Study?' *Anthropology of Consciousness* 4(1), 9–12.

Turner, Edith. (1998). *Experiencing Ritual: A New Approach to African Healing*. Philadelphia, PA: University of Pennsylvania Press.

Ulaney, David. (1989). *The Origins of the Mithraic Mysteries*. New York: Oxford University Press.

van Lommel, Pim. (2011). 'Near-Death Experiences: The Experience of the Self as Real and Not as an Illusion'. *Annals of the New York Academy of Sciences* 1234(1), 19–28. https://doi-org.ezproxy.canberra.edu.au/10.1111/j.1749-6632.2011.06080.x

von Franz, Marie-Louise. (1979). 'Archetypes Surrounding Death'. *Quadrant* 12(1), 5–23.

von Franz, Marie-Louise. (1984). *On Dreams & Death*. Boston, MA: Shambhala.

von Franz, Marie-Louise. (1998). *C. G. Jung: His Myth in Our Time*. Toronto: Inner City Books.

Villoldo, Alberto and Krippner, Stanley. (1986). *Healing States: A Journey Into the World of Spiritual Healing and Shamanism*. New York: Fireside Books.

Virgil. (1972). *The Aeneid of Virgil*, Books 1–6, ed. R. D. Williams. New York: St. Martin's Press.

Walker, Steven. (2002). *Jung and the Jungians on Myth*. London, Routledge.

Wehr, Gerard. (1990). *Jung and Steiner: The Birth of a New Psychology*. Great Barrington, MA: Anthroposophic Press.

Woolger, Roger. (1988). *Other Lives, Other Selves*. New York, Bantam Books.

Woolger, Roger. (2011). 'Understanding C.G Jung's *Red Book*, Part 1'. *Network Review*, Summer, 1–5.

Yates, Jenny, ed. (1997). *Jung on Death and Immortality*. Princeton, NJ: Princeton University Press.

INDEX

Note: page numbers in bold type refer to tables.

à Kempis, Thomas 112, 113, 116
Ackroyd, Peter 59
active imagination 3, 10n16, 20, 32, 60, 62, 150, 172; commentary on 130–131; and IADC (induced after-death communication) 169, 170; *see also* 'Instruction'; merry garden; 'Mysterium Encounter'; 'Resolution'; Siegfried murder
'Active Imagination and the Dead' (Stephens) 4
ADC (after-death communication) 12, 17; *see also* IADC (induced after-death communication)
Addison, Ann 166
Aeneas 58, 61n4, 75, 107, 131n6
Aeneid (Virgil) 58, 75, 107
Africa 81, 82
after-death communication (ADC) 12, 17; *see also* IADC (induced after-death communication)
after-death survival 28n30; denial of 119; Jung's beliefs concerning 6, 8, 26, 31, 32, 35, 42–45, 108
alchemy 113, 117; loggia dream 47–49; rubedo/red stage 73
Analytical Psychology 92–93
'ancestral souls' 166
ancestral spirits dream 40–42, 43, 45, 50
Anchorite, the 52n50
anima figure, Salome as 87–88
anomalous experiences 17

archetypes 6; row of tombs dream 49
auditory hallucinations 117
Austrian customs official/knight dream 45–47, 104, 109n4, 114, 149
aware unconscious 17

Baeur, E. 12
Bardo Thödal 154–155
Baynes, Cary 26
Belz, M. 11–12
bereavement dreams 10n16
bereavement process 7, 8, 38n2; after-death communication 12; continuing bonds research 14; *see also* grief therapy
betrachten 49, 66, 73, 88
bhumisparsha mudra 154, 155
'big' dreams 32
birth 71, 72; *see also* rebirth
Black Book 62
Blake, William 59
blood 74, 138–139, 142
Boddinghaus, Martha 144n9
Botkin, Allan 168–169, 170
brain, the, and NDEs (near-death experiences) 24
Brimo 110n17, 140
Brooke, Roger 170
Buddha 108, 154, 155
Bulkeley, Kelly 32
Burkert, Walter 70, 91–92
Burleson, Blake 81

Index **181**

Cameron, Rose 13–14, 15–16, 37
Cave, Nick 167n8
channelling 20, 141
chaos 119–120
Charet, F.X. 8, 42, 150
Christ 89–90, 113, 129, 141, 142
Collected Works 107
collective unconscious 30, 32, 44, 46, 49, 93, 100, 106, 119–120, 128
colours 101; greening of the desert 66; red 73–75
complexes 165–166
'Concerning Rebirth' 166
consciousness, birth of 148
continuing bonds research 14

Dannenbaum, S.M. 13
Dante 57, 58
dead, the: definition of 6–7; guidance of 149; individuation of 44, 150–151, 162; instruction for 120–121; Jungians on 7–8; Jung's early experiences 4–5; knowledge of 42–45; legacy of 139; and the moon 103; nature of 5–6; need for learning and knowledge 123, 147, 155–156, 161–162; 'Nox Secunda' commentary on 118–121; as objective presences in the psyche 36–37; and the psychoid realm 35–36; raising of 85, 91, 114, 123; as souls without bodies 6, 8, 150; and the transcendent function 7, 150–151, 152, 158n2, 165; and the unconscious 147–148; 'unfinished business' of 45; *see also* literal interpretation of the dead; symbolic interpretation of the dead
Death 106–108, 154, 160
death dreams 40–50, 73; 1911-1912 period 5; precognitive 17; *see also* ancestral spirits dream; Austrian customs official/knight dream; Jung, Emma; Jung, Paul; loggia dream; row of tombs dream; Wolff, Toni
deification 63
descent 70; descent into hell, Jung's 63, 69–77, 92
desert, the 66, 106
detachment model, grief therapy 14
devil, the *see* Red One, the
discarnate 5, 8; definition of 6
dissociation, and No. 2 aspect of Jung's personality 29
Divine Comedy (Dante) 57
'Divine Folly' 112, 116

doves, and spirituality 152, 153
dreams and dreaming: lucid 20, 46–47; visitation dreams 31, 32, 35, 41; *see also* ancestral spirits dream; Austrian customs official/knight dream; 'big' dreams; death dreams; loggia dream; metachoric visions (waking dreams); row of tombs dream

ecstasy, Jung's experience of 25–26
Elijah 30, 52n49, 52n51, 63, 76–77, 83, 85, 86–87, 88, 89, 90, 91, 92, 99, 101, 113, 114, 119, 123, 124, 129, 140, 147, 151, 152, 161
EMDR (eye-movement desensitisation reprocessing) 168–169
exceptional experiences (ExE) 11–12, 17
Ezechiel 6, 17, 106, 113–116, 119, 155
Ezekiel 38n5

female principle 48
figures of the unconscious 101, 102, 104–105
flooding vision 64–65
Freud, S., Jung's relationship with 42, 45, 46, 47, 52, 65, 70–71, 72–73, 74, 81

garden party dream 21–22
Gasparetto, L.A. 28n30
Gilmagesh 58
Grail studies of Emma Jung 34, 44
Greyson, Bruce 23–24, **23–24**
grief therapy: continuing bonds research 14; war veterans 168–169

Hanegraaf, W. 141
Hannah, Barbara 62, 69, 81, 82
HAP 138
Harding, Esther 110n18
Heaven and Hell (Swedenborg) 58
Hekate 110n17
Heisig, James 150
Hell 130; and the tramp 103, 104
Henderson, Joseph 70, 76
Hermes Trismegistus 47, 48
Hollenback, Jess 25, 124
Homans, Peter 81
Homer 58, 74–75
Hunter, Jack 14–15
hypnagogic vision 70

IADC (induced after-death communication) 168–169, 170; *see also* ADC (after-death communication)
Ihamba healing ritual, Ndembu people, Zambia 15

182 Index

Imitation of Christ, The (à Kempis) 112, 113, 116
immortality 92, 108; *see also* after-death survival
impending death 21–22
incest taboo 122–124
individuation 44, 150–151, 153–154, 162
induced after-death communication (IADC) 168–169, 170; *see also* ADC (after-death communication)
Inferno (Dante) 58
initiatory rites 70
inner heat, of Ezechiel 115
instruction 88–89
interpsychic rapport 20, 116, 150, 172; and IADC (induced after-death communication) 169, 170
intuition, Pilard's definition of 19n20
Izdubar, shrinking of 82

Jaffé, Aniela 17, 32–33, 41, 44, 137
Jarbuch für Psychoanalytische und Psychopathologische Forschungen 65, 110n27
journeys 57, 58, 71, 99
Jung, C. G.: Jung's myth, and his dead 42; relationship with Freud 42, 45, 46, 47, 52, 65, 70–71, 72–73, 74, 81; soul of 63, 64–65, 66, 69–70, 86, 91, 92, 121, 137–138, 143; *see also* No. 2 aspect of Jung's personality/spirit of the depths; No. 1 aspect of Jung's personality/spirit of the times
Jung, Emma 33–35, 36, 41, 44, 46, 47, 50, 140, 146n31, 156, 170
Jung, Paul 4, 5, 31–32, 33, 37, 40, 46, 49, 50, 140, 151

Kant, I. 60
karma 108
Kingsley, Peter 74
Kinnier, R.T. 13
Knight, Michelle 12
Kugler, P. 8, 35, 111n41

landscapes 99
Liber Primus 41, 62–66, 76–77, 99, 126n51, 131, 155–156, 161; conclusion to 92–93; *see also* 'Instruction'; merry garden; 'Mysterium Encounter'; *Red Book, The*; 'Resolution'; Siegfried murder
Liber Secundus 74, 83, 85, 89, 91, 94n28, 94n29, 99–100, 135, 136, 137, 143, 154; *see also* Death; 'Divine Folly'; Philemon; poisoner, the; *Red Book, The*; Red One, the; tramp, the

libido 51n43, 73, 90; serpents as symbol of 76; Siegfried murder 80, 81; and the tramp 105, 106
life of the dead 34, 116, 146n44, 156, 162
literal interpretation of the dead 11, 13, 14, 16, 18, 40, 50, 165; assistance of 17–18
loggia dream 47–49, 66n2, 72, 129, 153
lucid dreaming 20, 46–47
Luke, Helen 57

magic 129
Maillard, C. 20
Main, Roderick 22
Mann, Kristine 26
Mass for the dead 136, 141–143, 147, 162
Memories, Dreams, Reflections 3, 4, 5, 7, 11, 23, 32, 35, 47, 57, 62, 63, 70, 71, 81, 94, 108, 120, 135, 137, 139, 151; 'On Life After Death' chapter 32, 34, 42, 45
man: male principle 48–49; sexuality and spirituality 152
merry garden 82–83, 129
metachoric visions (waking dreams) 20, 22, 25
Miller, David 60
Mogenson, Greg 8, 34, 156n2
Moltzer, Maria 136
moon, the 74, 103, 110n17, 110n18, 110n19
Moore, Peter 8
mourning *see* bereavement process; grief therapy
mummification 49–50, 72–73
mysterium coniunctionis (sacred wedding) images 26, 48
'Mysterium Encounter' 63, 76–77, 85–88, 92, 102, 128

Nagy, Marilyn 154
NDE (near-death experience) 20, **23–24**, 23–27
necromancy 74
Nekyia scene, *Odyssey* 74–75, 138–139
Neumann, Erich 33, 148
No. 1 aspect of Jung's personality/spirit of the times 29, 41, 63, 65, 66, 70–71, 72, 74, 81, 92, 137; merry garden 82; Siegfried murder 80, 81, 83
No. 2 aspect of Jung's personality/spirit of the depths 29–30, 41, 53n59, 62, 63–64, 65, 69–70, 81, 92, 108, 137, 147, 153, 154, 155, 160, 161; descent of 15 November 1913 65–66; and Elijah 86, 88; merry garden 82, 83; Siegfried murder 80, 81
non-ordinary experiences 17

'Nox Quarta' 122–124
'Nox Secunda' 45, 108, 112–118, 137, 156, 166; commentary on the dead 118–121
'Nox Tertia' 121–122

Oakes, Maud 76
occult 16–17
Odyssey, The (Homer) 58; Nekyia scene 74–75, 138–139; Odysseus and the dead 75
Oeri, Albert 74
Olson, Susan 8, 9n9, 38n7, 44, 110n41, 158n26
'omniconsciousness' 43
ontological flooding 14, 15
Origins and History of Consciousness, The (Neumann) 148
out-of-body experiences 20, 23, 25–27, 160

paranormal 11, 14–15, 16–17
parapsychology 13
past life memories 108; past lifetimes 119
phenomenological bracketing (Husserl) 14
Philemon 30, 92, 108, 129, 135, 136, 141, 142, 143, 146n39, 162; in the Sermones 15, 147, 149, 150, 151, 153–154, 155, 156
philosopher's stone 48, 73; see also alchemy
Pilard, Nathalie 19n24, 19n31, 20
play therapy 50
poisoner, the 129–130, 152
post-traumatic stress disorder (PTSD) 168–169
Preiswerk, Helly 136, 138–139; life as a discarnate 139–141; mass for the dead 136, 141–143, 147, 162
prescient visions 20, 21
psychic projections: the dead as 6, 8; spirits as 5
psychoid realm 35–36
'Psychological Foundations of Belief in Spirits, The' 165
psychological model of Jung 3, 4, 6, 11, 172
Psychology of the Transference 71
Psychology of the Unconscious 41, 42, 45, 50, 76, 103; see also Symbols of Transformation
PTSD (post-traumatic stress disorder) 168–169

Raff, Jeffrey 35–36, 131n14
rebirth 71, 72, 74, 76, 83, 109, 123, 138, 142, 154, 156, 166; serpents as symbol of 76; and the sun 107–108; see also reincarnation

Red Book, The 3, 4, 16, 17, 21, 23, 26–27, 29, 32, 35, 40, 43, 45, 48, 49, 57, 59, 62, 69, 70, 71–72, 73, 75, 106; as a Book of the Dead for the Western psyche 171–172; hospital episode 28n19; literary predecessors to 57–60; see also Liber Primus; Liber Secundus; Scrutinies; Sermones (Septem Sermones ad Mortuos / Seven Sermons to the Dead)
Red One, the 100–102
reincarnation 108–109, 153
religious advisors, and after-death communication 12
remote viewing 20
resolution 89–90
resurrection 49
row of tombs dream 49–50, 66, 72
Roxburgh, Elisabeth 11, 12

sacred wedding (mysterium coniunctionis) images 26, 48
'Sacrificial Murder' 108
Salome 52n49, 52n51, 63, 76–77, 83, 85, 86–89, 90, 91, 92, 99, 102, 114, 119, 129, 140, 151, 152, 154, 161
Schopenhauer, A. 60
Scrutinies 76, 92, 108, 135–143, 168; final material 160–162; see also Red Book, The
Septem Sermones ad Mortuos / Seven Sermons to the Dead; Sermones (Septem Sermones ad Mortuos / Seven Sermons to the Dead)
Sermones (Septem Sermones ad Mortuos / Seven Sermons to the Dead) 4, 6, 17, 26, 42, 44, 58, 73, 100, 112, 118, 135, 136–137, 142, 143, 147–150, 161–162; final sermon 155–156; goal of 150–152; sermons 5 and 6 152–154; see also Red Book, The; Scrutinies
serpents 75–77; and the poisoner 129–130; Resolution 89–90; and sexuality 152–153
sexuality, and spirituality 152–153
shamanism 9n4
Shamdasani, Sonu 8, 41, 62, 65, 109, 120, 137
Siegfried murder 52n51, 63, 66n1, 66n2, 74, 76, 80–82, 83, 86, 92, 104, 105, 128, 129
Smith, Evans Lansing 42
Society of Psychical Research 165
solitude 64
soul, the 152, 165; 'ancestral souls' 166; finding of 121
soul, the, Jung's 63, 70, 92, 121, 128, 137–138; emergence of 66, 69–70; and

184 Index

meaning-making 64–65; and Philemon 143; and Salome 86, 91

soul-complexes 165

space: abolition of in the unconscious 22; spacelessness 32

Spielrein, Sabina 51n43, 136

spirit-complexes 165–166

spirit of the depths/ No. 2 aspect of Jung's personality 29–30, 41, 53n59, 62, 63–64, 65, 69–70, 81, 92, 108, 137, 147, 153, 154, 155, 160, 161; descent of 15 November 1913 65–66; and Elijah 86, 88; merry garden 82, 83; Siegfried murder 80, 81

spirit of the times/ No. 1 aspect of Jung's personality 29, 41, 63, 65, 66, 70–71, 72, 74, 81, 92, 137; merry garden 82; Siegfried murder 80, 81, 83

spirits, nature of 5–6, 166

spiritualism 6, 7, 17, 41, 141

spirituality: during lifetime 150–152, 162; and sexuality 152–153

spiritually transformative experiences, people with (STEs) 11

split-off parts of the psyche, spirits/the dead as 5, 7, 8, 86, 87, 123, 165, 166

'spontaneous foreknowledge' 22

Stein, Murray 42

Steiner, Rudolph 149, 151, 152, 157n16, 158n23

STEs (spiritually transformative experiences, people with) 11

sun 71, 73, 74, 81, 111n39, 145n19: rebirth of 107–108; symbolism of 76; veiling 162

sun beetle 138

sun disk 138

Swedenborg, E. 58–59, 61n8, 67n20

symbolic interpretation of the dead 11, 13, 16, 18

Symbols of Transformation 70, 71; *see also Psychology of the Unconscious*

synchronicity 22

Tabula Smaragdina 47, 48

therapists, and the dead 11–13; jelly bean case study 13–17, 37

Tibetan Book of the Dead, Jung's commentary on 42, 154–155, 159n46, 171

time: abolition of in the unconscious 22; timelessness 32

tramp, the 102–106, 114, 145n16, 149, 153

transcendent function 7, 37, 51n33, 90, 101, 104, 105, 116, 165; and the dead 7, 150–152

transrational experiences 17

Turner, Edith 15

unconscious, the: and after-life survival 17, 34; figures of the unconscious 101, 102, 104–105; space and time in 22

under-conscious 19n20, 19n31

underworld, in ancient mythology 107

'unfinished business' of the dead 45

van Lommel, Pim 23

van Waveren, Erlo 108

Virgil 58, 75, 107

visioning/visioning process 4, 7, 20–21, 60

visitation dreams 31, 32, 35, 41

von Franz, Marie-Louise 16, 17, 34, 35, 36, 37, 44, 48, 72, 73, 80, 81, 115, 131n14

Walker, Steven 81

war veterans 168–169, 170

Wolff, Toni 32–34, 41, 47, 50, 52, 95n37, 136, 140, 156, 158n39

woman: sexuality and spirituality 152

Woolger, Roger 58, 108, 109

World War I 69, 83, 137

Zofingia lectures 8, 31